PRACTICE & REVISION KIT

Professional Diploma

Marketing Planning

BPP Professional Education
September 2004

First edition September 2003
Second edition September 2004

ISBN 0 7517 1744 4 (Previous edition 0 7517 1261 2)

British Library Cataloguing-in-Publication Data
A catalogue record for this book
is available from the British Library

Published by

BPP Professional Education
Aldine House, Aldine Place
London W12 8AW

www.bpp.com

Printed in Great Britain by W M Print
45-47 Frederick Street
Walsall, West Midlands
WS2 9NE

We are grateful to the Chartered Institute of Marketing for permission to reproduce the syllabus and past examination questions. The suggested solutions to past examination questions have been prepared by BPP Professional Education.

Author
Neil Towers

Series editor
Paul Brittain

Contents

The headings indicate the main topics of questions, but questions often cover several different topics.

Tutorial questions, listed in italics, are followed by **guidance notes** on how to approach the question, thus easing the transition from study to examination practice.

Most of the questions and answers are taken from previous Marketing Planning and Control and Marketing Operations papers and are of an equivalent standard to those expected to be set on this new syllabus.

Questions marked by * are **key questions** which we think you must attempt in order to pass the exam. Tick them off on this list as you complete them.

ABOUT THIS KIT

You're taking your exams. You're under time pressure to get your exam revision done and you want to pass first time. Could you make better use of your time? Are you sure that your revision is really relevant to the exam you will be facing?

If you use this BPP Practice & Revision Kit you can be sure that the time you spend revising and practising questions is time well spent.

The BPP Practice & Revision Kit: Marketing Planning

The BPP Practice & Revision Kit has been specifically written for this paper by an expert in marketing education.

- We give you a comprehensive question and answer checklist so you can see at a glance which are the key questions that we think you should attempt in order to pass the exam, what the mark and time allocations are and when they were set (where this is relevant)
- We offer vital guidance on revision, question practice and exam technique
- We show you the syllabus examinable and the papers set so far
- We give you a comprehensive question bank containing:
    - *Tutorial questions* to warm you up
    - *Exam-standard questions*
    - *Full suggested answers* - with summaries of the examiner's comments
- A Test Your Knowledge quiz covering selected areas from the entire syllabus
- A Test Paper with full suggested answers, for you to attempt just before the real thing
- A Topic Index for ready reference

The Study Text: further help from BPP

The other vital part of BPP's study package is the Study Text. The Study Text features:

- Structured, methodical syllabus coverage
- Lots of case examples from real businesses throughout, to show you how the theory applies in real life
- Action programmes and quizzes so that you can test that you've mastered the theory
- A question and answer bank
- Key concepts and full index

There's an order form at the back of this Kit.

Passcards

BPP passcards enable you to revise at a glance by summarising key revision points in a card format.

Help us to help you

Your feedback will help us improve our study package. Please complete and return the Review Form at the end of this Kit; you will be entered automatically in a Free Prize Draw.

BPP Professional Education
September 2004

To learn more about what BPP has to offer, visit our website: www.bpp.com

REVISION

This is a very important time as you approach the exam. You must remember three things.

Use time sensibly
Set realistic goals
Believe in yourself

Use time sensibly

1 **How much study time do you have?** Remember that you must EAT, SLEEP, and of course, RELAX.

2 **How will you split that available time between each subject?** What are your weaker subjects? They need more time.

3 **What is your learning style?** AM/PM? Little and often/long sessions? Evenings/ weekends?

4 **Are you taking regular breaks?** Most people absorb more if they do not attempt to study for long uninterrupted periods of time. A five minute break every hour (to make coffee, watch the news headlines) can make all the difference.

5 **Do you have quality study time?** Unplug the phone. Let everybody know that you're studying and shouldn't be disturbed.

Set realistic goals

1 Have you set a **clearly defined objective** for each study period?

2 Is the objective **achievable**?

3 Will you **stick to your plan**? Will you make up for any **lost time**?

4 Are you **rewarding yourself** for your hard work?

5 Are you leading a **healthy lifestyle**?

Believe in yourself

Are you cultivating the right attitude of mind? There is absolutely no reason why you should not pass this exam if you adopt the correct approach.

- **Be confident** – you've passed exams before, you can pass them again
- **Be calm** – plenty of adrenaline but no panicking
- **Be focused** – commit yourself to passing the exam

QUESTION PRACTICE

Do not simply open this Kit and, beginning with question 1, start attempting all of the questions. You first need to ask yourself three questions.

Am I ready to answer questions?
Do I know which questions to do first?
How should I use this Kit?

Am I ready to answer questions?

1 Check that you are familiar with the material for a particular syllabus area.

2 If you are happy, you can go ahead and start answering questions. If not, go back to your BPP Study Text and revise first.

Do I know which questions to do first?

1 **Start with tutorial questions**. They warm you up for key and difficult areas of the syllabus. Try to produce at least a plan for these questions, using the guidance notes following the question to ensure your answer is structured so as to gain a good pass mark.

2 Don't worry about the time it takes to answer these questions. Concentrate on producing good answers. There are 7 tutorial questions in this Kit.

How should I use this Kit?

1 Once you are confident with the tutorial questions, you should try as many as possible of the exam-standard questions; at the very least you should attempt the **key questions,** which are highlighted in the **question and answer checklist/index** at the front of the Kit.

2 Try to **produce full answers under timed conditions**; you are practising exam technique as much as knowledge recall here. Don't look at the answer, your BPP Study Text or your notes for any help at all.

3 **Mark your answers to the non-tutorial questions as if you were the examiner**. Only give yourself marks for what you have written, not for what you meant to put down, or would have put down if you had had more time. If you did badly, try another question.

4 Read the **Tutorial notes** in the answers very carefully and take note of the advice given and any **comments by the examiner**.

5 When you have practised the whole syllabus, go back to the areas you had problems with and **practise further questions**.

6 When you feel you have completed your revision of the entire syllabus to your satisfaction, answer the **test your knowledge** quiz. This covers selected areas from the entire syllabus and answering it unseen is a good test of how well you can recall your knowledge of diverse subjects quickly.

7 Finally, when you think you really understand the entire subject, **attempt the test paper** at the end of the Kit. Sit the paper under strict exam conditions, so that you gain experience of selecting and sequencing your questions, and managing your time, as well as of writing answers.

EXAM TECHNIQUE

Passing professional examinations is half about having the knowledge, and half about doing yourself full justice in the examination. You must have the right approach to two things.

The day of the exam
Your time in the exam hall

The day of the exam

1 Set at least one alarm (or get an alarm call) for a morning exam.

2 Have something to eat but beware of eating too much; you may feel sleepy if your system is digesting a large meal.

3 Allow plenty of time to get to the exam hall; have your route worked out in advance and listen to news bulletins to check for potential travel problems.

4 Don't forget pens, pencils, rulers, erasers.

5 Put new batteries into your calculator and take a spare set (or a spare calculator).

6 Avoid discussion about the exam with other candidates outside the exam hall.

Your time in the exam hall

1 **Read the instructions (the 'rubric') on the front of the exam paper carefully**

Check that the exam format hasn't changed. It is surprising how often examiners' reports remark on the number of students who attempt too few – or too many – questions, or who attempt the wrong number of questions from different parts of the paper. Make sure that you are planning to answer the right number of questions.

2 **Select questions carefully**

Read through the paper once, then quickly jot down key points against each question in a second read through. Select those questions where you could latch on to 'what the question is about' – but remember to check carefully that you have got the right end of the stick before putting pen to paper.

3 **Plan your attack carefully**

Consider the order in which you are going to tackle questions. It is a good idea to start with your best question to boost your morale and get some easy marks 'in the bag'.

4 **Check the time allocation for each question**

Each mark carries with it a time allocation of 1.6 minutes (including time for selecting and reading questions). A 25 mark question therefore should be completed in 40 minutes. When time is up, you must go on to the next question or part. Going even one minute over the time allowed brings you a lot closer to failure.

5 **Read the question carefully and plan your answer**

Read through the question again very carefully when you come to answer it. Plan your answer to ensure that you keep to the point. Two minutes of planning plus eight minutes of writing is virtually certain to earn you more marks than ten minutes of writing.

6 **Produce relevant answers**

Particularly with written answers, make sure you answer the question set, and not the question you would have preferred to have been set.

7 **Gain the easy marks**

Include the obvious if it answers the question and don't try to produce the perfect answer.

Don't get bogged down in small parts of questions. If you find a part of a question difficult, get on with the rest of the question. If you are having problems with something, the chances are that everyone else is too.

8 **Produce an answer in the correct format**

The examiner will state in the requirements the format in which the question should be answered, for example in a report or memorandum.

9 **Follow the examiner's instructions**

You will annoy the examiner if you ignore him or her. The examiner will state whether he or she wishes you to 'discuss', 'comment', 'evaluate' or 'recommend'.

10 **Present a tidy paper**

Students are penalised for poor presentation and so you should make sure that you write legibly, label diagrams clearly and lay out your work neatly. Markers of scripts each have hundreds of papers to mark; a badly written scrawl is unlikely to receive the same attention as a neat and well laid out paper.

11 **Stay until the end of the exam**

Use any spare time checking and rechecking your script.

12 **Don't worry if you feel you have performed badly in the exam**

It is more than likely that the other candidates will have found the exam difficult too. Don't forget that there is a competitive element in these exams. As soon as you get up to leave the exam hall, forget that exam and think about the next – or, if it is the last one, celebrate!

13 **Don't discuss an exam with other candidates**

This is particularly the case if you still have other exams to sit. Even if you have finished, you should put it out of your mind until the day of the results. Forget about exams and relax!

The Examination Paper

Here is some advice from the CIM.

There are two basic question types:

1 **The mini case or scenario or article**

Part A is a mini case, scenario or article, with compulsory questions. This represents half of the paper, and students are required to make marketing decisions based on the information given. Spend time evaluating the material given in the case, but do not rewrite this for the examiners. This is a compulsory part of the paper designed to evaluate practical marketing skills. Make sure you allocate enough time to it, but do not take time from the other half of the paper.

2 The straightforward exam question

You are expected to make a choice from a number of questions. There is some skill necessary in selecting the questions which you are best prepared to answer. Read the questions through carefully before making your choice. Think about how you will tackle the question. Check you are answering the question in the context it has been set, then make a rough plan before you start writing. Remember that examiners are interested in quality answers.

Common Mistakes

- **Not answering the question set**

  The examiners are looking for both **relevant content** and its application in an **appropriate context**. You must be able to work flexibly with the material you have studied, answering different questions in different ways, even though the fundamental theory remains the same. Make sure that you answer all parts of the question.

- **Presentation and style**

  Both of these essential business skills are of great importance to a marketing practitioner. The examiners expect work to be presented in a well-written, professional manner. 'Report' style, using sub-headings and indented numbering for points is not only acceptable, but looks much more commercially credible than academic essays. This approach allows you to break the work up, highlight the key points, and structure your answer in a logical way. Take care with your grammar and use of language; small errors can change the sense considerably.

- **Timing**

  The scarce resource in an examination is time. You must control the allocation of this resource carefully. Read the instructions to the paper carefully, and identify what has to be done and how the marks are allocated. Spread your time proportionately to the mark allocation, ie. If the mini case = 50% of marks, allocate 50% of your time to it. Allow a few minutes at the end to read through your work.

  It is no good only completing two questions when you should have done three. It is so much harder for you to pass on just two questions. Have a clock or watch with you and be ruthless in your timekeeping. If you find you are spending too long on an answer, you are probably not answering the question specifically enough.

- **Theory without application**

  The examiners expect relevant theory to be illustrated with practical examples and illustrations. These can be drawn from your own marketing experience, or observations, or your reading. A theory paper without evidence of practical appreciation is unlikely to be successful.

APPROACHING MINI-CASES

What is a mini-case?

The mini-case in the examination is a description of an organisation at a moment in time. You first see it in the examination room and so you have 80 minutes to read, understand, analyse and answer the mini-case.

The mini-case (Part A of the paper) carries 50% of the available marks in the examination.

As mini-cases are fundamental to your exam success, you should be absolutely clear about what mini-cases are, the CIM's purpose in using them, and what the examiner seeks; then, in context, you must consider how best they should be tackled.

The purpose of the mini-case

The examiner requires students to demonstrate not only their knowledge of the fundamentals of marketing, but also their ability to use that knowledge in a commercially credible way in the context of a 'real' business scenario.

The examiner's requirements

The examiner is the 'consumer' of your examination script. You should remember first and foremost that a paper is needed which makes his or her life easy. That means that the script should be well laid out, with plenty of white space and neat readable writing. All the basic rules of examination technique discussed earlier must be applied, but because communication skills are fundamental to the marketer, the ability to communicate clearly is particularly important.

An approach to mini-cases

Mini-cases are easy once you have mastered the basic techniques. The key to success lies in adopting a logical sequence of steps which, with practice, you will master. You must enter the exam room with the process as second nature, so you can concentrate your attention on the marketing issues which face you.

Students who are at first apprehensive when faced with a mini-case often come to find them much more stimulating and rewarding than traditional examination questions. There is the added security of knowing that there is no single correct answer to a case study.

Suggested mini-case method

You have about 80 minutes in total.

Stage		*Minutes*
1	Read the mini-case and questions set on it very quickly.	2
2	Read the questions and case again, but carefully. Make brief notes of significant material. Determine key issues in relation to the questions etc.	5
3	Put the case on one side and turn to your notes. What do they contain? A clear picture of the situation? Go back if necessary and concentrate on getting a grip on the scenario outlined.	4
4	Prepare an answer structure plan for question (a) following exactly the structure suggested in the question, highlighting your decisions supported by case data and theory if appropriate. Follow the process outlined for question (b), etc.	3
5	Prepare a timeplan for each part of the question, according to the marks allocated.	1
6	Write your answer	60
7	Read through and correct errors, improve presentation	5
		80

A good answer will be a document on which a competent manager can take action.

Notes

(a) It is not seriously suggested that you can allocate your time quite so rigorously! The purpose of showing detailed timings is to demonstrate the need to move with purpose and control through each stage of the process.

(b) Take time to get the facts into your short term memory. Making decisions is easier once the facts are in your head.

(c) Establish a clear plan and you will find that writing the answers is straightforward.

(d) Some candidates will be writing answers within five minutes. The better candidates will ignore them and concentrate on planning. This is not easy to do, but management of your examination technique is the key to your personal success.

(e) Presentation is crucial. Your answer should be written as a final draft that would go to typing. If the typist could understand every word and replicate the layout, then the examiner will be delighted and it will be marked highly.

Handling an unseen mini-case or caselet in the examination

The following extract is taken from the Chartered Institute of Marketing's Tutor's/Student Guide to the treatment of mini-cases.

Tutors'/Student Guide to the treatment of mini-cases

'It needs to be stated unequivocally that the type of extremely short case (popularly called the mini-case) set in the examinations for Certificate and Diploma subjects cannot be treated in exactly the same way as a long case study issued in advance. If it could there would be little point of going to all the trouble of writing an in-depth case study.

'Far too many students adopt a maxi-case approach using a detailed marketing audit outline which is largely inappropriate to a case consisting only of two or three paragraphs. Others use the SWOT analysis and simply re-write the case under the four headings of strengths, weaknesses, opportunities and threats.

'Some students even go so far as to totally ignore the specific questions set and present a standard maxi-case analysis outline including environmental reviews through to contingency plans.

'The "mini-case" is not really a case at all, it is merely an outline of a given situation, a scenario. Its purpose is to test whether examinees can apply their knowledge of marketing theory and techniques to the company or organisation and the operating environment described in the scenario. For example answers advocating retail audits as part of the marketing information system for a small industrial goods manufacturer demonstrate a lack of practical awareness. Such answers confirm that the examinee has learned a given MIS outline by rote and simply regurgitated this in complete disregard of the scenario. Such an approach would be disastrous in the real world and examinees adopting this approach cannot be passed, ie gain the confidence of the Institute as professional marketing practitioners. The correct approach to the scenario is a mental review of the area covered by the question and the *selection* by the examinee of those particular parts of knowledge or techniques which apply to the case. This implies a rejection of those parts of the student's knowledge which clearly do not apply to the scenario.

'All scenarios are based upon real world companies and situations and are written with a fuller knowledge of how that organisation actually operates in its planning environments. Often the organisation described in the scenario will not be a giant fast moving consumer goods manufacturing and marketing company since this would facilitate mindless regurgitation of textbook outlines and be counter to the intention of this section of the examination.

'More often the scenarios will involve innovative medium sized firms which comprise the vast majority of UK companies and which might lack the resources often assumed by the textbook approach. These firms do have to market within these constraints however and are just as much concerned with marketing communications, marketing planning and control and indeed (proportionately) in international marketing, particularly the Common Market, as are larger enterprises.

'However, as marketing applications develop and expand and as changes take root, the Institute (through its examiners) will wish to test students' knowledge and awareness of these changes and their implication with regard to marketing practice. For example in the public sector increasing attention is being paid to the marketing of leisure services and the concept of "asset marketing" where the "product" is to a greater extent fixed and therefore the option of product as a variable in the marketing mix is somewhat more constrained.

'Tutors and students are referred to Examiners' Reports which repeatedly complain of inappropriateness of answer detail which demonstrates a real lack of *practical* marketing grasp and confirms that a leaned by rote textbook regurgitation is being used. Examples would include:

- The recommendation of national TV advertising for a small industrial company with a local market
- The overnight installation of a marketing department comprising Marketing Director, Marketing Manager, Advertising Manager, Distribution Manager, Sales Manager, etc into what has been described as a very small company
- The inclusion of packaging, branded packs, on-pack offers, etc, in the marketing mix recommendations for a service

'It has to be borne in mind that the award of the Diploma is in a very real sense the granting of a licence to practice marketing and certainly an endorsement of the candidate's practical as well as theoretical grasps of marketing. In these circumstances such treatments of the mini-case as described above cannot be passed and give rise to some concern that perhaps the teaching/learning approach to mini-cases has not been sufficiently differentiated from that recommended for maxi-cases.

'Tutors/distance-learning students are recommended to work on previously set mini-cases and questions and review results against published specimen answers. They are also advised to use course-members' companies/organisations as examples in the constraints/limitations of marketing techniques and how they might need to be modified.

'Students are also advised to answer the specified questions set and if for example a question was on objectives, then undue reference to market analysis and strategies would be treated as extraneous.'

THE EXAM PAPER

Format of the exam

	Number of marks
Part A: one compulsory mini-case	50
Part B: two questions from four (equal marks)	50
	100

Time allowed: 3 hours

Analysis of past papers

June 2004

Part A (compulsory question worth 50 marks)

1 You are marketing consultant to Beijing Olympic Organising Committee for 2006 Olympic Games.

(a) Macro-environmental influences on marketing plan
(b) Role of brand and its importance in attracting sponsorship
(c) Service quality and extended marketing mix

Part B (two questions 25 marks each)

2 Marketing plan for a small business looking for funds
3 Marketing audit, including macro-environmental factors, segmentation, targeting and positioning
4 Market penetration strategy, including pricing, in a recessionary environment
5 Reviving and repositioning a consumer product

This paper forms the Test Paper at the end of this Kit.

December 2003

Part A (compulsory question worth 50 marks)

1 You are marketing consultant to a global chain of coffee shops.

(a) Challenges in marketing environment and the role of marketing information
(b) Expansion opportunities
(c) Extended marketing mix for growth strategies

Part B (two questions 25 marks each)

2 Marketing budget for FMCG brand
3 Corporate and product branding, marketing communications mix and pricing
4 Marketing mix and activities to maintain stakeholder relationships
5 Role of innovation and NPD

Examiner's comments: summary

The first exams in the new syllabus. Overall, strengths included: use of appropriate examples and application to case study; layout and presentation; use of models; application of theory to case study and examples; time management. Weaknesses included: misinterpretation of the question requirements (a particular problem with question 1); some candidates had difficulties analysing and understanding the question; reproduction of lecture material; reluctance to comply with the precise requirements of the question; including everything on a subject even if not relevant; lack of practical examples.

Specimen Paper 2003

Part A (Compulsory question with 50 marks)

1 You are a marketing consultant to a bicycle manufacturer

(a) Components of the marketing plan
(b) Marketing environment. Market information
(c) Growth strategies
(d) Marketing mix decisions

Part B (two questions from four, 25 marks each)

2 Gap analysis and segmentation
3 Innovation, new product development and branding
4 Pricing strategy: role of forecasting, environmental factors
5 Service quality and internal marketing

Syllabus – Stage 2, Marketing Planning

Aim

The Marketing Planning module provides the essential knowledge and understanding for Stage 2 in the creation and use of operational marketing plans and the marketing process. It aims to provide participants with an understanding of the differences in the internal organisational and external contexts within which operational marketing planning and marketing are carried out and the different models of marketing used to meet these contingencies. The module aims in particular to ensure that the knowledge and understanding can be applied in the practical construction of appropriate and realistic marketing plans.

Related statements of practice

Bc.2 Create competitive operational marketing plans.
Cc.1 Create and build competitive brands.
Cc.2 Manage competitive brands.
Ec.1 Prepare a business case for a product/service and progress it to market.
Ec.2 Manage and maintain competitive produces/services or portfolio.
Fc.1 Create competitive and sustainable pricing policies.
Fc.2 Manage the implementation and monitor the effectiveness of pricing policies.
Gc.1 Establish and develop effective support for channels to market.
Kc.1 Define measurements appropriate to the plan or business case and ensure they are undertaken.
Kc.2 Evaluate activities and identify improvements using measurement data.

Learning outcomes

Participants will be able to:

- Explain the role of the marketing plan within the context of the organisation's strategy and culture and the broader marketing environment (ethics, social responsibility, legal frameworks, sustainability).
- Conduct a marketing audit considering appropriate internal and external factors.
- Develop marketing objectives and plans at an operational level appropriate to the internal and external environment.
- Develop the role of branding and positioning within the marketing plan.
- Integrate marketing mix tools to achieve effective implementation of plans.
- Select an appropriate co-ordinated marketing mix incorporating appropriate stakeholder relationships for a particular marketing context.
- Set and justify budgets for marketing plans and mix decisions.
- Define and use appropriate measurements to evaluate the effectiveness of marketing plans and activities.
- Make recommendations for changes and innovations to marketing processes based on an understanding of the organisational context and an evaluation of past marketing activities.

Knowledge and skill requirements – Syllabus content

Element 1: The marketing plan in its organisational and wider marketing context (15%)	
1.1	Describe the roles of marketing and the nature of relationships with other functions in organisations operating in a range of different industries and contexts.
1.2	Explain the synergistic planning process – analysis, planning, implementation and control.
1.3	List and describe the components of the marketing plan.
1.4	Evaluate the role of the marketing plan in relation to the organisation's philosophy or business definition.
1.5	Assess the potential impact of wider macro-environmental forces relating to the role of culture, ethical approach, social responsibility, legal frameworks and sustainability.

Element 2: Marketing planning and budgeting (20%)	
2.1	Explain the constituents of the macro environmental and micro environmental marketing audit.
2.2	Assess the external marketing environment for an organisation through a PESTEL audit.
2.3	Assess the internal marketing environment for an organisation through an internal audit.
2.4	Critically appraise processes and techniques used for auditing the marketing environments.
2.5	Explain the role of marketing information and research in conducting and analysing the marketing audit.
2.6	Evaluate the relationship between corporate objectives, business objectives and marketing objectives at an operational level.
2.7	Explain the concept of the planning gap and its impact on operational decisions.
2.8	Determine segmentation, targeting and positioning within the marketing plan.
2.9	Determine and evaluate marketing budgets for mix decisions included in the marketing plan.
2.10	Describe methods for evaluating and controlling the marketing plan.

Element 3: The extended marketing mix and related tools (50%)

3.1	Explain the role of strategy development in relation to developing market share and growth.
3.2	Explain how strategy formulation and decisions relating to the selection of markets impact at an operational level on the planning and implementation of an integrated marketing mix.
3.3	Explain the role of branding and its impact on the marketing mix decisions.
3.4	Describe the methods for maintaining and managing the brand.
3.5	Explain how a product or service portfolio is developed to achieve marketing objectives.
3.6	Explain the new product development process (including innovative, replacement, relaunched and imitative products) and the role of innovation.
3.7	Explain pricing frameworks available to, and used by, organisations for decision-making.
3.8	Describe how pricing is developed as an integrated part of the marketing mix.
3.9	Determine the channels of distribution and logistics to be used by an organisation and develop a plan for channel support.
3.10	Explain how the marketing communications mix is coordinated with the marketing mix as part of a marketing plan.
3.11	Explain the importance of customer relationships to the organisation and how they can be developed and supported by the marketing mix.
3.12	Describe how a plan is developed for the human element of the service encounter, including staff at different levels of the organisation.
3.13	Explain how the physical evidence element of the integrated marketing mix is developed.
3.14	Explain how a plan covering the process or the systems of delivery for a service is developed.

Element 4: Marketing in different contexts (15%)

4.1	Explain how marketing plans and activities vary in organisations that operate in an international context and develop an appropriate marketing mix.
4.2	Develop a marketing plan and select an appropriate marketing mix for an organisation operating in any context such as FMCG, business-to-business (supply chain), large or capital project-based, services, voluntary and not-for-profit, sales support (eg. SMEs).
4.3	Explain how marketing plans and activities vary in organisations that operate in a virtual marketplace and develop an appropriate marketing mix.
4.4	Determine an effective extended marketing mix in relation to design and delivery of service encounters (SERVQUAL).

Question bank

1 Tutorial question: Marketing and corporate planning

How does corporate planning differ from marketing planning?

Guidance note

Outline the stages of the corporate planning process and indicate how marketing contributes at each stage.

2 Marketing and corporate strategy 40 mins

What are the characteristics of strategic decisions at the corporate and marketing level, and how can a strategic perspective at the marketing level be developed? **(25 marks)**

3 Tutorial question: The synergistic planning process and components of the marketing plan

Define the marketing planning process, giving examples to illustrate the differences between each stage.

Guidance notes

In our solution we have identified three main stages of the process.

(a) Analysis of markets and trading environment opportunities

(b) Planning: Determination of core markets; competitive edge; differential advantage, statement of goals and desired brand positioning

(c) Determination of marketing programmes for implementation and control

4 Marketing planning and corporate mission/ philosophy 40 mins

What relationships does marketing planning have with corporate planning? Give practical examples of how marketing planning can contribute to corporate planning and the corporate mission. **(25 marks)**

5 Impacts of macro-environmental forces 40 mins

You are a freelance journalist working for the CIM *Marketing Business* magazine. You have been asked to write an article which discusses the growing number of constraints on marketing decisions. Write a summary of the proposed article, illustrating it with company examples. You should cover legal/regulatory, voluntary and ethics/social responsibility constraints.

(25 marks)

6 Constituents of macro/micro environmental audits

40 mins

Explain the constituents of the macro environmental and micro environmental marketing audit to the Board of an international hotel chain and how it can be developed into a SWOT analysis.

(25 marks)

7 Tutorial question: Assessing the external marketing environment

What are the environmental forces affecting marketing? Give examples of how these forces operate in a marketing context.

8 Tutorial question: Assessing internal capabilities

How would you assess an organisation's internal capabilities? Why are these capabilities important?

9 Critical appraisal of auditing techniques 40 mins

Critically appraise processes and techniques used for auditing the marketing environments.

(25 marks)

10 Role of information and research in auditing 40 mins

You have recently been appointed as a marketing manager for a marketing consultancy firm, and you have been asked to conduct a review of operations in your firm with a view to attracting new clients. In this context you have been asked to produce a brief report that gives details of:

(a) Possible sources of data that you will refer to in your review of operations. Internal and external sources should be identified.

(b) What types of information each data source will provide. Give specific examples of how the data will be used in the review. (Equal marks for (a) and (b))

(25 marks)

11 Relationships between corporate, business and marketing objectives 40 mins

What are the relationships between corporate, business and marketing objectives?

(25 marks)

12 Relationship management and the marketing mix (12/03) 40 mins

You are the marketing manager for a not-for-profit service organisation of your choice.

(a) Explain the importance of developing and maintaining relationships with your stakeholders. (10 marks)

(b) Recommend an appropriate extended marketing mix for your organisation to ensure that relationships are developed and managed. (10 marks)

(c) Justify how the marketing activities for this organisation may vary in an international context. (5 marks)

(25 marks)

13 The planning gap and its operational implications 40 mins

Explain the planning gap and its impact on operational decisions. **(25 marks)**

14 Gap analysis (Specimen paper) 40 mins

Your soft drinks manufacturing company has conducted a gap analysis.

(a) Explain the concept of 'gap analysis' as used in marketing planning. (5 marks)

(b) With reference to appropriate theory, recommend how such a 'gap' could be filled by an organisation. (5 marks)

(c) The organisation has realised that it needs to identify more domestic and international segments to target when planning its market development strategy. Evaluate the concepts of segmentation and targeting, including the benefits of segmentation. (10 marks)

(d) Recommend how the following variables for segmentation could be used for drinks products:

(i) Lifestyle
(ii) Benefits sought (5 marks)

(25 marks)

15 Segmentation, targeting and positioning strategies 40 mins

A publishing company specialising in marketing texts wants to publish a book made up of cases of marketing operations excellence. You have been approached to write a case history which illustrates excellence in the practice of market segmentation, targeting and positioning. Select an example of your choice and provide an outline case history for the attention of the editor.

(25 marks)

16 Determining and evaluating marketing budgets

40 mins

Determine and evaluate marketing budgets for mix decisions included in the marketing plan.

(25 marks)

17 Evaluating and controlling the marketing plan

40 mins

Describe methods for evaluating and controlling the marketing plan.

(25 marks)

18 Marketing budgeting (12/03)

40 mins

You have been assigned to manage an FMCG (fast moving consumer good) brand and you are rather concerned about the current marketing budgets, which have been set.

(a) Explain what factors influence the marketing budget for such a brand. (9 marks)

(b) Explain and evaluate the different approaches for setting the marketing budget for the mix decisions included in the marketing plan. (8 marks)

(c) Recommend methods for evaluating and controlling the marketing plan for this FMCG brand. (8 marks)

(25 marks)

19 Strategy development and market share growth

40 mins

You are the commercial director of a book publisher that specialises in producing car repair manuals. You have been asked by the Board of Directors to consider new strategies for growing the business. Produce a report for the Board which identifies options for growth in the short and medium term, and which sets out a process by which these options might be evaluated.

(25 marks)

20 Market selection's impact on the integrated mix

Show how strategy formulation and decisions relating to the selection of markets impact at an operational level on the planning and implementation of an integrated marketing mix.

(25 marks)

21 Tutorial question: The extended marketing mix

In what ways and for what purposes can the traditional marketing mix of the 4Ps be extended?

22 Branding: its impact on the marketing mix 40 mins

Branding is an important component of any organisation's marketing strategy. Provide the notes for a local CIM branch presentation which explains what is meant by brand positioning, and provides an example of excellent brand positioning in each of the consumer goods, service and not-for-profit sectors. You should also provide your audience with suggested follow-up reading sources. **(25 marks)**

23 Managing the brand 40 mins

A major supermarket chain is planning to enter the financial services market. Write a report identifying the key elements of a brand strategy and the criteria that should be used by the retailer in making a decision on whether to stretch its current brand name into this new market. Describe methods for maintaining and managing the brand. **(25 marks)**

24 Branding strategies and the communications mix (12/03) 40 mins

Acting as an advisor to the marketing director of a retail bank, write a report which:

(a) Assesses the role of branding at both the product and corporate level. (8 marks)

(b) Recommends the use of the marketing communications mix in developing a new product branding strategy. (9 marks)

(c) Explains how pricing is developed as an integrated part of the extended marketing mix. (8 marks)

(25 marks)

25 Product/Service portfolio's role in achieving marketing objectives 40 mins

Describe how a product or service portfolio is developed to achieve marketing objectives. **(25 marks)**

26 The new product development process 40 mins

Explain the new product development process and the role of innovation (including degrees of innovation). **(25 marks)**

27 New product development: innovation and branding (Specimen Paper) 40 mins

Your organisation has developed a new range of cosmetic products to be targeted at the 'grey' market.

(a) Explain and justify the role of innovation within organisations. (5 marks)

(b) Critically evaluate reactive and proactive approaches to new product development. (5 marks)

(c) Explain the following terms and offer examples for cosmetic products:

(i) Replacement products
(ii) Relaunched products
(iii) Imitative products (10 marks)

(d) Explain the role of branding in relation to the development of new products and its impact on marketing mix decisions. (5 marks)

(25 marks)

28 International new product development and innovation (12/03) 40 mins

Your organisation is hoping to develop a new range of products to be targeted at an international market of your choice. Using examples:

(a) Explain the role of innovation within organisations (10 marks)
(b) Propose and justify an approach to new product development (15 marks)

(25 marks)

29 Pricing frameworks 40 mins

Explain frameworks available to, and used by, organisations for making pricing decisions. Illustrate your answer with reference to an organisation of your choice **(25 marks)**

30 Pricing and the integrated marketing mix 40 mins

You are developing a marketing plan to launch a new restaurant in a city centre. You have the task of determining the pricing policy for the restaurant. Write the section of the marketing plan which outlines the factors you need to take into consideration when setting the price and your preferred pricing approach. **(25 marks)**

31 Price planning (Specimen paper) 40 mins

You are the marketing manager of a low cost air travel organisation and you are currently developing the marketing plan for next year.

(a) Recommend both qualitative and quantitative techniques for forecasting which could be used when preparing the marketing plan. (5 marks)

(b) Identify and justify the main external factors from the macro- and micro-environment affecting this organisation's pricing strategy. (10 marks)

(c) Critically evaluate the following approaches that this organisation will need to consider when setting its pricing strategy:

(i) Marginal analysis

(ii) Breakeven analysis (10 marks)

(25 marks)

32 Distribution channels and support 40 mins

As the marketing operations manager of a tour operations business that targets package holidays at the 55 and over age group, you have been asked by your marketing director to review your distribution strategy.

(a) Outline the various channels of distribution available. (9 marks)

(b) Identify a set of criteria for their evaluation. (9 marks)

(c) Recommend an appropriate strategy for your target market. (7 marks)

(25 marks)

33 Tutorial question: Co-ordinating the communications and marketing mixes 40 mins

Explain how the marketing communications mix is co-ordinated with the marketing mix as part of a marketing plan. **(25 marks)**

34 Customer relations: the contribution of the marketing mix 40 mins

As the relationship marketing manager at an airline of your choice, you have been given the task of identifying which aspects of the extended relationship marketing mix may be particularly effective in maintaining high customer retention rates for the company. In a report to the marketing director, illustrate how each element of the mix may be relevant to your airline in its efforts to keep its customers. **(25 marks)**

35 Planning the service encounter 40 mins

You are employed as a marketing manager by a service organisation that supplies cleaning products and services to commercial premises. Your Managing Director has asked you to prepare a presentation for junior marketing recruits explaining the characteristics of services marketing and how they apply to your organisation. Draft a document which details the areas you will cover in your presentation. **(25 marks)**

36 Physical evidence in the integrated marketing mix 40 mins

Explain how the physical evidence element of the integrated and extended marketing mix is developed. **(25 marks)**

37 Planning the service process/delivery 40 mins

Explain how a plan covering the process or the systems of delivery for a service is developed. **(25 marks)**

38 Tutorial question: non-business marketing

Use examples which explore charity, non-profit and non-business marketing and illustrate the marketing strategies adopted by organisations operating in these areas.

Guidance note

Non-business marketing covers the other two, but we have written about all three terms.

39 International context's impact on marketing strategy and mix 40 mins

Your managing director is about to attend a conference where the theme is global competitiveness. As a result, she has asked you to prepare a briefing paper evaluating the affect of globalisation on the development of an organisation's marketing strategy. **(25 marks)**

40 Marketing planning context: business-to-business 40 mins

As a consultant who specialises in advising industrial marketers, you have been approached to write a case history that illustrates excellence in the practice of business-to-business marketing. Select an example of your choice and provide an outline case history, which should include details of organisational buyer behaviour in the target market, and the marketing mix employed to meet the specified objectives of the business. **(25 marks)**

41 Marketing planning context: not-for-profit 40 mins

A publishing company specialising in marketing texts wants to publish a book made up of cases of marketing operations excellence. You have been approached to write a case history which illustrates excellence in the practice of not-for-profit marketing. Select an example of your choice and provide an outline case history for the attention of the editor. Your case should at least include details on market analysis, market segmentation and the marketing mix. **(25 marks)**

42 Planning and the mix in a virtual marketplace (1)

40 mins

You are an owner of a small agency specialising in Internet site development. Prepare a direct marketing leaflet outlining the possible marketing uses of the Internet and how the Internet is changing managers' thinking on marketing strategy and the marketing mix. **(25 marks)**

43 Planning and the mix in a virtual marketplace (2)

40 mins

In the business-to-business sector, discuss the areas of an organisation's marketing strategy that are likely to be affected by the development of the Internet and related e-commerce capabilities. **(20 marks)**

44 Service encounters and the extended mix (SERVQUAL)

40 mins

Determine an effective extended marketing mix in relation to design and delivery of service encounters. **(25 marks)**

45 Service quality (Specimen paper) 40 mins

The marketing manager of your university is worried about service quality.

(a) Explain the criteria that affect student's or customers' perceptions of service quality. (10 marks)

(b) Discuss the role of internal marketing and explain why it is important for services marketing. (10 marks)

(c) Recommend how the marketing mix for this university might be adapted for full-time international students who wish to attend the university. (5 marks)

(25 marks)

DO YOU KNOW? - MINI-CASES

- If you are in any doubt as to how you should tackle a mini-case go back to page (xiii)
- The mini-case is compulsory and comprises 50% of the marks. Ignore it at your peril.
- Consequently, all the mini-cases given below should be attempted.

46 The Lens Shop Ltd 80 mins

The Lens Shop Ltd (TLS) is a camera retailer based in the UK. It currently has 15 outlets based in the major centres of population.

There are two types of retailers selling cameras in the UK. On the one hand stores that sell a limited range of cameras amongst a range of other electrical and domestic appliances. These are mainly large department stores and electrical retailers that sell computers, hi-fi's, televisions and cameras. Then there are specialist camera stores that only sell photographic products. TLS is one of major retailers in this more specialist camera sector.

TLS sells the majority of the leading brands. it also is the largest and most well established outlet for discontinued products, used by all the distributors to clear their shelves of 'old' product lines. These products are discounted heavily by TLS. TLS are able to buy in bulk and as a result can negotiate extra discounts.

All TLS stores are small and are located on less expensive secondary sites in the city centre but away from the main, high rent, shopping centre locations. As the outlets are small they need less stock for display purposes and have very limited stock room space. Management feel that small stores have a better atmosphere, are less formal, hectic, yet friendly.

TLS's main promotional vehicle is a colour catalogue, which is described as '16 great pages of bargains'. This is very much seen as a 'fun' brochure promoting products in a positive light-hearted way by mixing illustrations, technical details and humour. The catalogue is distributed in a number of ways; to people coming into the stores, from racks outside the store, by 'freephone' telephone hotline and via a database of past customers. Media advertising is also used. Typically camera magazines will carry a five-page advertisement which highlights current bargains and often contains a promotional voucher for discounts or free accessories.

Prices are highly competitive, often discounted below recommended retail levels. The customer is provided with a price guarantee that TLS will beat any current local price by £10 for a similar brand of camera. TLS also offer a three year extended warranty at an extremely low price. Additionally, their warranty offers a unique guaranteed buy-back service for customers wishing to upgrade their photographic equipment. Management sees this as a genuine customer service which will hopefully encourage customer loyalty. All goods are subject to a 14-day exchange.

The company also aims to give high levels of customer service. Members of staff have a high degree of product knowledge. Sales assistants are particularly helpful, advising on the best purchases for any given budget. Staff are also happy to demonstrate the equipment. Selections of recent reviews from camera magazines are also available in the store to provide further information to customers.

To maintain required levels of customer service all customers are given a short questionnaire and asked to return them to the managing directors of TLS by freepost. The managing Director reviews all comments relating to customer service, and responds where appropriate.

As the new marketing manager for 'TLS' you have been asked to:

(a) Identify and explain the sources of the organisation's competitive advantage and whether their current position is sustainable. (25 marks)

(b) The managing directors of 'TLS' has heard that internal marketing might be a useful approach to adopt in her business. You have been asked to write a report illustrating how an internal marketing programme could be implemented. This report should also highlight the benefits of such a programme and the potential problems. (25 marks)

(50 marks)

47 The wet shave market 80 mins

Gillette is launching a new wet shave razor system, called Mach 3, onto the global market. This product cost £460 million and took seven years to develop. The company aims to spend around

£215 million launching this product globally of which approximately 10% will be spent in the UK. The main feature of this shaving system is that it has three blades. The key benefit is that it cuts 40% more hair than Gillette's previous shaving system Sensor Excel, and gives an extra-smooth shave. It also exerts less friction making shaving more comfortable. The Mach 3 is forecast to generate 17% category growth over two years, equivalent to selling 1.2 billion blades globally.

Wet shave customers can buy a shaving system or a disposable razor. With shaving systems the customer buys a razor handle which is refillable with blades that they can buy separately. The three main competitors in the wet shave market in the UK have the following market shares:

	Number of users of wet shave razors
	(Millions)
Gillette	9.0
Wilkinson Sword	2.8
Biro Bic	2.6

Note: Biro Bic concentrate on disposable razors.

The UK market is split between 54% on systems and 46% on disposables. 74% of blade and razor purchases (shaving systems and disposables) are made by men for themselves. The male grooming market has grown over the last two years by £50 million. The shaving systems market alone is worth £161 million. This is broken down as follows:

Gillette	£105m	65%
Wilkinson Sword	£32m	20%
Biro Bic	£11m	7%
Other brands, retailers own label	£13m	8%

When Gillette launched Sensor (a new razor system) in 1989 it went on to generate £3.65 billion in worldwide brand sales and sold nearly 400 million razor handles and eight billion blades. At the same time because Sensor was an innovative product Gillette was able to charge a high price for the product. The fact that there was little interchangability of the blades with other systems meant that the customer was restricted to purchasing Gillette blades. Previous launches of new systems have typically been priced 15% higher than the most expensive product available. The Mach 3 will be around 35% more expensive. Replacement blades will cost £1.12 each.

The aim with the Mach 3 is to capture new users into the Gillette franchise, to encourage millions of current Gillette users to trade up to the new system, and to move current users of disposables into the refillable shaving systems sector.

Advertising for the Mach 3 will be identical globally. Television advertisements will use the same film from Asia to Europe, with only minor modifications to the script. The aim of the campaign will be to steal customers from its competitors, (Wilkinson Sword in particular, as it is the only major competitor in the systems market) and to aggressively grow the sector. Prior to the launch of the Mach 3 Gillette ran a television advertising campaign with the aim of persuading customers to move from disposable razors to the Gillette system.

This mini-case study has been prepared from secondary sources.

(a) As a marketing manager for Wilkinson Sword write a briefing paper to your marketing director explaining why Gillette continue to spend large amounts of money on new product development and promotion. (25 marks)

(b) Outline and evaluate the strategic options that are available to Wilkinson Sword in this market. (25 marks)

(50 marks)

48 Easyjet 80 mins

EasyJet is a low fare airline that operates a number of routes within the European market. Stelios Haji-Ioannou, the owner of Easyjet, founded the airline based on the belief that reduced prices would lead to more people flying. EasyJet's prices are low, for instance a return flight from Luton to Amsterdam costs between £70 to £130. Flights, with an airline offering full customer service package, could cost around £315 upwards.

The organisation's main base is at Luton airport from where flights to European destinations such as Amsterdam, Geneva, Nice, Barcelona, Palma and Athens are available. The airline also flies UK domestic routes from Luton to Edinburgh, Glasgow, Belfast and Liverpool. Liverpool allows the company to gain access into the lucrative North of England market and is becoming a growing centre of activity for EasyJet. Flights can now be taken from Liverpool to Nice, Amsterdam and Belfast.

Luton airport is around 30 minutes by road from north London and only 15 minutes from London's main orbital motorway, the M25. The airport is ten minutes away from Luton railway from where a 27-minute rail connection to London is available. A shuttle bus to the station is available every 10 minutes. A return rail journey for EasyJet passengers is available at around £8 (sterling). Liverpool airport also has good motorway connections.

Connecting flights are not part of EasyJet's product offering. The airline merely carries passengers to and from single destinations. This allows the airline to eliminate costly ticketing processes as well as intermediaries, such as travel agents. The company operates a paperless office policy and non-ticket flights. Simply by ringing the company's telephone number or using the company's Internet site customers can book a seat immediately by credit card. In autumn 1998, 40% of bookings for a major promotion in *The Times* newspaper were via the Internet. Although a confirmation of the booking will be sent if requested, customers only have to produce identification at the airport and quote the booking reference number to be given a boarding pass for their flight.

EasyJet flights are 'free seating'. Passengers are not allocated a specific seat when they check-in, instead they are given a boarding card that carries a priority number. The first person to check-in gets boarding card No.1, the next passenger, boarding card No. 2 and so on. Customers are then asked to board according to the order in which they checked-in occupying whichever seat they wish. The result is that passengers board the plane faster and tend to sit down faster than is the case when they have to search for an allocated seat, as is the situation in the more traditional airline operations. The faster passengers board an aircraft the quicker the plane can take off and the less time it spends on the tarmac. This results in reduced airport fees.

The fact that EasyJet is not hindered by connections to other flights allows it to operate out of cheaper secondary airports such as Luton and Liverpool, rather than larger airports like Heathrow or Manchester. EasyJet also exploits the lack of competition for time slots at Luton and Liverpool to keep the length of time its aircraft are on the tarmac to a minimum. EasyJet's aircraft are therefore airborne longer, creating more hours of revenue earning per aircraft, than companies operating out of larger and busier airports.

Premium priced airlines offer business class seats, which take up more room on an aircraft, and will normally operate with 109 seats on a Boeing 737-300. These airlines also require additional cabin crew in order to provide the level of service business class passengers demand. EasyJet operates without offering business class seats, which allows it to create 148 passenger places on a Boeing 737-300. Catering consists of a trolley from which cabin staff will sell drinks and a limited range of snacks to passengers. The only 'freebie' on the flight is a copy of the airlines in-flight magazine called 'Easy Rider', which is printed on recycled paper. Cabin staff look more casual in orange polo shirts and black jeans than traditional airlines and have a more relaxed attitude. They appear equally safety conscious as staff on other airlines.

EasyJet's telephone number is promoted widely. The company's telephone number, in bright orange, dominates the sides of the aircraft, where it has almost become part of the EasyJet corporate image. The organisation's approach to advertising has been described as "a guerrilla promotional approach", distinguished by attacks on the airline establishment and a series of PR stunts. Press and magazine advertising is widespread. Sales promotional activity has included joint promotions in national UK newspapers such as *The Times* and *The Independent.* The airline has also been the focus of a documentary series on UK television. The owner, Haji-Ioannou, has been featured in many business articles in the press, particularly for his high profile campaign against British Airways launch of its own low cost airline operation called 'GO'.

EasyJet has also started targeting companies that wish to keep travel budgets under control. EasyJet emphasises that they do not offer a loyalty scheme where business customers can build up loyalty points and gain free flights. The suggestion is that although executives may like this perk the executive's company could be saving hundreds of pounds per trip by sending their staff on EasyJet flights.

The organisation's latest plan is to develop a family of companies with a common theme, beginning with the launch of a chain of cybercafes. Although the branding for this venture has yet to be decided, the working title is 'EasyCafé'. The company still has to make decisions, such as whether EasyJet's trademark bright orange colour is made a prominent feature of the cafés. Tony Anderson, who will oversee this new development, is quoted as saying that with these cafés 'We are targeting Joe Public, not the middle classes.'

This mini-case study has been prepared from secondary sources.

(a) As a consultant you have been asked, as an initial step, to identify the core capabilities of EasyJet that can be used to grow the family of companies that Haji-Ioannou envisages. In particular you have been asked to use the value chain as part of this analysis. (25 marks)

(b) EasyJet have decided to develop a group of companies beginning with the cybercafé concept. You have been asked to provide advice on issues that need to be considered when making decisions on the organisation's branding strategy, for the group as a whole and for the 'Easycafé' concept in particular. (25 marks)

(50 marks)

49 Weetabix 80 mins

The breakfast cereal market in the UK is estimated to be worth around £1 billion a year and has been growing at around 2%-3% a year in terms of value. Consumers in the UK eat 17lbs of breakfast cereal a year, more than in any other country in the world. The nearest rivals are consumers in the United States of America who eat 10lbs a year. This sector of the UK market is highly competitive with both Kellogg's and Nestlé - two of the world's biggest food companies - being actively involved ('Cereal Partners' being Nestlé's joint venture with General Mills). The market share breakdown is shown in Table 1.

Table 1: Share of the UK breakfast cereal market by company

Company	Market Share %
Kellogg's	43.5
Weetabix	15.2
Cereal Partners	12.0
Others	29.3

Source: Marketing

As well as having major global players active in market, retailer own label brands have been growing in strength. In the last three years alone retailers' own label brands have increased their share of the market from 22% to 33%.

Weetabix is a medium-sized company employing 2,000 people in the UK. Yet, against this market background in the year ending February 1999 Weetabix's turnover had risen 12% from £274 million to £308 million. Pre-tax profits had grown 23% to £52 million from £42 million. In fact Weetabix has shown steady growth for a number of years. Back in 1982 Weetabix have a turnover of just £55 million with profits of just over £1 million.

Weetabix (the product) was developed in Australia around 1900. It is a sugarless flaked wheat biscuit with a consistency that turns into a soft pulp once milk is poured over it. When eaten this biscuit delivers nourishment in the form of a strong mix of complex carbohydrates. Due to its consistency it can be eaten by any age group. In particular, it is ideal for weaning babies. It is currently the number two brand in the UK breakfast cereal market (see Table 2). Unlike the other leading brands, no other retailer or manufacturer has managed to launch successfully a 'me-too' product. The majority of own label flaked wheat biscuits are actually manufactured by Weetabix.

Weetabix (the company) has six major products which are: Weetabix (plus a variation, Frutibix), Alpen, Crunchy Bran, Weetos, Ready Brek and Advantage. This gives the company some advantages in concentrating investment and management effort over a small range of products. Some observers see this situation arising because Weetabix is poor at innovation and see the company as having a conservative new product development policy. This is especially noticeable given that the other major players in this market have launched a number of minor variations on their breakfast cereal products in recent years.

Table 2: The UK breakfast cereal market

Position	Brand	1998 Listing (£m)	% Change on Previous Year	Company
1	Kellogg's Corn Flakes	Over 90	-7.8	Kellogg's
2	Weetabix	75-80	0.7	Weetabix
3	Kellogg's Frosties	60-65	-5.9	Kellogg's
4	Nestle Shredded Wheat	45-50	14.2	Cereal Partners
5	Kellogg's Rice Krispies	35-40	-6.2	Kellogg's
6	Kellogg's Crunchy Nut Corn Flakes	35-40	-3.7	Kellogg's
7	Kellogg's Healthwise Bran Flakes	30-35	-5.2	Kellogg's
8	Kellogg's Special K	25-30	0.9	Kellogg's
9	Quaker Sugar Puffs	25-30	8.8	Quaker
10	Kellogg's Optima Fruit 'n' Fibre	25-30	-2.5	Kellogg's

Source: AC Nielsen MEAL

Weetabix does not compete in every segment of the market and does not have multiple products in each category. However, it does tend to dominate the categories where it chooses to compete. For instance, Alpen is the brand leader in muesli, Ready Brek created and still dominates the hot cereal sector and Weetabix leads the wholewheat biscuit category.

Table 3: Advertising spend, cereals

Company	**Advertising spend in £m (April 1998-March 1999)**
Kellogg's	55
Cereal Partners	19
Weetabix	15
Quaker Oats	1.7
Others	2.2
Total	**92.9**

Source: Media Monitoring Services

One of Weetabix's key strengths is its high level of service. The Federation of Wholesale Distributors awarded the company a gold medal for service levels in 1995. Weetabix has a reputation of having products in stock, delivering when they say they will deliver and of offering merchandising and marketing support. This is in an industry where wholesalers are using to being let down on as many as one in ten orders.

At the end of 1998 Kellogg's decided to increase its advertising expenditure by 40%. At the same time it cut its prices on six of its leading brands by 12%. This price war was started in retaliation to the growth of the own label brands - however, it has obvious implications for Weetabix. The chairman of Weetabix said in February 1999 that he was 'concerned that the tactics of our major competitors may harm the whole breakfast cereal sector'.

Trends are also changing in the breakfast cereal market. Fewer consumers are having a sit down breakfast and are instead eating food such as croissants that can be eaten while travelling. A number of manufacturers have developed products to address this market (see Table 4). Kellogg's in particular has been active in this area of product development. Kellogg's Nutri-Grain is a bar high in fibre that the company is branding as a 'morning bar'. This product is now being extended with the addition of Nutri-Grain Twists, containing separate sections of yoghurt and fruit puree that are twisted into the Nutri-Grain bar. Kellogg's is also extending three of its breakfast bar brands into cereal bars. The Kellogg's brands of Frosties, Coco Pops and Smacks are all being launched in a cereal and milk bar format. Cereal and milk bars are bound together with dried milk and are claimed to contain the equivalent amount of milk as in a traditional bowl of breakfast cereal.

Table 4: Estimated manufacturers' shares in the UK cereal bar market in 1997

	£m	%
Kellogg's	14.1	25
Jordan	13.9	25
Mars	11.4	20
Quaker	6.3	11
Other brands	0.8	1.5
Own label	9.8	17.5
Total	**56.2**	**100**

Source: Mintel

This mini-case study has been prepared from secondary sources.

(a) As a consultant, write a report to Weetabix outlining and evaluating the strategic options open to the company in responding to the developing price war initiated by Kellogg's.

(25 marks)

(b) Weetabix has decided to review the company's innovation activities. Prepare a report advising the board of Weetabix on the auditing process necessary to undertake this analysis successfully. (25 marks)

(50 marks)

50 Freeplay energy 80 mins

In the early 1980s Trevor Bayliss, the British inventor, developed the concept of a self-powered radio. Electricity for the radio would be provided by an integral wind-up generator. Bayliss's idea was that this self-powered ratio would allow people in remote villages across Africa to gain access to news and information from around the world. In 1994 the South African based BayGen Power company (later renamed Freeplay Energy) signed an exclusive agreement with Trevor Bayliss to develop and commercialise the product.

Although Trevor Bayliss no longer has an active involvement with Freeplay Energy, the partners who run the company are still driven by the desire to improve the lives of individuals in the developing world. The company's Cape Town factories are co-owned by local charities that represent the disabled, single mothers and former offenders. Around one third of the company's employees are from these disadvantaged groups.

The first commercial version of the wind-up radio was the FPR1 and this was distributed to villages by aid agencies. Very early on, it became apparent that the radio was too heavy, too fragile and more crucially too expensive for its intended market. Villagers appeared to be more willing to spend £2 to £3 a month on batteries, than an initial £29 on a radio that did not require battery replacements. The product however began to develop sales in more affluent markets. In the UK the Design Council awarded the wind-up radio 'Millennium Product', status. One national newspaper went as far as naming it the significant invention of a generation.

Freeplay Energy began to realise that volume sales could be developed by concentrating on the European and North American markets. Sales growth in these markets has allowed Freeplay to invest further in the technology, and as a result develop products that are smaller, lighter, more durable and less expensive. The FPR1 had to be wound for 20 seconds in order to produce 30 minutes of playing time. The FPR2, which Freeplay launched in 1997, weighs less, is more compact and supplies an hour of playing time after being wound for 20 seconds.

In 1999 the company added to the radio range with the launch of a new model, the Freeplay S360. The company also launched the 20/20 flashlight, which contains an integral energy storage unit to generate power for instantaneous or later use.

Currently Freeplay Energy has a £30m turnover and is forecast to produce around 1.2 million units in the year 2000. Around 70% of its sales are in the United States of America and 25% in Europe, with Africa and Middle East making up the balance. The company's promotional budget is around £3m.

Through market research the organisation has identified that the product is positioned differently in the various overseas markets. In Germany the product appeals to the consumers' strong environmental consciousness. In the United States of America and Japan, where there is a strong outdoor culture, the product is bought as a component of tornado or earthquake survival kits. In the UK, the company's biggest market per capita, the general public is proud of the fact that the product was invented there.

The company still has an aspiration to create products that will bring modern forms of communication to individuals in remote rural villages. However they believe that entering into the European and North American markets has allowed them to develop much larger manufacturing volumes which in turn has enabled them to gradually lower prices.

Freeplay Energy has a number of new product ideas under investigation. One initiative is the concept of a satellite telephone that can be charged with energy provided by a 'self-powered', generator rather than costly disposable batteries. The company believes this product would overcome some of the problems faced by African economies. African states cannot afford to develop the landlines and other facilities needed for a modern telecommunications infrastructure. This approach would allow these states to make a technology leap and allow individuals access to the global communications network. Other product ideas include self-powered pull cord lights, water purification systems and even foetal heartbeat monitors.

The company's philosophy is to attempt to create a range of products that will help improve communication across the developing world. This is reflected in its tagline, 'Powered by You'.

The company now has to consider how it plans to develop over the next five years. There are a number of strategic choices to be made. It could move away from making its own products or it could carry on some manufacturing but licence to its technology to mobile phone manufacturers such as Nokia, Ericsson and Motorola.

This mini-case study has been prepared from secondary sources.

(a) The managers of Freeplay Energy have asked you to write a report advising them of the issues they need to consider when developing the organisation's mission, goals and objectives. This report should specifically address Freeplay's unique situation and its current stage of development. (25 marks)

(b) The managers of the company have also asked you to write a report outlining the process the company should follow in order to successfully undertake market segmentation, targeting and positioning. This report should specifically discuss the segmentation variables that would be applicable in this market. (25 marks)

(50 marks)

51 Marks & Spencer — 80 mins

Over the last three decades Marks & Spencer (M&S) has been seen as the leading clothing retailer in the UK, operating around 300 stores. The quality and range of its functional and fashionable clothes combined with good customer service had proved to be unbeatable in the past. The retailer's position was so strong in the UK market that it could even refuse to take payments by credit cards from customers. The company also did not see the need to undertake any advertising.

Marks & Spencer's recent performance

M&S's fortunes however, have recently been in decline. This started initially with a poor year in the South East Asian market, which by itself should not have been too damaging. However, in the last few years there has been increasing competition in UK clothing from more aggressive middle market high street retailers such as Next and Gap, as well as revitalised department stores such as Debenhams and discount outlets such as Matalan. The result has been a sharp decline in annual profitability for M&S since 1998 with a consequent fall in the company's share price, dropping 70% from its peak in 1997 (see Table 1). In fact the share price fell as low as £1.70 at one point in the year 2000, sending M&S's market capitalisation to under £5 billion from its 1998 value of £17 billion.

Table 1 – Marks & Spencer's profits and share price 1996-2000

Year	Profit £m	Share price £ (high)
1996	996	5.31
1997	1,102	6.65
1998	1,115	6.20
1999	546	4.61
2000	418	3.32

Competition

Gap – This middle market company has taken market share by creating a high profile lifestyle brand, based on attitude and meaning.

Next – In May 2000, another middle market competitor, Next, demonstrated its increasing ability to attract consumers by reporting a 19% increase in sales. Next bases its business on giving 25-45 year old customers fashionable clothing at a reasonable price.

Matalan – Is a discount clothing and homeware retailer operating 111 stores, mostly out of town. Garment sales make up 82% of group profits. Matalan forecasts that it can continue to grow at 30% a year compound for the next three years. Matalan plans include entering the financial services market with its own credit card and personal loans and potentially, insurance products.

Debenhams – Has also been attempting to take market share away from mid-market retailers such as Marks & Spencer by focusing on the needs of working women. In the financial year 1999-2000 Debenhams increased its share of the UK lingerie market, previously an M&S staple, from 3.75 to 4.8%.

Marks & Spencer's responses

M&S has taken a number of measures in the last two years to regain its market position, in particular introducing more fashionable lines of clothing. These, however, have not been an overwhelming success. They were widely seen as alienating the company's traditional customers, mainly ABC1 housewives. At the same time younger, more fashion oriented customers did not associate fashion with the M&S brand.

M&S has also been undertaking a severe round of cost cutting measures. As part of this process the company has started to shift production of its clothing from the UK to cheaper factories internationally. This has led to large-scale redundancies in the UK clothing industry. The move to international production has also meant that M&S is no longer so able to place late orders for particular items or colours that are proving popular.

October 2000 saw a new management team announce a range of new initiatives. To accompany the women's designer collection, which features clothes designed by Betty Jackson, Julien Macdonald and Katherine Hamnett, M&S then also launched its first ever designer menswear collection in five stores in the UK.

Marks & Spencer Financial Services are to open in around 30 of the company's stores, offering customers confidential consultations on their personal finances. M&S's financial services are also planning to launch a range of new products. Both these moves are likely to lead to greater competition with the traditional banks. The company aims to launch a poster advertising campaign involving placing advertisements in areas near traditional banks stating 'Unhappy with your bank? Come to M&S'.

The company has taken a stake in the Confetti Network, a website business specialising in products bought for weddings. The aim is that M&S will become the leading retailer in the online retail site developed by Confetti.

M&S has also unveiled plans to open a chain of new lingerie boutiques in continental Europe, starting in Paris, Hamburg and Dusseldorf. The stores will operate under the brand name of 'msl'. Twenty five per cent of the lingerie range will be exclusively designed for the new stores; the rest will come from M&S's current range. There are no plans to open msl boutiques in the UK.

Finally M&S has also launched a £20 million advertising campaign, emphasising quality and wide range of products, under the slogan 'Exclusively for everyone'.

This mini case study has been prepared from secondary sources.

(a) As a marketing consultant you have been asked, using an appropriate model or models of your choice, to prepare a report analysing the current strategic position of Marks & Spencer in the UK clothing market. (25 marks)

(b) Evaluate the proposed actions that the Marks & Spencer management team is suggesting. Stating your reasons, outline the alternative options you believe Marks & Spencer should explore. (25 marks)

(50 marks)

52 Xbox 80 mins

In May 2001 it was announced that Microsoft, a company with vast resources, planned to enter the games hardware market in November 2001 with its new Xbox games console. Priced at $299, each console contains a hard disk, DVD drive and Internet connection. Microsoft believes that the introduction of broadband technology will change the nature of the game market. In particular, individuals who play games with each other over an Internet connection will be able to talk directly to each other rather than typing messages to each other. In order to facilitate online gaming, Microsoft has formed an alliance with the Japanese Internet and Telecommunications Company, NTT Communications.

Microsoft aims to have 15-20 games titles available by the time Xbox is launched; also all the major software programming houses such as Saga and Electronic Arts have agreed to produce games for their console. The company aims to sell between 1-1.5 million units over the Christmas period.

Sony launched the PlayStation 2 last year by May 2001 had already achieved sales of 9 million units and plans to sell another 20 million units by the end of the year. At the time of its launch 33 games were available and a further 63 have come on stream since. The console can also operate many of the games originally designed for the first PlayStation console, so that individuals can upgrade to the new console without having to replace all their games software.

In response to the impending increase in competition, Sony has taken several initiatives. It has formed an alliance with America Online (AOL) to enable fast Internet access through its games console. It has also linked up with the software company RealNetworks to allow its software product RealPlay 8 to be installed on the PlayStation 2 to allow access to video on the Internet. A Netscape browser for the console is also under development along with other developments such as a hard disk drive, LCD display, keyboard and mouse. PlayStation 2 will be able to offer instant messaging, chat and email.

Nintendo plans to launch its GameCube in the United States on 5 November, 3 days before Microsoft introduces it Xbox console. The GameCube will have wireless control and is aimed at a slightly younger market. The GameCube console will not have the ability to play CDs or DVDs. However, Nintendo is also a software producer and has a reputation for providing some of the best games on the market and will be able to offer popular games such as Super Mario Brothers and Pokémon with the new console. It is currently assumed that it will be slower than Xbox but will be priced at $199.95, which may be attractive to many parents.

At the beginning of 2001 Sega, which makes the Dreamcast console, announced that it was ending production of games hardware and concentrating its activities on creating software products for this market. The Dreamcast console offered online gaming.

The world console market is estimated to be worth $20 billion a year. Microsoft plans to spend $500 million on promotion in the first year alone. It is estimated that Sony has spent $750 million promoting the launch of the PlayStation 2.

The games console market has some interesting dynamics. When Sony launched the PlayStation, as a financially strong consumer goods company it was able and prepared to discount prices in order to buy market share. The company lost money on every machine it sold but gained the largest share of the market. However, through licensing deals with the software houses it made money on every game console and created large profits for Sony. The games companies were also content because they were making strong profits from a games market that was expanding due to lower priced consoles.

With the arrival of a new competitor to this market and three new product offerings, the outcome in this market over the next few years is far from certain.

This mini-case study has been prepared from secondary sources.

(a) Any development in the games hardware market will have a major impact on the software companies. Therefore, as part of a contingency planning exercise, an independent games software company has asked you to evaluate the appropriateness of the actions Sony has taken, over the last twelve months, to defend its leadership of the games hardware market. (25 marks)

(b) The software company has also asked you to write a report outlining what actions Microsoft will need to undertake to be a successful challenger in this market. (25 marks)

(50 marks)

53 Howden Joinery 80 mins

Based in the UK, MFI is a vertically integrated business, manufacturing and retailing kitchen and bedroom furniture and fittings. In 1999 the company's retail outlets were mainly large 'out of town' retail sites. MFI at this time had falling sales, rising losses, high debts and a low share price. In fact, in December 1998 the share price had reached a new low of 28.5 pence a share. Since then the company has implemented a number of initiatives to increase sales and ensure its factories are operating at efficient levels.

Firstly, by the end of 2001, MFI aimed to have opened 20 smaller High Street stores of about 370m^2. The aim was then to have 50 of this type of retail outlet by 2003. In a further development, in 12 stores, MFI are also currently testing the idea of selling bathrooms. Collaborative agreements are also being explored. The company has recently negotiated an agreement with an electrical goods retailer named Curry's, to sell kitchen fittings and furniture alongside electrical appliances. Currently this is taking place in 50 Curry's stores, with the aim of the idea being developed in a further 50 stores by summer 2002.

MFI is also expanding internationally. It is planned to expand its already profitable business in France, where it feels it can double sales and triple profits in a three-to-four-year period. The company also has a joint venture in Taiwan which operates four stores.

Despite these developments, the fastest growing venture within the MFI group is a business called Howden Joinery. This company is a chain of depots that supply kitchens to small builders. The idea of the business is to meet small builders' needs by supplying kitchens that are easy to install, whilst at the same time meeting the expectations of the builder's customers in terms of quality and design. The kitchens are supplied through local depots that hold stock and also contain a small showroom space. The depots are located on industrial estates which offer low rents. This also means they are often close to other suppliers which small builders use, such as plumbers' merchants and timber outlets. These depots can supply a builder with all the component parts needed to create a new kitchen. They can also supply other joinery items such as windows and doors. Rather than supplying the component parts that need assembling, all kitchen cupboards are carefully assembled by Howden joinery and ready for installation by the builder. This not only saves the builder time but also ensures that the final units are of a high quality.

Howden Joinery promote themselves by contacting local builders with mailshots and by staff ringing them directly. The relationship between local staff and local customers is seen as a crucial aspect of the business. Howden Joinery staff help the builders to draw computer designs of proposed kitchens, as well as providing builders with brochures which they can show to their customers. Howden Joinery's customers are offered trade discounts and easy credit terms. The normal MFI store reaches maturity after around eighteen months, however a Howden Joinery depot is still attracting new business four years after opening.

Two years ago there were 100 Howden Joinery depots. Now there are 200, and the aim is to have 350 outlets in the next two to three years. In 2000, Howden Joinery's operating profits were £8.9 m against the total group's profits of £44.9 m. In 2001, Howden Joinery's profits had grown to £15.3 m against what ING Barings Charterhouse Securities predicted would be profits of around £63 m for the MFI group as a whole. MFI is now considering international expansion of the Howden Joinery business.

This mini-case has been prepared from secondary sources and is intended as a basis for student discussion, and not as an illustration of good or bad management practice.

(a) As the newly appointed marketing director for MFI, you have been asked to identify and explain the sources of Howden Joinery's competitive advantage, and to make a judgement as to whether their current position is sustainable. (25 marks)

(b) Your senior management team has decided to evaluate the potential of franchising the Howden Joinery business into international markets, both in Europe and South-East Asia. As a first step you have been asked to write a report outlining the criteria that should be used in order to evaluate any new international market. (25 marks)

(50 marks)

54 Guinness in China — 80 mins

Guinness is one of the many brewers now exploiting the massive potential of the Asian drinks market. It is assisting the development of Irish themed pubs which are proving to be very popular in cities as far ranging as Casablanca and Reykjavik. China's first Irish themed pub, O'Malley's, was officially opened early in 1997 in Shanghai and was built from a £500,000 flat-pack self-assembly kit. Rather than directly invest in its own far-flung chain of Irish pubs, Guinness is working with individual entrepreneurs prepared to put up their own cash. The company initially invested £10m in this international expansion, the bulk of it on staff, marketing and promotion, but it provides only advice and support to potential investors. In the process Guinness sells an increasing amount of the famous stout and other products in emerging markets at very little cost to itself.

Guinness is working with a design company called the Irish Pub Company to help create authentic Irish pubs. Buyers can choose from three styles; the Dublin Victorian Pub complete with bevelled mirrors, stained glass and elaborate tiling, the Irish Pub Shop based on a tradition whereby the local grocery shop doubled as a pub; and the Irish Country Cottage adorned with tankards and crockery. The pubs take 8-12 weeks to build, cost an investor on average £200,000, although one bar in the US cost $1.5m, and have been built in over 36 countries. Irish bar and catering staff who are prepared to move around the world are also recruited by the company. O'Malley's in Shanghai is owned by a New Zealander and managed by an Irish couple.

However, Guinness is not just concerned with providing international job opportunities. With a population of 1.2 billion, China is a huge potential market, already the second biggest beer market in the world and by the year 2000 is expected to overtake the US. At the present time only about 120 million urban Chinese earn sufficient to buy the most modest Western brands such as packaged foods and detergent. The cost of a pint of Guinness is out of reach for most Chinese and is only purchased by the most wealthy trend-setters together with British, Americans and Australians working in Shanghai.

Guinness believes the Asian market will provide profitable returns and has set up seven co-ordinators across Asia to supply the demand. The company is directly investing in manufacturing Guinness stout in Malaysia, and through a licensed brewing agreement with the Putian Jinse Brewery in the Fujian Province of China, it is also producing a lower strength beer called Guinness Special Light. The country director for China says, 'It's early days for Guinness Brewing Worldwide in China. We want to learn about the market and perfect our strategy in a limited geographical area before rolling out locally brewed Guinness to other provinces. China is a complex and highly fragmented market and with a product like Guinness it's important not to rush the market entry until we have a better understanding of market dynamics.' O'Malley's is just one stage in furthering that market understanding, and similar pubs will open in other, newly-emerging markets. Nowhere, it seems, is immune to the charm of the Irish.

As advisor to the marketing director for Guinness Worldwide, prepare a report which does the following.

(a) Details the types and possible sources of information required to assess the relative attractiveness of the various emerging markets around the world for Irish themed pubs.

(25 marks)

(b) Describes the various market entry methods available to companies wishing to operate internationally and goes on to explain the advantages and disadvantages of Guinness's current approach (licensing and direct manufacturing) to market entry in Asia.

(25 marks)

(50 marks)

55 Cafédirect 80 mins

Cafédirect holds approximately three per cent of the UK fresh ground and freeze-dried coffee markets despite very little marketing spend. The company began trading in 1991 as a non-profit joint venture involving the following ethical trading organisations; Equal Exchange, Oxfam Trading, Traidcraft and Twin Trade.

Cutting out the middlemen is key to the organisation's success. The company buys coffee beans directly from small co-operatives in Latin and Central America and Africa. Cafédirect guarantees an agreed trade price for the coffee beans which means they have occasionally paid suppliers more than twice the normal market rate. If the international coffee price rises above the agreed trade price, they pay the international price plus a ten percent 'social premium' which the co-operatives distribute as they see fit. Cafédirect also provide an upfront subsidy of up to sixty per cent of the value of one contract. It also provides regular updates on world coffee prices. This is important because the fourteen co-operatives who supply the company only sell a quarter to one half of their beans to Cafédirect.

What does all this ethical trading mean for the consumer? The recommended retail price for a 227 gram jar of roast or ground Cafédirect is £2.09. A jar of the leading brand Kenco costs £1.99. Cafédirect's 100 gram freeze-dried product retails at £2.39; Nestlé Gold Blend sells for £2.19. The UK supermarkets have maintained their profit margins and have passed on the cost of ethical business practices to the consumer, a number of whom are clearly willing to pay a slight premium if they believe the company behind the brand is operating ethically.

The issue of ethical trading has been driven by publicity about poor working conditions in factories and plantations in some developing countries. A recent documentary focused on the relationship between a major supermarket chain, and one of its larger suppliers of peas in Zimbabwe where it revealed that out of the retail price of a 99 pence pack of peas, the pickers got less than 1 pence. Supermarkets have been prompted to initiate audits of their supply and production lines and make public statements about their commitment to ethical trading. For example, Tesco recently set up a team of ethical advisers to help monitor the goods it sells in its stores and develop an ethical trading policy. Other major chains, such as the Co-operative, have signed up to participate in a project with the Fair Trade Foundation to investigate the mechanics of implementing independent auditing procedures to meet international ethical trading standards. These include agreements to negotiate with independent worker organisations and to honour or better any locally agreed minimum wage.

As the profile of ethical trading increases, the retailers' position that consumers will have to pay a premium may become untenable - especially if one of the supermarket chains takes a more definite ethical stance to distinguish itself from the other companies.

In the role of an independent ethical advisor working for a large supermarket chain in a country of your choice, prepare a report which:

(a) Defines and explains the strategic approach taken by Cafédirect, the Co-operative and Tesco to the social responsibility issues raised by ethical trading. (15 marks)

(b) Outlines the marketing operations issues that should be included in the development of a code of ethical trading. (15 marks)

(c) Makes recommendations on how the chosen supermarket chain could take a definite ethical stance to differentiate itself from competitors. This should include details on the marketing strategy and mix to be adopted. (20 marks)

(50 marks)

56 Ford and Honda 80 mins

Rising costs and the worldwide spread of shared tastes in car styling have prompted the automobile industry's giants to exploit global economies of scale. However rivals such as Ford and Honda have approached the task very differently.

Ford was one of the world's first multinationals. Its first foreign production unit was set up in Canada in 1904 – just a year after the creation of the USA parent. For years Ford operated on a regional basis. Individual countries or areas had a large degree of autonomy from the USA headquarters. That meant products differed considerably, depending on local executives' views of regional requirements. In Europe the company built different cars in the UK and Germany until the late 1960s.

Honda, in comparison, is a much younger company which has grown rapidly from its beginnings as a manufacturer of motorcycles in the 1950s. In contrast to Ford, Honda was run very firmly out of Japan. Until well into the 1980s its vehicles were designed, engineered and built domestically for sale around the world. Significantly however, Honda tended to be more flexible than Ford in developing new products. Rather than having a structure based on independent functional departments, such as bodywork or engines, all Japan's car makers preferred multi-disciplined teams. This allowed development work to take place simultaneously, rather than being passed between departments, which speeded up time to market for new product launches.

In the 1990s both companies started to review their organisations to take advantage of the perceived strengths of other forms of organisational structures.

In 1993 the Ford 2000 restructuring programme replaced the old functional departments with multi-disciplinary product teams. The teams were based on five vehicle centres, responsible for different types of vehicles. Small and medium-sized cars for example, are handled by a European team split between the UK and Germany. The development teams comprise of staff from a range of backgrounds, with each taking charge of one area of the process, whether technical, financial or marketing based.

Honda, by contrast, has decentralised in recent years. While its cars have much the same names around the world, they are becoming less, rather than more, standardised. In fact 'Globalisation' – a global strategy with local management – is the most appropriate term. Eventually the group expects its structure will comprise four regions – Japan, the USA, Europe and Asia-Pacific – which will become increasingly self-sufficient. As a result, the latest generation Accord family car, initially launched in Japan, and recently in the USA and Europe, differs in all the regions.

Both Ford and Honda argue their new international structures represent a correct response to the demands of the global market. Much of what they have done is similar, but intriguingly, they have chosen to adopt the same strategies at different times.

As a marketing consultant in the automobile industry provide a report which:

(a) Reviews the advantages and disadvantages of the international structures of both Ford and Honda (ie centralisation versus decentralisation). (25 marks)

(b) Highlights the marketing mix implications of Ford and Honda's contrasting international marketing strategy (ie globalised versus customised). (25 marks)

(50 marks)

57 Air Products 80 mins

Air Products and Chemicals Inc is a leading supplier of industrial gases and related equipment, based in America but with operations worldwide. They are an example of an industrial organisation who practice excellence in the application of business-to-business marketing. This is rewarded by increases of 17% reported income from operations year on year and with sales of over $2.4 billion.

John Dodds, European Communications Director, is convinced that, 'you can't just make products and hope to sell them. You have to be far more customer focused than production focused'. In industrial gases, whose applications range from freezing in the food manufacturing sector to heating in the leisure industry, this means investing in marketing research to find out who your potential customers are, how they segment and what their different needs are - which in some cases they may not even be aware of.

Air Products follow-up this customer and market insight with a clear strategy of target marketing, effective brand positioning and joint new product development - the image and innovation elements of their planning process. The food sector has been identified as a key target market and as Dodds comments, 'It is fine knowing who your customer is in a country and what products and equipment you can supply, but you need a lot more. You have to know who the key individuals are in the organisation who will affect the purchase decision, their likes and dislikes, and what their particular problems and concerns are in relation to their freezing needs'. Once this has been determined the company uses its network of business development managers to establish and build a successful trading relationship. In addition to the essential one-to-one personal contact required in business-to-business markets, establishing a relationship is greatly facilitated by Air Products' strong brand.

The company have been pushing the company brand. 'What lives in customers minds is value from the brand', says Dodds. Rather than just following the traditional route of trade fairs and brochures, Air Products are active on the Internet, with direct mail and perimeter sponsorship at sports grounds. This promotional activity raises the awareness, stature and trustworthiness of the company. The basis of their branch position is customer value. The company strategy avoids the traditional industrial malaise of simply cutting prices. Instead, Air Products design offerings that create value and lower customer costs, without cutting prices as a key source of competitive customer advantage. For example, in the food sector products are designed that offer better freezing value so that customers can freeze more quickly and use less gas. So not only is Air Products an expert in industrial gases used in industry but also in the type of machinery that makes the process work. This has been achieved by integrating basic research with detailed customer knowledge, and by actively using the expertise forged through liaisons between the marketers and the technologists, both within the company and in joint initiatives with buyers and technologists in customer organisations. That way innovative applications have been developed quickly.

In addition to Insight, Image and Innovation, Air Products focuses on effective implementation of its strategic vision. The company has a top down and bottom up planning process where broad sector focus and direction is set by senior management, and annual marketing plans are devolved to Strategic Action Teams, comprising the business development managers, technologists, customer service, product managers and finance personnel, who have to make the strategy happen in each target sector. Each group is given their own annual budget and tasked with developing an effective marketing mix to achieve objectives.

This marketing orientated approach is working well, 'the challenge now is not to rest on our laurels. We need to continue to satisfy existing customers and attract new ones', says Dodds.

In the role of an applicant for the job of General Sales and Marketing Manager for the Food Sector, in a worldwide region of your choice, develop a presentation which:

(a) Details the differences between industrial and consumer markets and shows how these differences are likely to influence Air Products' marketing mix. (25 marks)

(b) Examines the likely composition of the Decision-Making Unit (DMU) in a prospect organisation, and suggests how each member of the DMU can be persuaded to select Air Products as the preferred supplier. (25 marks)

(50 marks)

58 ICI Dulux Trade Paints 80 mins

In recent years there has been a dramatic growth in the popularity of broken colour decorative paint effects with publicity in magazines, books and television programmes creating interest in special effects. As a result more and more decorators are being asked by customers to produce broken colour effects such as colourwashing, ragrolling, woodgraining, marbling and sponging.

Dulux Trade recognised this increased demand for special effects and launched Duette, Sonata and Acrylic Scumble Glaze products targeted at trade customers in the UK. Duette is a water-based system that produces a unique broken effect using Duette Classic and Duette Nouveau patented rollers. As it is water-based it has low odour, is quick drying and non-yellowing. It comes in an extensive colour range - 50 two-tone colourways are available on the Dulux Trade tinting system. Sonata is a trade paint that produces a fleck finish. Acrylic Scumble Glaze is also uniquely water-based and provides a topcoat that is distressed to produce broken colour effects. This product offers all the benefits of traditional glaze without the drawbacks. Oil based glazes are awkward to handle, can take several days to dry, have high odour levels and are prone to yellowing.

Since its launch in 1997 Acrylic Scumble Glaze sales have continuously grown but recently at a slower rate. Duette sales have reduced for the first time and some of this downturn can be attributed to competitors' recent investments in special effect ranges.

A major competitor, Crown, has spent a lot of time and money relaunching its special effects product range in both the trade and retail markets with its brand Coloufects, targeted at the professional specifier. A smaller competitor, Polyvine, produces an extensive range of special effects products that are popular with experienced, accomplished and more traditional decorators.

The markets that Dulux serves can be segmented as follows.

- Decorator - many have the knowledge of special effects but lack the confidence in their ability to achieve them although they know they are a way of adding value to their work.
- Domestic specifier/homeowner - special effects provide the homeowner with a means to making his/her home unique. Communications should provide inspiration to those planning to employ decorators and there are possibilities for spin-offs and links between trade special effects and retail activity.
- Professional specifier - includes architects, interior designers, local authorities and facilities managers. Special effects can provide a unique look for interiors and can be used to create textures which can provide cost savings compared to using alternative materials.
- Contractor - special effects are an additional offering that can be made to clients and generate the potential to make higher margins on more specialist work.

Distribution is split between independents (builders' merchants and some retailers) and Dulux Decorator Centres of which there are around 130 outlets in the UK. However there still remain relatively low levels of awareness of the Dulux Trade special effects products.

Required

In the role of a marketing consultant reporting to the marketing manager for Dulux Trade Paints, produce a report which:

(a) Explains, using relevant examples, the aspects of a marketing audit the senior brand manager should monitor and how these factors may be summarised into a SWOT analysis. (25 marks)

(b) Develops a marketing strategy and tactical plan to increase sales of the brand over the next 3 years. (25 marks)

(50 marks)

59 Volvo cars 80 mins

The Volvo Group provides a range of transportation related products and services with a focus on quality, safety and environmental care to customers in selected market segments. The company began in 1927, when the original models where designed to withstand the rigours of Sweden's rough roads and low temperatures. Since then safety is built in to the quality of Volvo's products, production processes and services. Today the Volvo Group is among the world leaders when it comes to heavy commercial vehicles such as trucks, buses, construction equipment and propulsion systems for marine and industrial applications. Volvo cars occupy a strong position as a car producer in the upper segment of the global market.

Volvo Cars has set itself the vision of becoming the 'most desired and successful speciality car brand and the most customer focused organisation in the world, achieving exemplary standards and support which will match or exceed customer expectations'.

One aspect of building the brand to become the most desired speciality car brand in the world is the company's sponsorship of a CNN music programme. 'World Beat' airs weekly to a combined audience of more than 213 million households. An upbeat global music show, 'World Beat' features music news and information from around the world offering insight into the international music scene. The half-hour show covers a full range of stories and artists from contemporary music, jazz, world music, classical and fusion. Regular features include a Gig Guide and World Top Ten Albums, charting the best selling albums around the world.

Volvo's commercial branding on the programme includes opening and closing credits, programme break bumpers and spot advertising, as well as Volvo branded vignettes running on the CNN Airport Network to extend the programme reach. An online version of 'World Beat' is available on CNN.com, the network's worldwide website, with Volvo as the exclusive partner and sole car advertiser. CNN and Volvo are also developing marketing support to drive appointment viewing to 'World Beat', including programme promotion among Volvo customers worldwide.

As an additional part of the strategy to achieve its vision, Volvo Cars has two relationship building programmes aimed at two different customer groups. The first is Corporate Account Relationship Experience (Care) which has the specific purpose of ensuring that everyone involved with corporate customers (fleet buyers) delivers a level of service consistent with the vision statement. The second is One Customer One Relationship (Oncore) which is aimed at the dealer network to ensure the end customer (the driver) experiences a differentiated experience that matches the new products and services that Volvo continually launches. These two programmes work together to satisfy the business needs of the corporate customer and the human needs of the driver. Both programmes concentrate on developing the skills of all the people who influence the customer experience, whether they are directly employed by Volvo or by a dealer. Dealers are involved pre- and post-sales through their business centres run by a business sales manager, whose main objective is to build business-to-business relationships.

In order to secure corporate sales Volvo has to manage a number of different relationships:

- Volvo and its corporate customers. This determines inclusion in entitlement lists.
- Volvo and its dealers. Involves maintenance and improvement of service standards.
- Volvo and Volvo drivers. A direct marketing relationship is maintained.
- Corporate customers and their employees. Involves which models are available.
- Corporate customers and Volvo dealers. Involves delivery and servicing.
- Volvo dealers and Volvo drivers. The front line for meeting drivers' expectations.

The Oncore and Care programmes are designed to achieve a consistently high standard of service across all these relationships.

This combined with the investment in brand building over the last few years has increased business purchases above individual consumer purchases for the company.

In the role of a marketing consultant reporting to the senior vice president for marketing at Volvo cars produce a report which:

(a) Outlines the opportunities, strengths and weaknesses of programme sponsorship as a communicator of brand values. (25 marks)

(b) Outlines a corporate customer retention plan for a Volvo dealership. You should include details on analysis, objectives, relationship marketing mix and implementation activities required. (25 marks)

(50 marks)

60 The BBC goes digital 80 mins

The British Broadcasting Corporation (BBC) is the UK's main public service broadcaster providing TV, radio and online services to listeners and viewers at home and around the world. A Royal Charter and Agreement governs its constitution, finances and obligations. The Corporation is financed by a licence fee paid by viewers, plus the commercial revenues from its BBC Worldwide operations. The BBC provides a range of domestic broadcast services including BBC 1 and BBC 2 TV channels and BBC Network Radio Channels 1, 2, 3, 4, and 5 Live. In addition, BBC Worldwide is a major international broadcaster, operating the BBC World and Prime Channels, and acts as a publishing house for BBC publications of magazines, books, video and audio recordings, and CD-ROMs. The BBC also operates an online channel accessed via the Internet and has a small portfolio of existing digital channels, which includes BBC Choice and BBC Knowledge. The BBC World Service supplies free radio broadcasts to millions of people throughout the world.

As part of its current mission 'to met its public service obligations and operate effectively in a competitive market' the BBC recently announced that it was going to spend more than £300 million on new digital TV and radio channels. Digital represents the latest technology and is regarded as superior to the existing analogue broadcasting systems, enabling better quality sound and vision and the availability of additional channels. As a result of its largest every public consultation exercise, which involved nearly 7,000 responses via its website and Freepost address, and 1,000 interviews undertaken by the independent research agency BMRB, the Corporation claimed that its plans for the introduction of new digital channels had wide public support.

The BBC made a formal application to the UK Government in January 2001 to replace its existing digital TV channels with four new digital TV services to be launched over the next two years. One of the new TV channels, BBC 3, is aimed at 16 to 34 year olds and will focus 'exclusively on the young and young at heart'. Another channel, BBC 4, is aimed at 'everyone interested in culture, arts and ideas'. A further TV channel (provisionally called Playbox) is aimed at pre-school children and will be mostly educational. The fourth, which has the working title Children's B, is for 6-13 year olds and will have an interactive element. The corporation also wants to launch five digital radio services, including a music station aimed at a young black audience, a speech radio station, as Asian network, a station focusing on music from the 1970s to the 1990s and a sports network provisionally titled Five Live Sports Plus.

The BBC Director General, Greg Dyke, said viewers and listeners would get 'imaginative and distinctive services'. The proposal is designed to raise the take-up of digital television and radio. Without a wide choice of free-to-air channels on digital platforms, many viewers may not give up their existing analogue service. The UK Government wants to switch off analogue services between 2006 and 2010, but there are signs that insufficient viewers will have gone over to digital to allow the switch in that period. The BBC's Comerica rivals aim to lobby hard against the plans, particularly the proposals for the two children's channels. They believe that the BBC should not spend licence fees on services already provide elsewhere.

You have been retained as a marketing consultant to advise the UK Government on the proposals presented by the BBC. Present a report which:

(a) Identifies the main challenges in the marketing environment that are likely to affect the BBC and specifies the constraints that it is likely to face as a not-for-profit organisation when implementing its proposals. (25 marks)

(b) Proposes an approach for developing one of the new channels further and presents an outline plan for its launch in 2002. (25 marks)

(50 marks)

61 Reebok International 80 mins

Reebok International Ltd is one of the world's largest sports and fitness brands. From its humble beginnings in Bolton, UK in 1895 the company has become a challenger to Nike and Adidas in the global marketplace for sports footwear, apparel and equipment. The global headquarters of the company are now located in Boston, USA, which is the centre for the planning and execution of its global brand marketing activities. According to a recent company press release Reebok (named after a small fast-running gazelle) has a reputation for 'cutting-edge products, innovative technology, extraordinary athletes, and impactful marketing'.

However, it is not only in its product development that Reebok has been innovative, but it has also developed a long-standing reputation for innovative and differentiated brand positioning. In particular it has established itself as a socially responsible company through its Human Rights programme which it has pursued for many years. It pulled out of South Africa in 1986 in support of the anti-apartheid movement and subsequently sponsored the Amnesty International 'Human Rights Now' world concert tour in 1988. A key element of its ethical stance is the annual Reebok Human Rights Award, which is also enacted through its corporate culture, and supported by its policies on child labour, fair wages, and factory safety standards. Unlike some of its competitors, it sees itself as a brand that is honest and human, and being about fun and enjoyment.

In addition to its core value positioning, Reebok has to meet the challenge of its rivals through additional brand building activities in a growing but fiercely competitive industry. In 2001 the company launched its new re-energising 'Defy convention' brand campaign. The global TV and print campaign features endorsements from its contracted athletes who fit the positioning of 'defying convention in their pursuit to be the best ... individuals who are strong and confident – undeterred by obstacles, unfazed by stereotypes'. One of the featured athletes is the tennis star Venus Williams who has a 5-year, £28 million contract with the company. Advertisements in the campaign are designed to speak to a specific target audience and her role is to target the young female consumer who 'incorporates style and fashion into her active lifestyle'.

Against the background of its global brand development strategy Reebok is planning to launch stand alone retail stores in the UK in the near future. The company, which has until now only sold its merchandise in Europe through concessions, already runs retail outlets in the US and regards retail development as a cornerstone of its growth strategy. The venture, which will include new Reebok fashion lines in the stores, is regarded as a step towards fashion retailing for Reebok, while remaining true to its sportswear heritage.

The first flagship retail store in the UK will include an interactive console that will permit customers to access descriptions, sizes and colours of merchandise.

The company feels confident about its initial penetration of the European retail market with this concept in the UK, as brand awareness is high due to its local connections. This is further enhanced by its high profile sponsorship of UK Athletics and Liverpool Football Club. However, Reebok has yet to finalise its plans for entry into additional European markets outside the UK.

As an advisor to Reebok Retail Developments, prepare a report that:

(a) Identifies the types and sources of information that should be gathered to assess the attractiveness of different European markets outside the UK for the launch of further Reebok retail outlets. (25 marks)

(b) Proposes an outline marketing plan for the launch of a chain of Reebok stores in a European market of your choice outside the UK. (25 marks)

(50 marks)

62 Derby Cycle Corporation 80 mins

The Derby Cycle Corporation (DCC) is a bicycle designer and manufacturer which holds the leading market share in Canada, Ireland, the Netherlands and the UK and is a top supplier in the US. Formed in 1986 to acquire Raleigh, Gazelle, and Sturmey-Archer from TI Group, the company markets under those brands and others, including Derby, Nishiki, Univega and Diamondback. DCC has manufacturing operations in five countries and produces mountain, city, hybrid, British Motorcross (BMX) and racing bicycles. The company plans to expand through acquisitions in the US and Europe and by offering accessories and apparel.

The UK bicycle market has seen the rise of global brands and competition on the back of different bicycle types targeted at different market sectors. In the 1980s mountain bikes from US manufacturers became popular and Raleigh became a follower rather than leader with such products. Despite Raleigh's 98% brand recall scores with UK customers, the popular mountain bikes have US heritage and today's parents are not necessarily buying Raleigh for themselves and their children. In addition, as the mountain bike market matures a wider product range is available, with some bikes selling for as little as £99 (40% of the mountain bike sector is below £120). Own label bikes are available from retailers, mail order and the Internet.

The Diamondback brand was acquired by DCC in 1999, and the UK bicycle manufacturer Raleigh was later appointed as the distributor for UK and Ireland. This was significant for Raleigh as Diamondback was a global brand with consistent West Coast USA youth imagery. This gave it credibility in the product sectors of BMX and mountain bikes where Raleigh's older, British and family oriented brand equity was less appropriate.

With both brands, Raleigh needed to establish distinct positions in the market. This would have an impact on new product development, pricing, distribution and communication activities. Focus groups were conducted in the USA and UK with male/female, urban/rural and serious/leisure cyclists in order to develop a detailed understanding of both the Raleigh and Diamondback brand essence and values. This would form a blueprint for all communication agency briefings in order to provide consistency and focus.

(NB. This paper has been written using the case study from the Marketing Operations paper, June 2001.)

You are acting as a marketing consultant to the DCC marketing manager

(a) Identify and briefly explain the components of the marketing plan for DCC. (10 marks)

(b) Identify and critique the main challenges in the marketing environment that are likely to impact on the Raleigh and Diamondback brands in the next two years, and explain the limitations of the market information used when conducting an external audit. (15 marks)

(c) DCC plans to expand through acquisitions in the US and Europe and by offering accessories and apparel/clothing. With reference to appropriate theory, explain these planned growth strategies and the potential associated risks for the company if they implement these strategies. (15 marks)

(d) DCC has decided to launch a range of Diamondback clothing in your country. Recommend the marketing mix decisions for this range of clothing. (10 marks)

(50 marks)

63 Starbucks (12/03) 80 mins

In some countries, the coffee market has expanded more than threefold since 1995, with a range of coffee outlets, located on high streets in main towns, modelling themselves on successful American and Italian style coffee shops. People can go into a coffee shop and buy one of a range of specialist coffee beverages and enjoy a very relaxing atmosphere to drink their coffee. Consequently, there has been an expansion in the market and a growth in high street coffee-houses. In the UK alone, there is a range of providers:

- **Costa Coffee** – has 250 outlets and there are plans to have 500 outlets by 2004/5. It also supplies coffee to low-cost airlines. The company is planning to launch a change of sandwich style shops that also serve coffee.
- **Coffee Republic** – this is the largest independent operator in the UK. The company has almost doubled the number of its outlets from 36 to 61 in 2000, increasing to 82 in 2001. It has recently hired marketing specialists to develop its brand identity and is seeking to develop its food offer to capture a growing lunchtime trade.
- **Coffee Nero** – this has 62 outlets in the UK and plans to expand to 250 outlets by 2004.

- **Madison's** – has 48 coffee shops under the Madison brand and four under the name of its newly acquired chain Café Richoux. The company has developed an anglicised format which incorporates American style and an Italian coffee offer. Its open bars and lounges are designed to appeal to female customers.
- **Starbucks**

Starbucks coffee shops have been operating since 1971 and the company is US based. As a global company, The *Starbucks Experience* is about passion for a quality product, excellent customer service, and people. Starbucks has nearly 900 coffee-houses in 22 markets outside North America.

Internationalisation began in 1996 for Starbucks, with the first coffee shop in Tokyo, 'We have been amazed by the global acceptance and visibility of our brand in all our international markets,' says Peter Maslen, president of Starbucks Coffee International.

Starbucks purchases and roasts high-quality whole bean coffees and sells them along with fresh, rich-brewed, Italian style espresso beverages, a variety of pastries and confections, and coffee-related accessories and equipment (primarily through its company-operated retail stores). In addition to sales through its company-operated retail stores, Starbucks sells primarily whole bean coffees through a speciality sales group, a direct response business, supermarkets, and online at Starbucks.com. Additionally, Starbucks produces and sells bottled Frappuccino® coffee drink and a line of premium ice creams through its joint venture partnerships and offers a line of innovative premium teas produced by its wholly owned subsidiary, Tazo Tea Company.

The Company's objective is to establish Starbucks as the most recognised and respected brand in the world. To achieve this goal, the company plans to continue to rapidly expand its retail operations, grow its speciality sales and other operations, and selectively pursue opportunities to leverage the Starbucks brand.

Coffee Shop Consumers

During the last few years there has been an increasing trend among people towards the consumption of healthy food and drink products. This has lead to a decrease in coffee consumption, which is considered as an unhealthy product, especially among those between 15 and 24 years old. Indeed, 13% of 15-24 year olds do not drink coffee at all. Furthermore, club culture has also made bottled water and juice products a more fashionable choice of drink.

Mintel (2001) research indicates that the use of coffee shops has become a habit among distinct sections of the public, notably the mobile, affluent professional. Women are particularly attracted to the non-threatening singles-friendly environment that coffee shops offer.

The success of the coffee shop has been based on a youth friendly, aspirational clientele. However, long-term trends show that non-coffee drinking is on the increase among young people. Older consumers have not been specifically targeted, yet these adults are among the most likely to be consumers of specialised coffee products. High growth within the sector indicates that greater diversification is possible to meet as yet unsatisfied consumer demand among these groups.

The location of existing coffee shops has become a key factor which influences the way some people choose to visit branded coffee shops. Adults from socio-economic groups A and B are now four times more likely than C2 category adults to visit branded coffee shops, because they value highly a relaxed store design and ambience.

The above data has been based on a real life organisation, but details have been changed for assessment purposes and does not reflect the current management practices.

You have been appointed as a consultant specialising in retail marketing to advise Starbucks on their brand.

(a) Assess the main challenges in the marketing environment which are likely to impact on the Starbucks brand in the next two years, and explain the role of marketing information in conducting an external audit. (20 marks)

(b) With reference to appropriate theory, explain how Starbucks could expand their business within the next two years. (10 marks)

(c) Specifically considering the role of the brand, recommend the extended marketing mix decisions for your chosen growth strategies. (20 marks)

(50 marks)

Answer bank

1 Tutorial question: Marketing and corporate planning

Planning for the future, whether for the short, medium or long term, is a vital element of a manager's job. The future cannot be foreseen with certainty, of course, but while planning does not ensure success it does reduce the risks of failure and it does give the organisation direction and purpose.

In business, there is a standard, formal marketing planning process that operates at all management levels. Similarly we all get involved in planning activities in our non-professional lives. The general steps one would take when planning a house purchase, a holiday or a dinner party are the same.

Once you are clear about the level you are working at the rest is straightforward, because whoever you are and in whatever context you are working the principles of the planning process remain the same.

Where are we now?

The starting point must be a clear **assessment of the current position**. So for a house move you need to identify **resources and constraints**. Do you have a house to sell first? How much money can you afford to spend? In which geographic area must it be? What sort of house are you looking for? It is much the same when developing a corporate or marketing plan – both start with an **audit** and clarify the **mission statement.**

A **corporate audit** involves examining the strengths and weakness in each functional area: finance, production, personnel and marketing. Opportunities and threats of the corporate audit come predominantly from the marketing audit as it is here that the macro and micro environments (including PEST, customer and competitor analysis) are examined.

The **marketing audit** focuses on the external environment and the strengths and weaknesses of marketing strategy, functions, systems, structure and productivity. It is therefore less extensive than the corporate audit but in reality contributes greatly to this due to marketing's role as the customer/company interface.

Where are we going?

Planning can only have purpose if there is an agreed destination – an **objective** – what do you want to achieve from your plan? So for a holiday, do you want a relaxing holiday or an active holiday? Is it for one, two or three weeks? Will it be in Europe or elsewhere?

Corporate objectives are concerned with the whole firm and primary objectives relate to key financial factors for business success.

- Profitability (ROCE)
- Growth (sales)
- Reduction (increase in the product, customer, market base)
- Cash flow

All functions are deployed strategically towards achieving these objectives. For example, the production function can reduce costs, the finance function can manage funds more efficiently, the personnel function can recruit better people at less cost or increase their productivity and the marketing function can grow sales profitably. Because marketing's role is concerned with customers and products, marketing objectives are related to sales volume and market share and these are then translated down to tactical objectives for the marketing mix.

How do we get there?

Developing **strategies** involves making decisions about the best route to take. Without overall strategic direction everyone may set off from the same place but then veer off onto their own preferred route. So for the dinner party it involves decisions about who to invite, what menu to develop, how much to spend and such like. Strategies should be devised after careful evaluation of the alternatives. The final choice should be the one that capitalises on the organisation's strengths and exploits opportunities identified at the first stage of planning.

Strategies are **how** you will achieve your objectives. Corporate strategy involves decisions regarding which businesses to be in. Portfolio analysis is employed to assess the attractiveness of the company business portfolio and decisions regarding what new business to enter, which to develop and which to harvest or divest are taken. Marketing strategy involves decisions concerned with what competitive advantage, positioning, customer segments and broad outline of the marketing mix to pursue in each target market.

How do we ensure arrival?

This involves **implementing the strategy** and checking that the objectives are being achieved.

The strategic statement is not a detailed route map. Its purpose is to put everyone on the same track. Action (tactical) plans are the responsibility of those further down the management ladder who provide the detail of how their department will achieve its part of the plan. Control information allows the manager to assess progress towards the objectives and to monitor any developments which require a change of plan. The tactics for the dinner party would be sending out the invitations and cooking the lasagne and pavlova – control would be checking that the lasagne doesn't burn (with a good contingency idea being buying a Vienetta in case the meringue goes wrong).

Corporate tactics are the strategies of each of the functional areas and control involves ensuring that the corporate turnover and profit objectives are met. Marketing tactics are the details of the marketing mix and control involves checking that sales volume and market share targets are achieved within budget.

So whilst the general principles of planning remain the same, the specific activities of corporate and marketing planning differ. However, of all the functional areas, marketing most closely relates to corporate planning because of the central importance of customers and products to corporate success.

2 Marketing and corporate strategy

Planning occurs at different management levels.

Level	Management	Time Scale
1 Corporate	Top	Long term
2 Business/Functional	Middle	Medium term
3 Operational/Action	Junior/staff	Short term

Clarifying the level of analysis within the overall framework of a business plan causes some students and managers alike difficulty. Confusion arises because there are a number of different terms used in the literature for the same thing.

To help understand these levels imagine you are on a staircase, as you move up from one level to another the strategy of the lower level is the tactics of the higher. So for example, marketing strategy is part of corporate tactics. Similarly, sales strategy is marketing tactics.

A strategic perspective centres around planning for the future, either planning for the whole organisation or just for the marketing aspects of the organisation.

Johnson and Scholes in *Exploring Corporate Strategy* outline the characteristics associated with the word strategy and strategic decisions at the corporate level.

(a) **The scope of an organisation's activities.** Does it focus on one area of activity or many? For example should BAe focus on defence?

(b) **The matching of the activities of an organisation to its environment**. In Europe, defence firms are seeking to collaborate to compete internationally, not just serve the home government.

(c) **The matching of an organisation's activities to its resource capability**. Strategies need to be rooted in an adequate resource base.

(d) **The allocation of major resources** (often to do with major acquisitions or disposal of resources). BAe significantly rationalised its operations and workforce.

(e) **Affecting operational decisions**. Strategic decisions set off waves of lesser decisions. BAe's decision to rationalise the operation resulted in human resource issues for personnel, revised product and manufacturing plans which inevitably resulted in changes to the sorts of day-to-day problems faced by a production manager or a sales manager.

(f) **The values and expectations of those who have power**. Strategy can be thought of as a reflection of the attitudes and beliefs of those who have most influence in the organisation, this being related to the mission of the organisation. The expectations of the Government to maintain BAe as a major international competitor are influential in its mission.

(g) **The long term direction of the organisation.** The decision to privatise BAe affected its long-term future.

(h) **Implications for change and thus are likely to be complex in nature**. This arises for three reasons: strategic decisions usually involve a **high degree of uncertainty**, require **an integrated approach** to managing the organisation (including a cross-functional perspective) and thirdly, **involve change**, not only planning change but also in implementing it.

Marketing planning represents the strategic approach to marketing. *Lancaster and Massingham* (*Marketing Management*), outline three key reasons for what they see as an increasing need for a strategic approach to marketing.

(a) The pace of change and environmental complexity – environmental issues, technological change, social change etc.

(b) Increasing organisation size and complexity – a move from functionally structured to matrix and strategic business units, internationalisation.

(c) Increased competition (deregulation, globalisation, technology).

Kotler (in *Marketing Management*) highlights the characteristics of a strategic perspective in his definition of marketing management:

> 'The marketing management process consists of analysing market opportunities, researching and selecting target markets, designing marketing strategies, planning marketing programmes and organising, implementing and controlling the marketing effort.'

At the strategic level we see that marketing involves four processes.

(a) **Analysis**: the antecedent of decision making and plan formulation.

(b) **Planning**: analysis forms basis of plans, plans represent decision making.

(c) **Implementation**: having made plans they need to be put into action.

(d) **Control**: this completes the cycle of functional management as it feeds into the analysis and planning stages and the cycle starts again.

The tangible outcome of a strategic perspective to marketing is the marketing plan which outlines the current marketing situation, sets marketing objectives, strategies and tactics and outlines how the plan will be controlled.

Empirical research by *Greenley* and *McDonald* indicates that very few firms actually have formally written marketing plans, and this is particularly the case within the small business and not-for-profit sectors. Many organisations find it difficult to develop a strategic approach to marketing because of a lack of resources, marketing knowledge, skills, time and probably most importantly a lack of marketing orientation or culture.

Many prescriptive approaches have been developed, often as a checklist of activities needed to be done to write a marketing plan. However, changing an organisation's culture is not a simple or quick task. It requires top management support, internal communications and training on an on-going basis related to marketing skills and cross-function co-ordination.

However, the reality is that many organisations still do not adopt marketing planning practices at all. Therefore the first challenge for marketers working in these types of companies will be to introduce successfully a simple planning system which has the support of senior management.

3 Tutorial question: The synergistic planning process and components of the marketing plan

> Tutorial note. The marketing plan is a written document covering all an organisation's marketing activities, their implementation and control. There should be a plan for each major strategy. Because people and the marketing environment are in a state of continuous change, marketing planning is also a continuous process.

The marketing planning process defined

Marketing planning is a systematic process that involves the identification and assessment of marketing opportunities, the assessment of current and likely future resources and distinctive competences, the development of objectives and strategies and the implementation of detailed marketing programmes. In the syllabus, this process is defined and categorised in three main stages as follows.

(a) Analysis of markets and trading environment opportunities.

(b) Determination of core markets; competitive edge/differential advantage, statement of goals and desired brand positioning.

(c) Determination of marketing programme for implementation.

Further insights into how the market planning process actually works are afforded by *Dibb, Simkin, Pride, Ferrell:*

> 'The marketing planning process *combines* the organisation's overall marketing strategy *with* fundamental analyses of trends in the marketing environment; company strengths, weaknesses, opportunities and threats, competitive strategies; and identification of target market segments. Ultimately the process *leads to* the formulation of market programmes or marketing mixes *which facilitate* the implementation of the organisation's strategies and plans.'

The emphases in key words (which are added, not the authors') serve to highlight the nature of the process, which is also cyclical.

Stage 1 is analytical rather than decisive. We can't decide where we want to be until we know where we are now. Examples of the sort of analyses required start with sales, market share and environmental analysis. We should also want to know our position relative to competitors, and so competitor analysis is also pertinent.

Stage 2 is more decisive than analytical and moves us deeper into the planning process. However, coming to the right decision depends upon further analysis, both of the opportunities emerging from stage 1's environmental scanning and of our organisation's strengths, weaknesses, resources and distinctive competences. This part of the process is the **combines** stage referred to in the Dibb *et al* definition and leads to the setting of achievable/realistic objectives.

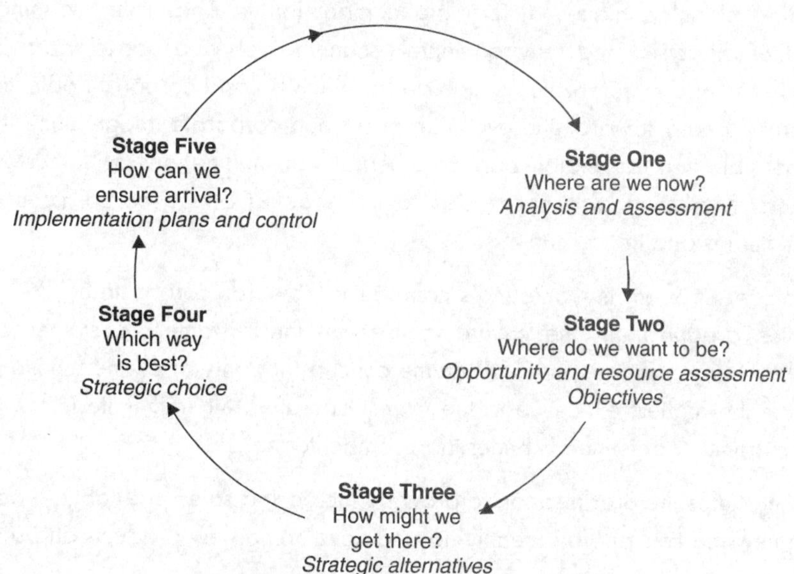

Stage 3 involves achieving of objectives and now we are at the heart of the process. Achieving objectives is normally split into two sub-stages.

(a) How are we going to get there in broad terms **strategy**

(b) How are we going to get there in detailed terms: **tactics (or operations)**

There are choices at both of these stages which have to be evaluated and decisions made. At strategic level a suitable choice framework might be Ansoff, whereas at the more detailed level it is likely to be the marketing mix (which *facilitates* the implementation of strategies)

We can see from these examples that all the stages of the planning process, although being distinctive, tend to merge into the process as a whole, which is in itself iterative in nature.

4 Marketing planning and corporate mission/philosophy

> Tutorial note. Corporate planning shares with marketing planning (or indeed any other form of planning) the same general framework, ie analysis → objectives → strategies → tactics → budgets → controls.

Corporate planning

Corporate planning covers all the organisational functions: production, marketing, R&D, finance and personnel, determining how these are utilised and balanced so as to achieve the overall corporate objectives. Corporate strategy determines the nature of the business, deployment of resources, competitive positioning and the overall co-ordination of the business functions. Corporate planners will also embrace the wider issues of organisation and control such as takeover and merger and the separating out and co-ordination of strategic business units (SBUs): they tend to take a longer-term approach than functional planners.

Marketing planning is part of corporate planning and could be said to have stronger relationships with corporate planning than any other function, since corporate planning is essentially concerned with products and services and markets. These elements govern revenue, profit and the very survival of the organisation.

Marketing planning's contribution to corporate planning

Marketing planning makes a very big contribution to corporate planning. Market analysis, competitor analysis and environmental scanning play a large part in determining the opportunities and threats which shape a firm's mission and corporate objectives. Marketing also contributes greatly towards the evolution of a good corporate image since it is marketing which is responsible for the major part of external communications with customers and potential customers. Marketing also contributes to the shaping of the corporate image by conducting attitude studies and image surveys.

Most important of all, is marketing's contribution towards corporate culture. In a truly marketing orientated organisation, the culture focuses on the customer. Customer care pervades right through the organisation and is the prime concern not only of all the functions but also of all the staff from the highest executive to the lowest operator. All staff unite in the prime endeavour to satisfy customer wants/needs better than competitors.

Marketing helps the organisation to grow by increasing sales profitably. It does so essentially by finding new markets and by identifying and developing new products and services.

Sales forecasting, normally conducted or orchestrated by marketing, sets the corporate objectives and also indirectly all the functional objectives. Marketing SWOT analyses contribute to corporate planning by aiding the development of strategies designed to exploit strengths, correct weaknesses, capitalise on opportunities and negate threats.

Sales analyses helps to determine trends and particularly to identify when products appear to be entering the decline stage of their life cycles. This triggers action aimed at arresting decline and/or developing replacement products so as to prevent potential corporate catastrophes. Similarly portfolio analysis assists in determining winners and losers and the allocation of resources more effectively to SBUs.

The marketing information system makes a major contribution to the corporate or management information systems which provide data essential to the corporate planning process.

The relationships between marketing planning and corporate planning may be expressed diagrammatically as follows.

Relationships between marketing and corporate planning

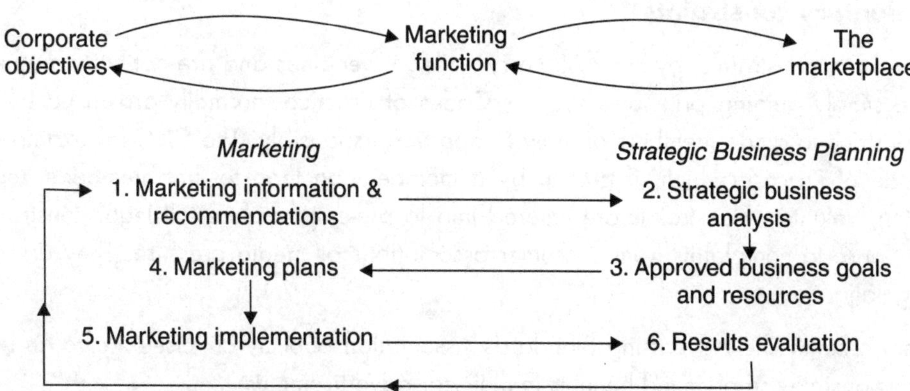

5 Impacts of macro-environmental forces

> Tutorial note. Good answers adopted a punchy journalistic style. Poor answers gave few examples.

Article for CIM *Business Marketing* magazine. Proposed title: Shackles on the CIM (with suitable illustration)

Introduction

As if it isn't bad enough having to take tough decisions in an increasingly volatile marketing environment, CIM members need to be on their guard against an increasing number of shackles or constraints. These shackles vary from handcuffs (you can't sign that!) to gags (you mustn't say that!) to chains/leads (you can't go there!). The modern marketer needs to be a veritable Houdini to be able to break free of these constraints and make the necessary decisions.

Looking more closely at this vast array of constraints we can see that they fall conveniently into three categories - the most binding (legal/regulatory), less binding (voluntary constraints) and constraints of conscience (ethical and social responsibilities).

Legal/regulatory constraints

Legal constraints are those imposed by law, mainly by competition legislation and consumer protection laws, contained in Acts of Parliament in the UK. Regulatory constraints normally arise from legal constraints and comprise the rules which are drawn up for enforcement by regulatory agencies in the UK such as the Ministry of Agriculture, Fisheries and Food, and the Department of the Environment.

Other regulatory constraints can arise from legally binding agreements in contract such as conditions of sale and conditions of purchase. The essential point about the first group of constraints is that organisations have to abide by them or suffer legal penalties such as fines or even imprisonment, and the second group raises issues of being sued for damages (compensation).

A senior city 'watchdog' (IMRO - The Investment Management Regulatory Organisation) last year handed down fines totalling £405,000 plus costs of £225,000 on four of the UK's largest financial broking houses for mis-selling personal pensions.

This year the UK government acting on recommendations by the Monopolies and Mergers Commission have abolished the practice by which manufacturers of electrical goods ranging from televisions to fridges fixed prices by threats/actions of refusal to supply non-cooperating stores.

Voluntary constraints

Voluntary constraints, by contrast, carry no legal penalties and are not enforceable in law. They are simply guiding principles such as Codes of Practice, normally drawn up by institutions or industries to guide members on how to operate responsibly. The CIM, for example, has its own Code of Practice which, if broken by a member can lead to that member's expulsion. Quite often, voluntary constraints are entered into to pre-empt or forestall legal constraints and/or in response to complaints from consumer associations or media pressure. They are a form of self-regulation.

Very recently the Advertising Standards Association publicly criticised *Volvo* and *Audi* for their irresponsible use of speed benefits in their car advertisements.

More and more companies publicise voluntary constraints in their mission statements. *The Body Shop's*, for example, reads 'The Body Shop's international business is in the manufacture and retailing of skincare and haircare preparations and cosmetics. Our business policies are defined by our core values: care for the environment, concern for human rights and opposition to the exploitation of animals'. Such a mission constrains marketing decisions on product, packaging and promotion.

Ethical and social responsibility

Ethics relate to moral values and commonly accepted principles of right and wrong. Organisations which offend these values are likely to receive *adverse publicity* in the media and by word of mouth. Social responsibilities are akin to ethics but involve the impact of an organisation's behaviour upon society. For example, a company like *Boots the Chemist* considering selling off its pharmaceutical division to a German company will offend no laws but places 2,000 jobs in jeopardy. This would reflect upon Boots' caring image and long-standing record of social responsibility. Social responsibility is like an unwritten contract with society, both locally and at large, whilst ethics are reasoned-out rules based on moral values that guide individual/group decisions.

Neither ethics nor social responsibilities are written down in 'tablets of stone' like Codes of Practice or Acts of Parliament. They differ from both legal/regulatory constraints and voluntary constraints by being non-specific and rooted in culture/tradition rather than contractual documentation.

Examples abound and multiply. The mighty Shell Oil company felt obliged to abandon its plans to sink its Brent platform in the North Sea following protests led by Greenpeace which included the mobilisation of ethical and social responsibility issues.

Ethical concerns underlie many simple economic issues such as the payment of a minimum wage with its implications for jobs and prices. Tobacco companies are expected to refrain from encouraging the young to smoke and the brewers are vilified for positioning their 'alcopops' at under-age drinkers.

Conclusions

Whilst the more masochistic marketers might welcome the proliferation of such bondage as described above, others will perhaps reflect upon Wordsworth's 'Shades of the prison-house begin to close upon the growing boy'.

In the end it boils down to the fact that one person's constraint is another person's opportunity.

6 Constituents of macro/micro environmental audits

> Tutorial note. Answers to this question need to explain what is a marketing audit, and how it can be used to produce a SWOT analysis. It is not necessary to explore the mechanics of carrying out the audit.
>
> *Examiner's comments.* Generally quite well answered although some lost marks by failing to answer the SWOT part of the question.

Outline Presentation - The Marketing Audit

By: The marketing manager
To: The board of directors
Time: 30 minutes
Equipment: OHP/slides, laser pointer, handouts

(a) **Introduction**

Ladies and gentlemen of the Board, it is my pleasure today to address you on the subject of a marketing audit for our company. You will need no reminding of the growing importance of environmental concern, having recently amended our mission statement to take this into account. Today we shall be looking specifically at a comprehensive *marketing* audit (show SLIDE).

In order to be comprehensive our audit needs to examine both the external and the internal marketing environments, and as we shall see each of these has several sub-sections (SLIDES). Some notes have been provided for you to study later at your leisure.

(b) **Definition**

We shall start in the time-honoured way with a definition, which is: (SLIDE)

A **marketing audit** is a systematic examination of the marketing group's objectives, strategies, organisation and performance within the prevailing environment. Its primary purpose is to identify weaknesses in ongoing marketing operations with a view to their correction and to monitor changes in the external environment for opportunities and threats arising (adapted from *Dibb, Simkin, Pride, Ferrell*).

(c) **External environment**

(i) **Macro environment**. A popular aide memoire used for grouping the various factors under this main heading is PESTLE standing for: political, economic, social, technological, legal and environmental ('green' issues) (SLIDE).

All of these factors impact upon our hotel chain in some way. For example, the massacre of tourists by terrorists in Luxor, Egypt (a political factor) is affecting our hotel occupancies in that country considerably; the recent windfall payments in the UK combined with a strong £ (both economic factors) have led to increases in holiday hotel bookings; we are experiencing increasing difficulties in obtaining planning permission to build new hotels due to environmental concerns and even physical interference from protest groups (legal/green/social factors).

(ii) **Micro environment**. This part of the audit embraces customers, competitors, suppliers and distributors (SLIDE). Clearly we need to know how we are doing against our competitors and what our customers and distributors think about us, our products and services. You will of course be aware of our **continuous** customer satisfaction survey but perhaps not know of our mystery shoppers - a device by which we directly experience actual customer service and also use to monitor travel agents' performance. Then there is the need to check out our many suppliers as well as to be aware of new products coming onto the hotel market. At present we are particularly looking for software to alleviate the problem of dating on our computer programs in the new millennium.

(d) International environment

There are a number of sub-audits under this heading which are concerned with evaluating our internal marketing performance. These are: (SLIDE)

(i) **The marketing strategy audit** demands answers to such questions as: are our marketing objectives appropriate? and are our strategies effective?

(ii) **The marketing organisation audit** queries our functional efficiencies with regard to such things as communications/relationships within the department and with other functions.

(iii) **The marketing systems audit** which critically examines the efficacies of our marketing information, new product development and our planning and control systems.

(iv) **The marketing productivity audit**. This involves rigorous cost-effectiveness and profitability analyses to ensure minimum waste.

(v) **The marketing functions audit** basically questions all the elements in our marketing mix - products/services, prices, promotion (advertising, sales promotion, PR and personal selling) and distribution - with regard to their effectiveness, how they compare with competitors in our customers' eyes.

(e) **The SWOT analysis**

All these external and internal analyses are brought together in the so-called SWOT analysis (SLIDE). This categories the internal factors into Strengths and Weaknesses and the external factors into Opportunities and Threats, so as to form the basis of our future marketing plans. For example: (SLIDE)

Strengths

- An international chain
- Marketing orientated
- Progressive/involved board of directors
- Profitable
- Group synergies

Weaknesses

- No clear growth strategy
- Marketing plans not communicated throughout the organisation
- Low calibre/untrained staff on customer interfaces
- Some poor hotel locations (relative to competitors)
- Over-systemised and impersonal (music, television, meals)

Opportunities

- Growth in holiday markets (UK, Eastern Europe, Far East)
- Marketing on the Internet (virtual hotel tours, booking)
- Higher per capita incomes and upwardly moving tastes

- Global warming

Threats

- Computer systems breakdown (millennium dating)
- Political unrest (Middle East, Eastern Europe, Far East)
- EU regulations and monetary union
- Decline in business traffic due to telecommunications

The above is indicative only. Items need to be allocated scores and degrees of importance to facilitate prioritisation. Some issues arising are: (SLIDE)

(i) Should we sell hotels at the low end of the market and invest in better albeit more expensive locations?

(ii) To what extent can we personalise products and services without lowering standards and increasing costs?

(iii) How can we exploit new technology?

(iv) How should we balance the decline in business markets with increases in consumer holiday markets?

(f) **Summary** (SLIDE)

Ladies and gentlemen of the board, I hope you would agree that no effective marketing plans can be drawn up without knowing where we are now, in order to decide where we want to be (that we can realistically achieve) in the future.

These critical decisions need to be based on the most thorough understanding of the facts and trends.

The more thorough the marketing audit, the better knowledge and understanding shall we possess, enabling this board to ensure that the right decisions are made with regard to sustaining the profitable growth of our company. Thank you for listening.

7 Tutorial question: Assessing the external marketing environment

> Tutorial note. The marketing environment consists of a number of external forces that affect an organisation's operations. An organisation's operations can usually be viewed as the acquisition of inputs with the purpose of generating particular outputs. Inputs are likely to be finance, personnel's time/expertise, information, raw materials, production processes etc. Outputs might be primarily products but also packaging, services, information and ideas. The marketing environment is normally in a state of flux or continuous change.

Marketing environment forces

Dibb, Simkin, Pride and Ferrell suggest that the marketing environment consists of external forces that affect an organisation's inputs and outputs. These forces are categorised as follows.

- Political
- Legal
- Regulatory
- Societal/green
- Technological
- Economic and competitive

These forces act directly or indirectly upon an organisation's marketing decisions and their outcomes in a variety of ways, as illustrated in the following examples.

(a) **Political factors**

Government responds to powerful lobbies and pressures from all sorts of groups. For example the anti-smoking lobby has succeeded in getting cigarette advertising banned from television by the Government. This clearly affects the promotional decisions of the manufacturers as well as the future sales forecasts of advertising agents and television advertisement production companies involved in the process.

(b) **Legal factors**

Various Acts of Parliament and, increasingly, European laws operate to constrain marketing decisions. Competition laws are intended to preserve competition and to prevent restrictive practices deemed to be against the public interest. Thus the Office of Fair Trading referred the major UK brewers to the Monopolies and Mergers Commission which then ordered the six major brewers to 'untie', ie free, thousands of tied public houses. The effect intended was to allow the public access to a greater variety of beers instead of being restricted to particular brewers' beers, usually the only ones on offer at their tied outlets.

(c) **Regulatory factors**

Closely allied to Government and legal forces are the regulatory agencies set up by national and local governments. For example the Department of the Environment may preclude the placing of new hypermarkets in particular areas. Ministry of Health inspectors police the hygiene standards of food shops, particularly butchers and fresh fish shops.

(d) **Societal/green factors**

Although non-legal, societal pressures can and often do oblige marketers to change their marketing decisions for fear of backlashes of adverse publicity in ever-vigilant media, prompted by various consumer interest groups. Increasingly in Europe, multiple retailers are giving preference to goods from manufacturers wrapped in environmentally friendly or recyclable packaging. Most professional bodies now have their own published codes of conduct or professional guidelines which forbid members from pursuing particular marketing practices, upon penalty of exposure and dismissal from membership.

(e) **Technological factors**

This is perhaps the most obvious force affecting an organisation's product/service decisions. The increasing rate of advances in technology are causing shorter and shorter product life cycles. Organisations therefore need to monitor technological change and must be prepared continuously to update their products/services to prevent these becoming obsolete. For example, a BPP Practice & Revision Kit would cost too much and take too long to produce on out-of-date letterpress equipment, and would no longer be competitive in a modern world of computerised printing technology.

(f) **Economic and competitive factors**

These two forces have particular effects on consumers' willingness to spend and on how much they are prepared to pay. They affect sales forecasting and pricing decisions to a marked degree. They also affect product and service design in that, during protracted periods of economic recession, customers are likely to give precedence to lower priced offerings. The degree of competition clearly affects marketing strategy decisions for organisations in the market and the various positions adopted.

It can be seen from the above that these six primary environmental forces together affect every aspect of marketing, from the setting of marketing objectives through strategy to details of the marketing mix.

8 Tutorial question: Assessing internal capabilities

> Tutorial note. Any organisation has limited internal capabilities. These include finite resources such as capital and staff. An organisation's employees have limited expertise and skills, limited time and limited equipment.

Having identified a marketing opportunity an organisation has to decide whether it is capable of exploiting it. In making this decision the organisation has to assess its resources both currently and in the future. Clearly an organisation is constrained by its resources and will normally have set overall objectives in light of these. An organisation's internal capabilities can conveniently be categorised using the normal business functions framework, as follows.

(a) **Financial capabilities**

Clearly there are limits to what an organisation can afford. An organisation's financial capability might be defined as its cash reserves, working capital and its capability to borrow money to invest.

(b) **Production capabilities**

An organisation is constrained in the types of goods or services it can supply by the limitations of its plant, machinery and the skills of its operatives.

(c) **Marketing capabilities**

A company's marketing capability is limited by its marketing mix, namely its products, prices, promotion and place (distribution outlets). Within the promotion element, an organisation may only have a certain number of salespeople, with limited product knowledge, limited selling skills and limited contacts. Marketing managers' expertise may not be particularly broad. For these sorts of reasons an organisation operating in industrial markets, if faced with an opportunity to move into consumer markets, may decide that it does not possess the right marketing capabilities to achieve this.

(d) **Personnel capabilities**

An organisation employs a limited number of staff, each of whom has limited expertise and skills. It may not be able to expand its staff quickly enough (or be able to train existing staff into acquiring new skills) to take advantage of a short-term marketing opportunity such as a sudden rise in demand for heating equipment during a particularly cold spell in the weather.

The above examples show that it is extremely important that a company analyses its internal capabilities. Failure to recognise the constraints imposed by limitations in these capabilities could lead to the grasping of a wrong marketing opportunity with catastrophic results.

9 Critical appraisal of auditing techniques

It could be argued that unless an organisation knows clearly where it is and where it has come from, it is difficult to aim and justify where it wants to be in the future. The basis of most forward planning is a degree of extrapolation of past trends, modified by a forecast of those factors most likely to impact on the organisation's performance. Auditing techniques are therefore essential to the drawing up of viable objectives.

However, most of the various auditing techniques, whilst found useful, have some drawbacks of which the planner should be aware, since these could materially affect the probability of the plan's success.

It is not possible here within the time limits to cover all the auditing techniques in use but the following examples are pertinent:

1 **PESTLE**

Most planners accept that these factors affect the organisation's future to some degree. A commercial business will particularly be affected by the economy whilst a global aid organisation such as the Red Cross will be affected by the incidence of war. The problem is that these factors are not always easily predictable, for example, the economy is subject to booms and depressions, whilst armed rebellion can break out suddenly in various parts of the world.

2 **SWOT**

Almost all organisations employ this technique in their marketing audits, which is a tribute to its general utility. However, it should be recognised that the assessment of the SWOT factors is largely subjective. The question has to be asked – how many people should participate in these assessments and what are their qualifications for doing this?

3 **Portfolio analysis**

Although the BCG matrix offers several advantages, their practical value rests on the quality of the data input, many of which are difficult to define and measure. These difficulties have led to further development such as the GE multifactor matrix, the Shell directional policy matrix and the Arthur. D. Little strategic condition matrix.

4 **The product life cycle**

Very little information is needed – just company, market and industry sales. It obliges marketing managers to consider changes to the marketing mix.

However, over the years there have been many critics of the PLC such as Day, Dhalla and Yspeh, and O'Shaughnessy, who say that:

- There is no empirical evidence to support the idea of products moving through the various stages
- It is dangerous to regard the decline stage as the end of the product
- The stages do not necessarily follow each other
- The life cycle is the dependent and not the independent variable

5 **The balanced scorecard**

This approach by Kaplan and Norton has a number of benefits including:

- Widening the view of managers beyond financial data
- Forcing managers to become involved in other areas and to interact
- Ensuring consistency between objectives – sales and profit objectives may become unrealistic when seen in conjunction with customer service and resource issues

6 **Porter's generic strategies**

Porter's thesis that there are three generic strategies open to an organisation wishing to achieve sustainable competitive advantage – Cost Leadership, Differentiation, Focus/Niche – and the necessity of choosing one or risk being stuck in the middle – has rightly gained popular support over the years.

However, the situation is not always so clear cut: it could for example be the case that some small companies in particular achieve both a cost advantage and a degree of differentiation while trading successfully and growing. In short, it can be argued that Porter's generic strategies are not mutually exclusive (Fulmer and Goodwin). Some measure also needs to be put on the interpretation of 'sustainable'.

In summary, the use of techniques for auditing is to be encouraged but some caution needs to be exercised. The techniques' strengths and weaknesses should be considered when choosing which of these are most suitable for the organisation and situation concerned.

10 Role of information and research in auditing

> *Examiner's comments.* There were a significant number of poor answers to part (a) that failed to recognise data sources and described research instead. Part (b) was well done by those candidates who had discussed data sources in part (a).

Data required to review marketing consultancy operations

To: The Board of Directors
From: Marketing Manger
Subject: Review of Operations
Date: December 20X1

(a) Our department has been asked to conduct a review of all of our consultancy operations with a view to attracting new clients. Please find below an outline of the sources of data that we will be reviewing, and how this data will be essential to our review. The list is split into the two major sections of internal and external data.

Internal data

Internal data is information and records that we hold in-house. Although these data have been produced for other purposes they can be applied to the new client project.

- Sales records
- Customer records
- Purchase records
- Complaints
- Accounts
- Customer tracking data
- Quotation database
- Sales Enquiry Records
- Customer feedback reports
- Corporate strategy

External data

External data is information which has been collected by outside agents together with information published by competitors. These can be in the form of census data or data specifically collected and analysed for market research purposes. This information is often chargeable.

- Competitor information
- Government statistics
- Market reports
- Trade journals

(b) Each of the above **data sources** will provide useful information for our new client review. The table below shows the type of information provided and gives specific examples on how the data will be used in the review.

Internal records

Sales records	*Use for the review*
Information on past sales and current sales activity. Sales will be split by: ■ Customer type ■ Customer size ■ By service/product type ■ New customers ■ Lapsed customers ■ By month and year	This information can be used to: ■ Analyse the source of our turnover ■ Identify any trends and make judgements about potential future activity ■ Assess which markets we are performing in ■ Identify poorly performing areas for additional study prior to decisions being made as to whether to drop them from the product portfolio or to develop them into other new markets.
Customer records	*Use for the review*
■ Customer type/sector ■ Size of organisation by employees and turnover ■ Geographic location ■ Historical data on individual customers. Project scoping documentation. ■ Inventory on work carried out. ■ Duration of project ■ Purchase patterns ■ Lapsed customers	■ To identify the characteristics of a good' customer. ■ Reveal market specific needs ■ To identify the most appropriate service/products to be offered to different segments. ■ To reveal seasonal trends to contribute to promotional/marketing campaign planning. ■ Identify areas of poor performance which are losing customers
Accounts	*Use for the review*
Profitability ■ Split by customer type ■ Split by product/service *Expenditure* ■ Allocation to each product/service type ■ Allocation to each customer type *Debtor days* *Bad debts*	■ To identify our most profitable services/products. ■ Identify most profitable customer types ■ Highlight poor performing or non-profitable services
Customer tracking data	*Use for the review*
How many phone calls, mailshots, personal visits and presentations did it take to convert the sale?	■ Determines the cost of making a sale in different markets and different customer types

Customer tracking data	*Use for the review*
	■ Determines the cost of making a sale for different service types
Quotation database	*Use for the review*
Project outline, client type and whether won or lost.	■ Indication of price sensitivity amongst markets ■ Use to highlight poor performance for further investigation
Sales enquiry records	*Use for the review*
Who enquired, where did they get our information from, type of enquiry, services requested, contact information and outcome.	■ Highlight areas for new service development ■ Identify whether enquiries are being followed up ■ Monitoring advertising effectiveness ■ Monitoring promotional effectiveness
Customer feedback reports	*Use for the review*
What we do well, areas where we need to improve, how we compare to our competitors.	■ Highlight areas for improvement ■ Provide examples of unique selling propositions for marketing

External data

Competitors	*Use for the review*
Numbers, size, structure, market position, product portfolio, client portfolio. Pricing, future intentions and likely reaction to pro-active marketing from our organisation. Gap analysis could be performed to find a competitive advantage.	■ This will give information for how we compare to the competition ■ Market share ■ Use for the development of USPs
Government statistics	*Use for the review*
Performance of particular sectors of the markets and economy.	Background information to aid selection of new market sectors.
Trade journals	*Use for the review*
Wealth of information on markets, competitors, forthcoming legislation and events.	■ Use for background information on the market ■ Reveal threats and opportunities for the consultancy ■ Identify potential new customers ■ Background information on customers ■ Information on competitors

Market reports	*Use for the review*
Industry specific reports with information on market size, structure, growth, spend on consultancy by market sector, trends and developments.	Background information to highlight the best opportunities for new market development or product/service development.

We have a large amount of **in-house information** which will allow us to review our current operations. Using this we will be able to gauge which products/markets are profitable and worth developing and which ones we need to review. This kind of information also contributes to decision making on which products/services to target to which new markets.

It is likely that we do not have all of the information which we require in a format which we can use, in which case additional recommendations may be made to review our internal records systems.

The external data can give clues to external influences on our company, together with valuable ideas for new product developments or new markets to target. Collecting this kind of data should become an ongoing process and all sources should be documented and referenced to facilitate future operational and strategic reviews.

11 Relationships between corporate, business and marketing objectives

Lecturers and students alike can get confused by the lack of clarity in differentiating between the levels of objectives by many authors, some of whom avoid the issue entirely. Others refer to strategic objectives or even tactical objectives, just to add a little further confusion.

Objectives are where you want to be, whereas strategies are how you get there in general terms and tactics are how you get there in more detailed terms, ie. specific actions. Objectives are the ends and strategies/tactics are the means.

An American author once wrote that without being quantified and time-scaled you don't have an objective, you have a delusion, because if you can't measure it you can't know whether it had been achieved or when. Today we have qualitative as well as quantitative objective but strenuous efforts will succeed in establishing appropriate measures for the former. An objective 'to increase sales' is not very helpful. If the outcome was actually by 0.0001% after 20 years, you would have achieved this but to what avail? A qualitative objective of 'to increase customer satisfaction' can be quantified by adding 'from the current overall rating of 4.6 to a minimum of 6.0 (on a scale of 7) by end 2004'.

Confusion can to some extent be cleared by reference to what is known as the hierarchy of objectives, or the cascade effect. For example, marketing objectives are in effect corporate strategies, since they are the means of achieving corporate objectives. An advertising objective is a marketing strategy...and so on downwards.

Kotler therefore counsels us to arrange objectives hierarchically from the most important to the least important. For example, the business's key objective might be to increase the rate of return on investment. This could be accomplished by increasing the profit level and reducing the amount of invested capital. Profit itself could be increased by increasing revenue and reducing expenditure. Revenue can be increased by gaining market share and increasing prices. In this way the business unit proceeds from broad to specific objectives for specific departments and individuals.

Most authors agree that for most objectives to be effective, they should be SMART, ie. **S**pecific, **M**easurable, **A**cceptable, **R**ealistic, **T**ime-scaled. Objectives must also be consistent. For example it is not possible to maximise both sales and profits simultaneously.

Trying now to distinguish between corporate, business and marketing objectives and their relationships, we should first acknowledge that organisations as well as businesses have overall or corporate objectives which are long-term and need to address stakeholder groups which may comprise customers, employees, shareholders, suppliers, governmental/regulatory bodies and so on. For these reasons specific SMART objectives tend to be avoided and broad aims substituted in conjunction with a mission statement. The latter can be defined as a 'statement of the organisation's purpose – what it wants to accomplish in the wider environment' (Kotler).

Most organisations associate expansion with success and these will set broad corporate objectives accordingly. A company is likely to set broad corporate objectives of profitable growth and the business objectives will then be specific and SMART: for example, 'to achieve a ROCE of X by Y'. Growth can be defined in a number of ways – increased numbers of employees, SBUs, retail outlets, number of markets entered and so on. Marketing objectives' major contribution to the corporate and business objectives are likely to be growth in market share and revenue, both of which may improve profit and reduce risk. The market share and revenue objectives do of course need to be quantified.

Service companies such as IBM recognise that customer satisfaction is essential for profitable growth and so maintain regular detailed surveys as a mechanism for setting SMART objectives and maintaining control of this important facet of their marketing strategy.

So perhaps authors are wise to avoid being too prescriptive in distinguishing between types of functional objectives and to treat these hierarchically. The most important relationship of the different objectives is that they should all work together to a common end.

In summary:

- Corporate objectives tend to be broad, long-term and less specific, concerning the organisation as a whole (which may not be a company) and defining the organisation's main purposes for the benefit of all stakeholders
- Business objectives are those made mainly by companies or SBUs and concerned with improving the financial and functional well-being of the business such as profitability, return on investment, production efficiency and so on. These business objectives will be SMART and shorter-term than corporate objectives.
- Marketing objectives will support the business objectives and be set in terms of market share, sales revenues, customer satisfaction. Lower down the hierarchy will be communications objectives, advertising objectives, pricing objectives and so on.

12 Relationship management and the marketing mix

> *Examiner's comments:* This question covers relationship marketing for not-for-profit organisations. It considers the marketing mix adaptation for relationship marketing and the influence that an international context may have on the organisation.

From: Marketing Manager
Date: December 2003

(a) **Report on relationships with stakeholders**

Introduction

Relationship marketing involves the use of a wide range of marketing, sales, communications and customer care techniques and processes. These identify named individuals, create a relationship between the company and these customers and manage that relationship to the benefit of both customers and company. To be successful relationship-marketers companies must develop a supportive organisational culture, market the relationship marketing activity internally and intimately understand customer expectations. It must create and maintain a detailed customer base and organise and reward staff in such a way that the objective of relationship marketing, customer retention is achieved.

For a not-for-profit service organisation such as a government department or public service provider, volunteers for charity or a local community project the relationships and stakeholders are just as important. We have chosen a national charity that protects dogs from abuse.

Importance of Customer Relationships

Relationship marketing is applied in different sectors but emerged in the service sector due to the inseparable and often longitudinal nature of the exchange as could be found in the charity sector. The notion of a relationship marketing loyalty ladder aims at moving the customer up the rungs of the ladder from a prospect to a partner. Stages in the ladder are shown below:

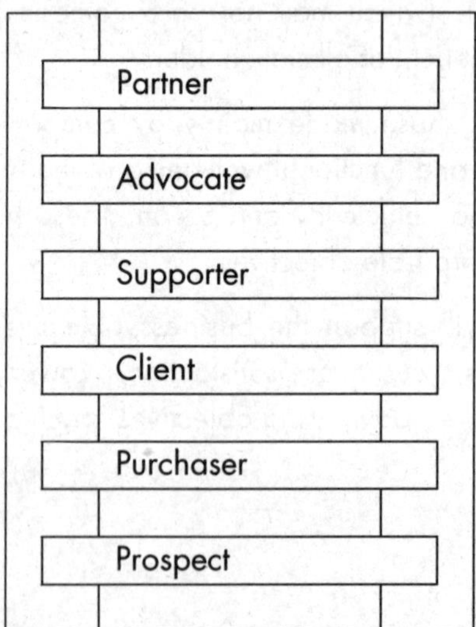

The first rung on the ladder represents a potential customer for the charity that the marketer could possibly persuade to do business with the charity. The other stages culminate with the top rung where the customer is viewed as a partner to the charity. The intention is that by consistently good customer service delivered by the charity the individual progresses through the intermediary stages to the top level. That will ensure that there is a high level of commitment by the customer to the charity with extensive use of all the different services on offer. This will ensure that there is an efficient and targeted use of costs from within the charity towards its customers.

The stakeholders include everyone who an interest in the charity organisation and listed below are some of the reasons to maintain a relationship.

Stakeholder	Reason to maintain relationship
Employees & Volunteers	Keep employees and volunteers informed on progress of organisation objectives as a whole
Management	In a Not-for-Profit it is easy to become detached from the organisation as there is no profit motive to converge thinking. This is substituted by the charity objectives and therefore communication and dialogue is vital throughout the organisation.
Customers	Our customers are the charity centres that care for the animals. Through good relationships and understanding we can tailor our activities when suitable for certain areas eg Christmas
Suppliers (Donations)	We rely entirely upon donations from the public. Contact must be maintained to ensure continued donations and charity loyalty. Feedback & benefits gained from their donations is vital for long term relationships.
Suppliers (Goods & Services)	As a charity all our costs have to be carefully monitored. Through good relationships with our service suppliers we can negotiate lower rates in exchange for good publicity for their business. Through these channels we can also seek sponsorship.

(b) **Marketing Mix adaptation for Relationship Marketing**

The following are the recommendations for an appropriate extended marketing mix for our charity to ensure relationships are developed and managed.

Product	Continue development of our services, new centres and vans for animals. Communicated to all stakeholders once opened and active.
Price	Review of donations. Setting of an acceptable monthly, yearly or one-off cost to suggest to donators as a guide. Research rival charities price setting
Promotion	Continued issuing of promotional collateral for donation requests (brochures, adverts and e mails) and to increase success stories and promote positive work. Encourage perception of social contribution
Place	Use of facilities that are suitable for the charity. Key account management must be available at the centres.
Physical evidence	Centres must be smart and functional. They must give the impression that the dogs are well cared for and well treated.
People	Training is important and donator focused. Staff need to be ambassadors of the charity and understand the charity's objectives.
Process	The adoption of suitable operating procedures is important. The ease of donations is very important. Use of banks, post office, selected stores, charity centres, affinity credit card and on-line via the Internet.

(c) **Considerations of marketing activities for international context**

The marketing of the charity internationally must allow for differences with different countries. Not all countries have the same level of respect or care for animals. This is often embedded in the different national beliefs and is based on cultural and religious differences. Developing countries may not be able to divert resources or funds to pet and veterinary care. Further the laws protecting animals will vary dramatically in an international context.

Marketing activities will have two approaches internationally

Educate for animal welfare – economically poor countries need education on the correct care for their animals. Animals are their workforce and livelihood and the promotion of care will help increase the quality of life for the animals

Donation appeals - countries of similar position as the UK and similar beliefs can be targeted for donations. Donations are more likely to be received for a nationally recognised charity. Campaigns to stop live animal transportation across the EU, which receives significant public support.

Conclusion

We will need to segment the market clearly and identify customers with potential and then assess reasons for customer churn at present. We will need to develop a plan to increase retention levels and need relationship marketing plan with a focus on internal marketing.

13 The planning gap and its operational implications

> *Examiner's comments.* Good answers outlined both the causes of strategic wear-out and how the planning gap can be filled by marketing operations. Poor answers were limited to explanations of the planning gap only.

'Strategic wear-out occurs when an organisation no longer meets customer needs and the pursued strategy is surpassed by competitors.' (*Ensor and Drummond*) This is a danger faced by most organisations which can come about by neglecting the changing face of the environment in which they are operating. Recent examples have included Marks and Spencer who to some extent lost touch with what their customers wanted. At a more extreme level, some businesses have suffered because they failed to use the new technology. For example, Encyclopaedia Britannica did not recognise the benefits of the CD-ROM.

If an organisation does not match its strategy to the environment then a strategic gap will occur between where the organisation should be and where it actually is:

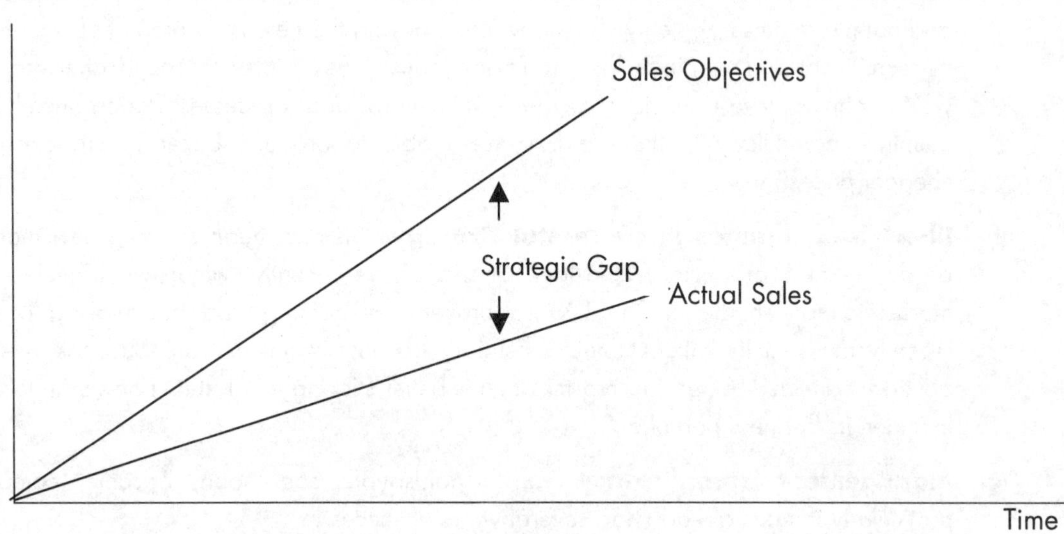

The Strategic Gap

Where a business position deteriorates such that the strategic gap widens then this is known as strategic drift and will eventually lead to strategic wear-out.

The causes of strategic wear-out

Davidson summarises the main causes as follows:

(a) **Changes in customer requirements and expectations**: An example of this is in the Pubs and Hotels sector where many of these outlets now have to cater for families and have to provide food and a range of non-alcoholic drinks. Many pubs have gone out of business because their traditional market has gone and for one reason or another have not adapted to this changed market place.

(b) **Changes in distribution systems**: many parts of the economy have been affected by these changes. The growth of large supermarkets has led to the demise of smaller retail outlets and wholesalers. The internet, with opportunities for on-line shopping, had led to many businesses in the music, books, financial services and travel markets, either having to change their marketing strategy or to close down and leave the industry.

(c) **Innovation by competitors**: here both existing and new competitors have used innovatory strategies which have forced companies to change their ways or face the consequences. In the no frills airline business, Easyjet and Ryanair have introduced many innovations. For example, ticketless systems, on-line booking and frequent services with short turnarounds. Many traditional competitors are at last now doing the same, but they have lost market share. In the Personal Computer retailing business, Time Computers were one of the first companies to offer direct sales to the home backed up by considerable customer service.

(d) **Poor control of company costs**: unless tight control is kept on costs then a business can soon become uneconomic and uncompetitive. Many banks have had to rationalise and change their business models. This has been in the face of new market entrants eg Tesco and competition from overseas banks eg MBNA. Although there have been public objections, many banks have closed branches and centralised their operations. They have also offered more cost efficient services (eg Telephone banking in order to compete more effectively).

(e) **Lack of consistent investment**: it is important for organisations to invest consistently and not just in times of plenty. This may mean buying the new technology but also investing in recruitment and training. The UK Textile Industry never saw the need after the second world war to invest in new factories, machines and processes. Consequently, other countries particularly in the Far East were able to produce better quality products at cheaper prices.

(f) **Ill-advised changes in successful strategy**: this can mean entering new markets or producing new products. Marks and Spencer have recently withdrawn from the French market to concentrate on the UK. Ladbrokes, the gaming and bookmaking company, recently divested its Hilton Hotels subsidiary because it felt its core business was being adversely affected. Often, an organisation is better sticking to what it knows than looking to broaden its business portfolio.

(g) **Management complacency**: an organisation can soon become complacent, particularly if it has already had several years of success.

The consequences of strategic wear-out can be loss of market share, loss of profitability and perhaps most important of all, damage to the confidence of customers, employees and suppliers. All of these consequences can take many years to regain. In many cases the organisation goes out of business or is taken over.

The planning gaps' impact on marketing operations

Clearly action needs to be taken to fill the planning gap, ideally without reducing the sales objectives. McDonald suggests how marketing operations can help to do this both at the strategic and tactical levels.

(a) Improved productivity by, for example, increasing prices, improving the return on the sales/products mix, reducing costs

(b) Market Penetration strategies, for example, increasing product usage, increasing share market, cross-selling

(c) Market Development strategies, for example finding new user groups, entering new segments, geographical expansion

(d) New Product/Service Development strategies, from cosmetic improvements, through product modifications to full-blown new products

(e) Redeployment of the extended marketing mix so as to achieve a more favourable positioning

(f) Diversification – new products for new markets, acquisitions, partnerships, strategic alliances.

Conclusions

Strategic wear-out is a real danger becoming increasingly so as markets fragment and competition increases. Only by remaining firmly committed to satisfying customer needs can organisations avoid this danger. This involves constant monitoring of the environment and constant analysis of how changes in the environment will impact on the business. This in itself necessitates a strong commitment by the organisation to the workforce, suppliers and customers in order to achieve effective market orientation.

14 Gap analysis

Report to: Soft Drinks Company Management
From: A N Other
Date: 7 December 200X
Subject: Gap analysis, segmentation and targeting

(a) **The concept of gap analysis**

Most companies, including ours, look forward to increased sales and profits so as to fulfil responsibilities to the stakeholders. However, when projecting future sales realistically, there is often a gap between projected sales and those desired by corporate management, as illustrated in the diagram below.

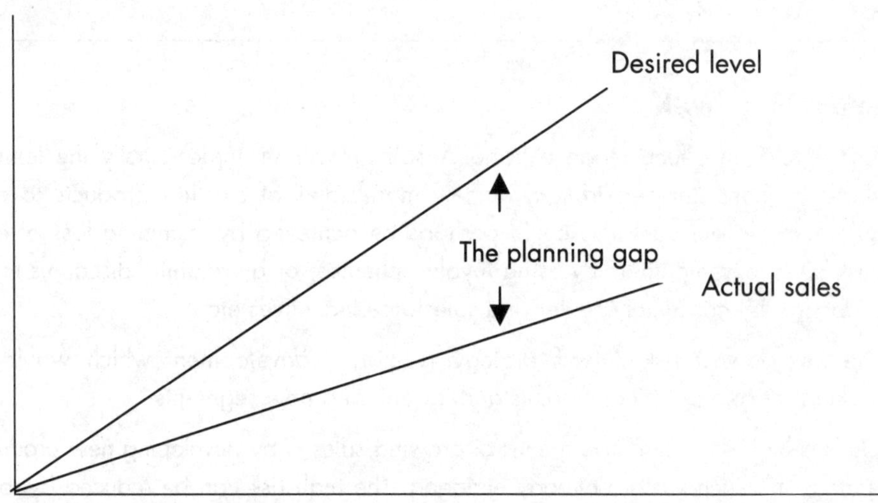

This is usually called the Planning Gap or the Strategic Planning Gap and can be defined as occurring where corporate financial and sales objectives are greater than the current long-term forecasts by marketing planning.

(b) **Filling the strategic planning gap**

Obviously the gap could be closed by simply reducing the sales required by corporate management but this would be an undesirably negative approach.

A more positive approach would be to try to close at least some of the gap by operational means such as increasing prices, promotional campaigns or improving the sales mix.

Kotler suggests there are three main ways of closing the gap, as illustrated below:

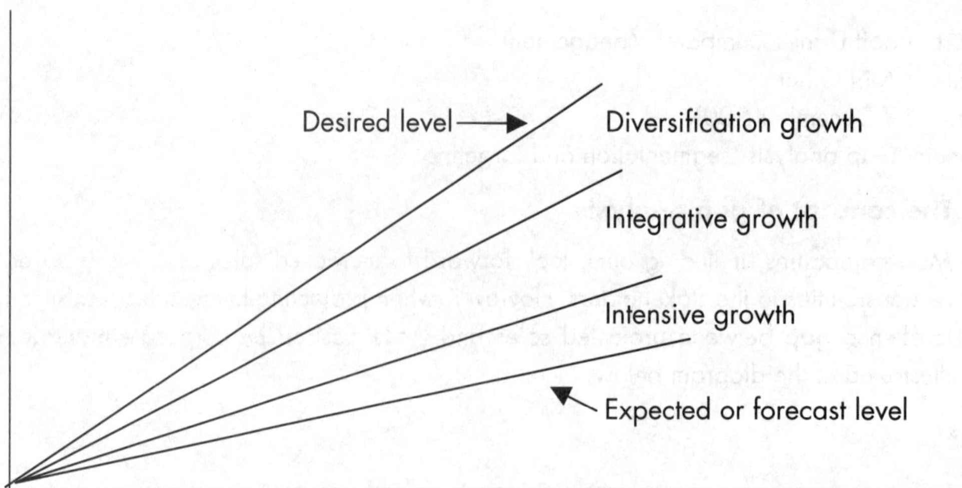

1 **Intensive growth**

This would, in effect, mean utilising Ansoff growth strategies, firstly the lowest risk strategy of *market penetration*, namely more sales of existing products to existing customers. In our case this could perhaps be achieved by stemming loss of existing customers to competitors by using loyalty schemes; or by quantity discounts for large orders; or by consumer/dealer and salesforce incentives etc.

The next lowest risk Ansoff strategy is *market development* which would mean looking for geographical markets and/or entering new segments.

Quite a high risk alternative means of growing sales is by developing new products – a strategy in which we are already engaged. The high risk can be reduced by lowering the degree of newness ie making modifications to our existing products such as improving the design of our bottles, the labelling, the strength of some of our flavours etc.

The last and highest risk Ansoff strategy of *diversification* has been separately addressed below.

2 **Integrative growth**

Our company's sales could be increased by backward, forward or horizontal integration within the industry. Backward would mean buying up some of our suppliers; forward would mean acquiring wholesalers or retailers; and horizontal would mean taking over competitors.

3 **Diversification growth**

In Ansoff terms this means new products for new markets. Three types of diversification can be considered:

- new products with technological or marketing synergies with our own
- new products without the above synergies but which would appeal to our customers
- new business acquisitions which have no product/customer relationships

(c) **Concepts of segmentation and targeting**

Segmentation recognises that not all people are the same, ie that not everyone wants a car coloured black. Children can have different wants and needs to adults, as can women to men. Thus we can identify a need of sports people for stamina-enhancing, energy-boosting soft drinks. This represents an opportunity for entrepreneurs like this company to exploit, providing the segment is identifiable, measurable, large enough to yield the desired profits, and accessible.

A segment is therefore a portion of the whole. No one company can hope to satisfy all the wants/needs of all the people in the world and so has to choose in which markets to operate and then whether to focus on particular segments.

There is an increasing array of characteristics used to define segments but the main ones are as follows:

- **Socio-Demographic** eg age, sex. This helps us to determine whether for example, young people prefer particular flavours in drinks. We are investigating an apparent social class distinction in preference for still as opposed to fizzy bottled water.
- **Geographic**. Regional as well as national preferences can emerge such as for cider in the South-West and the old 'Irn Bru' in Scotland.
- **Psychographic/Behavioural**. These can be used to focus on, for example, loyal customers, heavy users, influencers and so on.

Targeting is the selection of which segments, from the total available, upon which to focus. These are known as the target market segments. A decision then has to be made whether to differentiate the marketing mix for each of these segments and if so, to what extent. For example, if we were to target a low income segment, we could offer lower prices for products with artificial flavouring, in less expensive packaging, distributed through selected supermarkets.

The process of segmentation → targeting → positioning

Kotler carries segmentation and targeting through to positioning ie determining the most propitious position or mix to offer to a given target segment, relative to competitors, as follows:

1 Identify segmentation variables and segment the market
2 Develop profiles of resulting segments
3 Evaluate the attractiveness of each segment
4 Select the target segments
5 Identify and research potential positionings for each target segment
6 Select, develop and communicate the chosen positioning concept

The advantages of segmentation (Dibb *et al*)

Customer analysis

A better understanding of customer needs and wants and other characteristics which improves responsiveness. A better understanding than competitors offers a potential competitive advantage

Competitor analysis

Analysing which segments competitors are targeting and their positionings facilitates decisions in these areas with superior resources

Effective resource allocation

All companies have limited resources. Targeting the entire market is usually unrealistic. Operational effectiveness can be greatly improved by focusing upon a particular segment.

(d) **Recommended segmentation variables for drinks products**

Purchase occasion

This is an important variable in that people's thirst normally demands instant gratification and it is therefore essential that drinks are available in as many outlets as possible, ideally around the clock.

People will also purchase quite large quantities of drinks for special occasions such as parties and weddings. These purchase occasions will also influence the types and qualities of drinks sought – from mineral water through to champagne.

Benefits sought

Apart from slaking thirst, drinks can have other benefits. Alcoholic drinks offer an opportunity to lose inhibitions. Health drinks can help patients to recover more quickly. Sports drinks offer a potentially better performance for a longer period.

Other variables

The above cannot be completely separated from other variables, particularly those of **demographics** and **lifestyle**. For example, being seen drinking an expensive champagne can confer a certain cachet on the social climber, whereas 'alcopops' are targeted at younger people.

15 Segmentation, targeting and positioning strategies

> *Tutorial note.* Overseas students are encouraged to use examples from their own country's educational system rather than the UK. Segmentation, targeting and positioning are at the heart of modern marketing. No organisation can possibly hope to cater for all the needs/wants of all the people and so it has to select a group which offers the best opportunity to meet its organisational objectives. A company has to target the group at which to aim and with which to communicate.
>
> *Examiner's comments.* A popular question and generally answered well. Poorer candidates, though, provided theory without application.

(a) **Definitions**

(i) **Market segmentation** is the process by which customers in markets with some heterogeneity (such as buyers of books) can be grouped into smaller, more homogenous segments with similar needs and wants (such as people needing academic textbooks for study purposes).

(ii) **Targeting**. Once segments have been identified, decisions can be made as to which groups to concentrate on or target. There are three main options.

- Concentrate on just one segment with one product
- Offer one product to a number of segments
- Target a different product at each of a number of segments

(iii) **Positioning**. A product's positioning is the place a product occupies in a given market, as perceived by the relevant group of customers: that group of customers is known as the target segment of the market.

(b) **BPP Publishing**

Part of BPP Professional Education, a group which specialises in business education products and services including publications, professional training and language courses.

Market segmentation

BPP Publishing's chosen market segments are the professions and within these the people who are hoping to obtain professional qualifications by examinations. BPP offer a range of texts especially written for each of a number of professional examinations, eg accounting, secretarial, insurance and marketing. In addressing these segments, BPP works closely with the professional institutes concerned, the bookshops and other outlets, and of course the colleges and universities which offer courses in the professions.

The range of specifically tailored products include study texts, revision kits (comprising a compendium of previous exam questions and specimen answers like this one you are reading), passcards, audio and video tapes, and CD-ROMs.

Targeting

BPP aim mostly at young ambitious people of both sexes usually with prior qualification levels in appropriate subjects, age range 18-21 who have not long started work in one of the professions and who need to qualify at the professional certificate level.

A smaller but important target market segment comprises of more mature people seeking continual professional development for promotion or security reasons.

A growing target segment are university graduates mainly in business and professional studies who can gain exemptions from some of the subjects and who tend to enter at the professional diploma level.

The smallest target market segment, but not the least important, are the course tutors and subject lecturers in the teaching institutions who might use BPP products for teaching/revision purposes and therefore endorse them or specifically recommend them to the students.

Positioning

BPP's products are positioned on the medium-price, high quality, good value spectrums as illustrated on the following maps. (It could however be argued that because BPP products save busy professionals valuable time in assimilation and revision, they could command a premium price.)

The study texts and revision kits are all produced in a common corporate style/house colour which is easily recognised and in a common-sense A4 paperback format. The study texts and revision kits can be marketed collectively as an effective study package.

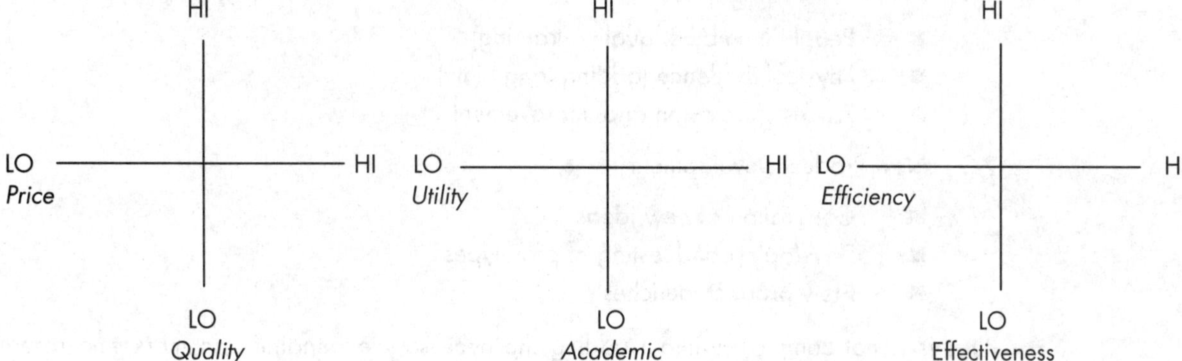

(c) **Summary**

As can be seen from the above analysis, BPP have a very well thought out marketing segmentation, targeting and positioning strategy in which all three elements work together harmoniously. The proof of this is the esteem in which BPP is held by its target market segments on its chosen brand attributes; the very satisfactory levels of profitability and ROI; and the continuous growth which has been enjoyed over a long period. Retrospectively, BPP has enjoyed a sustainable competitive advantage from the deployment of these strategies.

16 Determining and evaluating marketing budgets

1 **Methods of determining marketing budgets**

This is something of a fraught question in that budgets for future marketing expenditure are sometimes based on a percentage of sales, the forecasts for which are likely to be inaccurate to some degree. Companies can avoid this by using the previous year's sales but this can result in inappropriate budgets.

The literature advises against using a percentage of sales approach in favour of the objective or task approach which more logically assesses what expenditure is needed in order to achieve the marketing objectives set.

Yet a third method of determining marketing budgets is to base these on matching or exceeding competitors' spends. Although this approach has some merits in particular markets, it relies on being able to assess competitors' spends with some accuracy and is necessarily post-hoc.

2 **What are we trying to determine?**

Basically we are trying to determine what to spend on the extended marketing mix in order to achieve the marketing objectives set for the planning period. More specifically this will be:

2.1 The Promotional Mix spend

- Advertising
- Personal Selling
- Sales Promotion
- PR
- Direct Marketing
- Emarketing

2.2 The Service spend

- People (numbers, quality, training)
- Physical Evidence (adding tangibility)
- Process (provision and improvement

2.3 New Product Development

- Generation of new ideas
- Developing and testing of prototypes
- New product launches

But this is not complete without adding the necessary expenditure on marketing research and/or improvements to the MkIS.

3 **Evaluating the marketing budgets**

If the budgets have been set against SMART marketing objectives the evaluation will be a relatively simple matter of checking actual performance against these. Whilst sales/market share may be regarded as the bottom line, it is more realistic to measure the effectiveness of the promotional spend in terms of the increased levels of awareness and conviction, number and quality of PR articles published, take up of promotional offers, and so on.

In the case of expenditure on new product launches, there might be objectives of numbers trying the product, percentage repeat purchasing and so on.

Attempts should be made to evaluate the value of expenditure on the MkIS by the quantity and quality of the data generated and by the increased effectiveness of decision taking by using the data.

Use of the percentage of sales and matching competitors spend approaches will render evaluation more difficult and may be limited to the broad bases of sales/market share performances. Since these will be affected by other factors such as PESTLE this is a somewhat crude basis for evaluation.

Agencies used for promotion, market research and so on should be asked to evaluate their own outputs as an added measure.

As marketing becomes more sophisticated and scientific, more effort should be put into determining and evaluating the marketing budgets.

17 Evaluating and controlling the marketing plan

Tutorial note. The three major ways in which marketing activities may be evaluated could be said to be sales analysis, market share analysis and cost analysis. However there are other analyses which could be almost as important in particular product-market situations. For example when launching a major new FMCG product, it would be crucial for us to evaluate awareness, trial and re-purchase during the test market. In achieving sales there may also be caveats such as the number of customer complaints received or the number of new customers gained.

1 Marketing activities can be evaluated as follows.

(a) **Sales analysis**

Month	*Actual sales*	*Budgeted sales*	*Variance ±*	*Cumulative variance*
	£'000	£'000	£'000	£'000
1	90	100	– 10	– 10
2	115	120	– 5	– 15*
3	150	140	+ 10	– 5

In the above table we can see that at the start of the period, sales were well below the performance standard. At the point asterisked remedial action was taken which boosted sales above budget for month 3, so that at the end of the quarter the cumulative adverse variance has been greatly reduced.

(b) **Market share analysis**

Brand	*Sales 20X4*	*Est market share % 20X4*	*Position 20X4*	*Est market share % 20X3*	*Position 20X3*
	£m (est)				
Ours	12	20	3	15	3
Brand X	20	33	1	30	2
Brand Y	18	30	2	32	1
Others	10	17	-	23	-
Total	60	100		100	

In the above table we can see that our position is unchanged from 20X3 but that we have increased our market share by 5% over 20X3, largely at the expense of the minor players. We can also see that Brand Y has lost its brand leadership to Brand X (20X4 versus 20X3).

In order to make this analysis more meaningful we should want to know what our market share objective was for 20X4. It would also help to know sales for 20X3 so that we can establish whether the total market has risen, fallen or stayed about the same. (Care should be taken with interpretation: it is possible that in fact we have taken 5% from Brand Y and that Brands X and Y have each taken 3% from 'others'.)

(c) **Marketing cost analysis**

Period	*Cost item*	*Actual expenditure*	*Budgeted expenditure*	*Variance ±*	*Cumulative ±*
		£'000	£'000	£'000	£'000
Quarter 2	Advertising	100	110	–10	–10
	Exhibitions	50	40	+10	-
	Literature	40	80	–40	–40
	Marketing research	20	5	+15	+5
	Other prom	15	10	+5	+15
	Salesforce	400	440	–40	–60
	Totals	625	685	–60	–90

The above table illustrates some of the difficulties in controlling marketing costs. At first sight it appears that the performance standards have been poorly set but it should be noted these are only one quarter's figures. Some of the variances might well disappear over the year and some might be easily explained, eg the salesforce is temporarily below establishment, literature is underspent because a new catalogue is late in delivery etc. Also, it is good practice to have a contingency reserve, which would normally be added to the year's total at, say, 10% of the total budget.

(d) **Special analyses: major new product launch**

Launch of Product X - research results

Note. All figures are percentages of a total target market of 15 million 'home makers' (see separate profile)

	Awareness Target	*AwareNess Actual*	*Trial purchase Target*	*Trial purchase Actual*	*Repurchase Target*	*Repurchase Actual*
Pre-launch period Weeks 7 and 8	40	30	-	-	-	-
Launch period Weeks 9 and 10	75	60	50	55	-	-
Post-launch period Weeks 11 to 20	80	70	-	-	40	40

The table shows that the awareness level achieved is less than that targeted. This could indicate a fault in media reach which needs investigation with the media research department of the advertising agency.

However, despite having reached a smaller target audience than planned, trial purchase was higher than targeted, indicating highly effective advertising content. Due to this and a repurchase rate which is about on target, we have achieved our total sales objective.

However, it seems clear that if we can improve awareness then we should be able to achieve repurchase sales above target.

2 Principles of marketing control

Marketing controls are similar to the financial controls you are familiar with in the form of balance sheets and profit and loss accounts. That is to say they include figures for sales and market shares and costs which compare current performance against previous performance and against targets. However, there is a great more to it than this.

Perhaps these diagrams taken from *Kotler* will clarify the marketing control process.

The Control Process

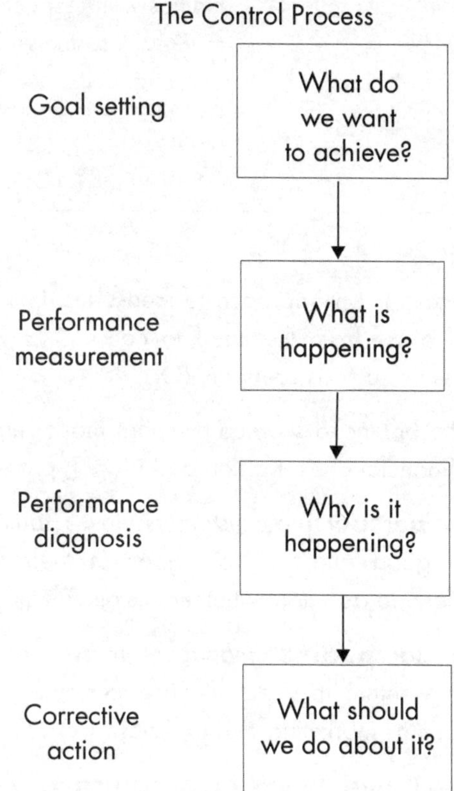

Types of Marketing Control

TYPE OF CONTROL	PRIME RESPONSIBILITY	PURPOSE OF CONTROL	APPROACHES
I Annual-plan control	Top management Middle management	To examine whether the planned results are being achieved	■ Sales analysis ■ Market share analysis ■ Expense-to-sales analysis ■ Financial analysis ■ Market-based scorecard ■ Analysis
II Profitability control	Marketing controller	To examine where the company is making and losing money	Profitability by: ■ product ■ territory ■ customer ■ segment ■ trade channel ■ order size
III Efficiency control	Line and staff management	To evaluate and improve the spending efficiency and impact of marketing expenditures	Efficiency of: ■ sales force ■ advertising ■ sales promotion ■ distribution
IV Strategic control	Top management Marketing auditor	To examine whether the company is pursuing its best opportunities with respect to markets, products and channels	■ Marketing-effectiveness rating instrument ■ Marketing audit ■ Marketing excellence review ■ Company ethical and social responsibility review

The Balanced Scorecard

The balanced scorecard is an approach to measuring business performance across a range of important factors. It arose from the need to consider a wider picture than that provided by simple financial measure such as profit an ROI.

The basic idea of the balanced scorecard is that managers should look at a broader range of objectives than just financial ones. Kaplan and Norton propose four key perspectives:

(a) **The customer perspective**: customers view a business from various points of view. Is the product of good quality? How good is their service? Customers' views must be measured regularly to ascertain whether customer objectives are being achieved.

(b) **The internal perspective**: managers must analyse the internal processes of their business to see whether they are meeting customer needs. This perspective includes key competences such as marketing and logistics.

(c) **The innovation and learning perspective**: this relates to how an organisation continually improves through learning in order to deliver improved value.

(d) **The financial perspective**: this is the traditional area associated with objective setting-return on capital, profitability etc. However, it is important that managers also consider implementation issues such as investment costs and cashflow. Here also financial objectives and measures will be set for various stakeholders such as shareholder, bankers and employees.

18 Marketing budgeting

Examiner's comments: It is important to discuss the key marketing budget influences and evaluate the different approaches in setting the marketing budget. Crucial for an FMCG is the evaluation and control of the marketing plan.

(a) **Report on Marketing Budgets**

From: Brand Manager – FMCG
Date: December 20X3

Introduction

The marketing budgeting is the planned allocation of costs within each product type for all the resources to be consumed in delivering the planned sales. It is important that the marketing budget relates directly to the business objectives and in particular is dovetailed into the overall business plan. Budgets should be flexible to allow for changing conditions or unforeseen circumstances. It can then be quickly changed to cover for such eventualities. The marketing budget acts as the foundation for the marketing planning process and identifies all the resources necessary to fulfil the business plan, which in turn will deliver the planned profit for the company. The importance of it cannot be underestimated.

Explanation of factors which influence the marketing budget

There are a number of factors which influence the marketing budget. They vary from controllable activities and decisions to human interactions in the business context. These will include all staff, materials including raw materials and consumables, and equipment to sustain the marketing activity. The equipment would also included company cars, office equipment, mobile phones and computer (IT) equipment. There will be budgets for both the purchase of the capital equipment and for its use as revenue expenditure. The budgets will need to be phased over the period of time of the marketing plan. The phasing will take into account the increased activity in the introductory and growth stages but will act as a constraining mechanism for expenditure during the maturity and decline stages as profit is planned to reduce.

The factors that influence the marketing plan are:

Power – power of the marketing function relative to other players in the organisation, in terms of structures and status. This can be extremely important in the bidding process for finite resources during the construction of internal budgets. Power will result in influence to secure vital resources of staff, equipment and materials.

Strategic contingencies – consideration of importance which a company believes its market problems and customers are embedded in decisions. Accepting a marketing orientation within the business will enhance support for the marketing budget.

Process control - who sets the rules and agenda for the budgeting process.

Political influence - who controls the information and exerts control over what people think. Support at senior levels within the business will assist in securing necessary funds for the marketing budget.

Bargaining and advocacy - how good people are at building cases and doing deals to get resources is an important skill set to support the marketing budget.

Corporate culture - acceptability of resource claims and the historical frame of reference contribute to expediting necessary budgets.

(b) **Explanation of Budgeting Approaches**

There are a number of different approaches for setting the marketing budget. There are a range of qualitative and quantitative approaches based on discrete scientific analysis and individual intuition and personal judgement. Often there is a mixture of approaches: a combination of a critical rational analysis and also an often apparently illogical but nonetheless valid assessment. The better-grounded budgeting approaches include elements from both approaches, although tempered by common sense and experience of the sector or industry. The different approaches include:

Calculation models - these normally include such methods as a rule of thumb, affordability, maintaining a share of industry spend, maintaining parity with the competition, objective and task approach.

Experiential - this approach is often seen to be quite risky and based on an exploratory interpretation of future performance. It is normally associated with situations where there is little or no information upon which to base a budget.

Negotiation - this occurs within larger businesses where different functions are competing for the same resource or funds. A skilled marketing professional will be required to gain the greatest possible budget whilst not alienating their activity from the rest of the business. It is important to retain the cohesive approach within the organisation as a whole.

Bottom-up budgeting - this approach is based on the situation where the initiative lies at the product management level and resource demands are pushed up through the organisation. The net result is to aggregate the different requirements into a unified budget and has the benefit of retaining the support and commitment of the junior members of the organisation as they can identify their contribution to the marketing budget.

Top-down budgeting - this approach involves greater control by top management. It normally results from discussion by senior managers at executive board level and provides for an agreed consensus that is disseminated throughout the organisation.

(c) **Methods for evaluating and controlling the FMCG brand marketing plan**

The normal assessment will relate to actual versus planned performance shown as variance reporting for each of the listed budgeted activities. These will indicate performance to date and predicted alterations, if necessary to achieve year end plans. The reporting system will normally highlight where there are better and worse performing product lines as a separate report so that further analysis can be undertaken. There are a number of methods for evaluating a marketing plan, and these are listed below.

Management control - these will include specific performance appraisal but will also include benchmarking measures. These benchmarking measures will include industry or sector related values, process dependant measures for similar activities and comparative macro economic analysis.

Financial control - these will include trend analysis, comparison, liquidity ratios, debt ratios and activity ratios. Examples would be sales turnover, % product margin and monthly cash flow and profit and loss account.

Efficiency control - optimum values from marketing assets normally presented as ratios and shown as percentages. These controls will have a target and an actual value. A percentage greater than 100% means that the target has been exceed and, whereas a shortfall will be shown as a number less than 100%. Examples would be factory production output and warehouse product throughput.

Strategic control - measures marketing activities against market performance. Often these are measures that are identified in the business plan and form the basis of the strategic marketing direction of the business. Such measures as business growth and market share are typical examples.

Conclusion

The most effective and logical approaches for an FMCG brand have to take into account the fast moving nature of the business and the short time scale of the product life cycle. The marketing plan has to be extremely reactive to product sales performance and to seasonality associated with the FMCG marketplace. For instance with higher sales in the run up to Christmas and the lower sales during the summer months the phasing of the marketing plan is important. A balance between financial controls and efficiency controls are particularly relevant at the product level, but the overall strategic controls for the business must be managed.

19 Strategy development and market share growth

Report to: Board of Directors
From: Commercial Director
Date: 7 December 200X
Subject: Business growth strategies

1 **Introduction**

I have been asked to identify new strategic options for growing the business to achieve our short and medium term targets. In doing so I shall present a process by which these options can be evaluated. A useful framework under which to identify growth options is the *Ansoff* matrix as follows:

Growth strategies

Product

			Market
Diversification 16	Market development 2	New	↑
Product development 4	Market Penetration 1	Existing	↓

The numbers shown in the boxes indicate the degree of risk associated with these four basic strategies, which you can see increases exponentially.

2 Application of above strategic options to our publishing company

2.1 Market Penetration

There are three main ways of increasing sales of existing products to existing customers:

2.1.1 *Gain more purchase and usage from existing types of customers*

- We could update our car repair manuals more frequently so as to stimulate extra demand.
- Grow our market share of increasing advertising expenditure and perhaps a change of agent.
- Introduce new sales promotions, for example extra manuals to SMEs at reduced prices.

2.1.2 *Gain customers from competitors*

- Reduced price incentives
- Introductory offers
- Salesforce incentives
- Recruit sales people with good contacts from our competitors

2.1.3 *Convert non-uses into users*

- Libraries might be persuaded to stock our manuals for the most popular makes of car.
- Motor clubs and enthusiasts could also be approached.
- Finally members of the general public could be encouraged to buy from us direct.

2.2 Market Development

2.2.1 *New market segments*

- We could encourage colleges to offer courses based on our manuals with volume discounts for orders over a minimum quantity.

2.2.2 *New distribution channels*

- The Internet offers us a promising opportunity to market direct at very little cost.
- Alternatively we could approach a Emarketing company like Amazon to feature us.

2.2.3 *New geographical areas*

- For example, Eastern Europe which h is buying more western cars and has a need for our existing manuals.
- We could produce repair manuals for American cars and market these in the USA.

2.3 Product Development

2.3.1 *Product Modification*

- Change the product slightly to meet the different needs of segments of the existing customers eg a simpler/reduced size manual for relatively amateur motor car mechanics or hard plasticated covers for manual used in greasy pits.

2.3.2 *Different quality levels*

- Change the product more drastically eg produce the manuals in CD ROM versions.

2.3.3 *Entirely new products*

- For example, a hand-held electronic diagnostic/fault finding tool or videos showing people how to repair common faults.

2.4 Diversification

2.4.1 At its simplest, new products for new markets could mean us producing books on motor bike development or transport related themes (eg biographies of motor sports personalities.)

However, diversification is often more quickly achieved through acquisition of other businesses. There are four main types of acquisition/integration:

2.4.2 *Horizontal Integration*

- Buy a similar business or competitor.

2.4.3 *Vertical Integration*

- Buy backwards or forwards into the distribution channel – in our case into motor cars repair/maintenance.

2.4.4 *Concentric Diversification*

- Buy another business with technical or marketing synergies such as agricultural vehicle repair manuals or with marketing expertise in garage equipment.

2.4.5 *Conglomerate Diversification*

- Seek a completely fresh challenge for our own marketing skills in say retailing.

3 Evaluation of options

A fundamental criterion in the evaluation of options is the degree of risk involved – see 1 above. The figures in the Ansoff Matrix are general and need to be modified according to our own assessments. The process recommended by *Johnson and Scholes* is to take each strategy in turn and assess its attractiveness on a scale of 1 to 10 using the criteria below.

3.1 *Acceptability*

- To what extent is this option acceptable to the Board, its shareholders and stakeholders?

3.2 *Suitability*

- To what extent does this option match our current strengths and weaknesses – based on a SWOT analysis conducted by a representative sample of qualified respondents.

3.3 *Feasibility*

- We need to assess whether we have the resources to carry out the strategy effectively based on a full external/internal audit, possibly supported by some marketing research. Having acquired the necessary data we can then apply this using a suitable model such as the GE multifactor matrix which plots each strategy on axes of Market Attractiveness (size, growth, competition, technological requirements, barriers to entry., potential profits) versus Business Strengths (brand, assets, competencies, financial resources, NPD capabilities, distributor relationships). It is important to remember that weightings need to be applied before calculating the final score for each option since a criterion such as the finance availability may be twice as important as the lack of a skill that can easily be outsourced.

4 **Timescale considerations**

Market Penetration is the easiest and quickest option to action, although not always the most effective. It is therefore most applicable to the achievement of short-term targets.

Market Development/Product Development take longer to achieve and can be considered as means to achieve our medium term objectives.

Diversification being the most radical of all the options is normally thought of as being a longer term strategy but if we adopted the lowest degree of Product/Market Development – see 2.2 and 2.3 above – then these strategies might be feasible in achieving our medium-term business growth objectives.

20 Market selection's impact on the integrated mix

Strategy formulation and decisions relating to the selection of markets covers quite a wide area and includes:

1 **Porter's generic strategies**

Porter suggests that companies should choose from three basic strategies or risk being 'stuck in the middle'. These three strategies are Cost Leadership, Differentiation and Focus/Niche.

All three strategies impact at an operational level on the planning and implementation of an integrated marketing mix. Clearly, the Cost Leadership option impacts most heavily on price. However, in order to achieve lowest price through economies of scale, a company may have to simplify the product and improve the efficiency of its marketing operations – particularly promotion and distribution. In short, product, promotion and place have to work with price to form an integrated and effective marketing mix.

2 **Ansoff's growth strategies**

Ansoff holds that there are four basic strategies for growth, namely Market Penetration, Product Development, Market Development and Diversification. Again all four options impact on the formulation of the integrated marketing mix:

- **Market Penetration** (existing products for existing markets) may sound like more of the same, but in order to achieve growth will mean deploying the integrated marketing mix appropriately. For example, to increase usage of a consumer good by existing customers may entail pricing offers, alterations to packaging and promotion and perhaps physical re-location in store.

- **Product Development** (new products for existing markets) has an obvious impact on product but the cost of NPD will impact on price and NPD itself may enable the developer to enter new distribution channels. Furthermore if the new consumer product represents a substantial move up-market, then the price, the type of distribution outlet and the nature of the promotion (eg. the media used) will all need to be integrated accordingly.

- **Market Development** (existing products for new markets) impacts upon all four elements of the integrated mix, especially when the new market is that of a different country (international marketing strategy) and the company decides it needs to tailor the mix to a differing cultural environment. This can mean quite radical changes to promotion and distribution as well as product and price changes.

- **Diversification** (new products for new markets) does of course posit the greatest change to the marketing mix and a great deal of care to its integration. Taking as an example a British manufacturer designing a car for a third world country, the product would be unique. The distribution system in the third world country could be completely different from that in the UK. The price would no doubt have to be relatively low and the product designed down to a price. Infrastructure and climate (place) would have product ramifications. Promotional changes could include language, target audiences, messages. Similar media to the UK may not be available.

3 **Segmentation, targeting and positioning strategies**

When an organisation segments its markets and decides on its target market segments, it also has to decide whether to differentiate the marketing mix for each of these segments or to have a common mix or a mixture of these. The decision as to whether or not to differentiate the mix will to a largest extent be based upon the degree to which the segments' needs are different.

Taking two contrasting segments for watches – that of affluent, fashion conscious adults and that of relatively poor young sportspeople, it is likely that quite a large amount of mix differentiation would be required. The first segment would be likely to expect high price, high quality, attractive appearance, image enhancing products whilst the second segment would be more concerned with performance, accuracy, suitability for their sports (eg. deep sea diving) and value for money.

Distribution outlets and the promotional mix would differ in detail such as outlets and media as well as products and prices.

4 **Conclusion**

There are of course other strategies which affect the integrated marketing mix, such as the military ones advocated by Kotler and Singh, but there is insufficient time here to cover them all.

However, the examples selected above clearly demonstrate that strategic formulation and decisions relating to the selection of markets do impact upon the planning and implementation of the marketing mix and its integration.

21 Tutorial question: The extended marketing mix

A number of authors have criticised the standard 4Ps approach to the marketing mix as being too limiting and have proposed extensions. In the developed world, services now formed increasing proportions of gross national product relative to the manufacture of goods.

As services have grown in importance, so have techniques of service marketing developed. It is no longer tenable to say that services are no different to products in their marketing requirements.

Analysis of services has revealed the following main differences when compared to products, for which additional elements of the marketing mix are required.

Intangibility

Kotler tells us that unlike physical products, services cannot be seen, tasted, felt, heard or smelled. However, there are different degrees of intangibility between a pure product and a pure service as can be seen in the following continuum:

The tangible-intangible spectrum

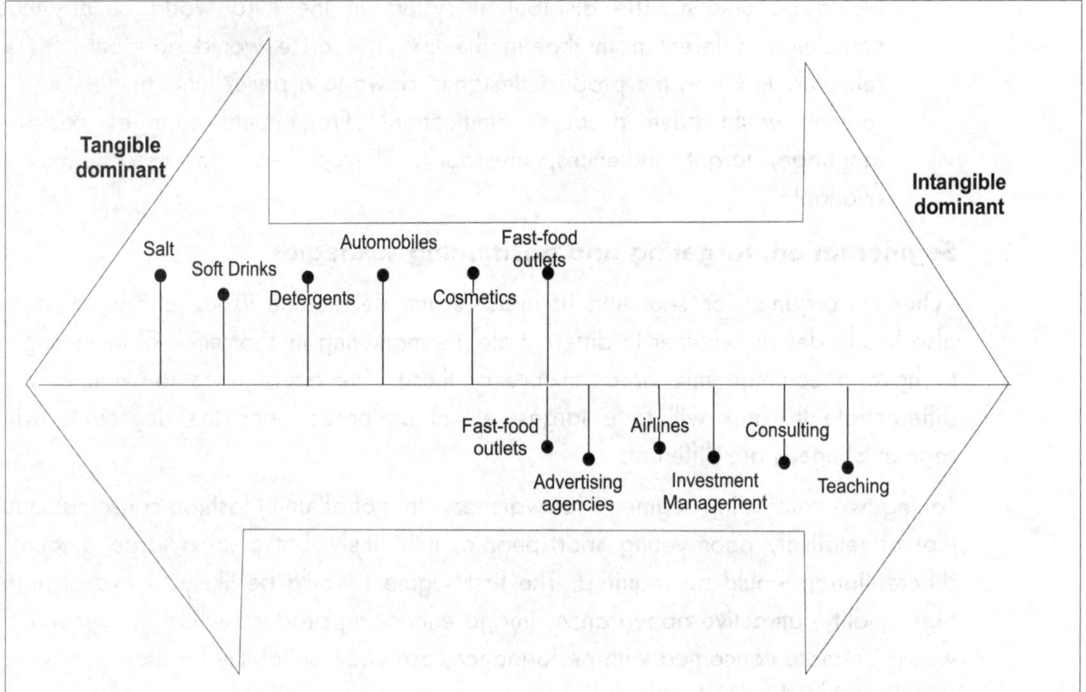

Source: Shostack G L (1977)

For services which are intangible dominant, marketers can try to add tangibility. This is known as a fifth P – **Physical Evidence**. Business Consultants can convey and image of quality to their service through the use of office location/furniture and expensive clothing and in the form of report/presentational materials, refreshments and so on.

Inseparability and Variability

Services cannot normally be separated from the provider in the same way as a product. Services are usually provided for people by people. Equally most services are subject to variability. Unlike a production line which delivers almost identical products continuously, it is difficult if not impossible to provide the same service to the same person, by the same person, at the same time and in the same environmental conditions. Imagine you have enjoyed excellent service and food at a restaurant to which you return to find yourself being served food cooked by a different chef, by a different waiter, at a different table, with different background music in different ambient conditions. You might well be very disappointed.

For these reasons, marketers of services realise that a further element of **People** – a sixth P – is all important. Efforts can be made to train different members of staff to provide a more consistent service to the same high standards.

Ownership and perishability

Whereas the legal title to a good is transferred from seller to buyer, the purchase of a service only confers the right of access or use. This tends to make service buyers more apprehensive. Also whilst goods can be stocked, service cannot be stored. Timing is very important. A passenger aircraft's empty seats represents an irretrievably lost opportunity to earn revenue.

A seventh P of the extended marketing mix intended to address these issues is that of **Process**. Processes and systems can be designed to confer reassurance at each service encounter. Perishability can be reduced by cybernetic systems that react in people terms to peaks and troughs in service demands – more check-outs manned, limited item checkouts converted to full service and so on. A hairdresser can work in a pattern designed to flatten demand and keep records of customer needs/wants/interests so as to lessen apprehensions.

Summary

So there are a variety of reasons why the marketing mix for services should be extended and a number of ways in which to do this. In closing, we could perhaps consider an eighth P – that of **Probe** to consider the essential operation of asking purchasers of services what their needs and wants are, and how we might best satisfy these.

22 Branding: its impact on the marketing mix

1 **Introduction**

Good evening, ladies and gentlemen. I am very pleased to have been invited to talk to you, the East Midlands Branch of the CIM, on the subject of brand positioning. Knowing that you come from a variety of different organisations, I will provide examples of excellence in brand positioning from the consumer goods, services and not-for-profit sectors and illustrate my talk with slides and short videos. There will be ample time at the end for questions, comments and perhaps further examples from yourselves.

2 **Definitions**

We should perhaps start by distinguishing between a product and a brand. A **product** is anything which meets the functional needs of consumers or users. For example a watch is bought to tell the time and a bank is used to save, borrow or transfer money.

A **brand** is a name, symbol, design or a combination of these which identifies and distinguishes the product of a particular organisation. For example here is a watch (show slide) and here is a Rolex watch and here are some Swatch watches (show slides).

A successful brand not only meets the functional requirements of consumers, it also has added values which meet certain of their psychological needs, so perhaps Rolex satisfies a need for esteem whilst Swatch addresses a need for fun and variety.

Getting a bit technical here, *Doyle* suggests that a successful brand (S) = P times D times AV, where P is product effectiveness, D is distinctive identity and AV equals added values.

3 **Brand positioning**

Brand positioning is part of brand strategy. Different authors (*Arnold, de Chernatony, Macrae, Hankinson and Cowking*) suggest different components but taking Arnold's definition, brand strategy comprises target market, **brand positioning**, brand name and brand extension decisions. Within this, brand positioning is a combination of brand personality (functional and symbolic values) and consumer proposition (or strap line).

The company has to effectively signal to the target market how its brand differs from competitors. It must not only develop a clear positioning strategy for its brand but it must also communicate it effectively. The brand's advertising packaging, promotion, pricing, channels etc must collectively communicate and support the brand's image and positioning (*Kotler*).

3.1 **Consumer products**

All this can sound a bit vague but we can make it become more realistic by looking at some brand positioning statements or maps. Here are some positioning maps covering famous brands of liqueur whiskies including Chivas, *Jack Daniels* and *Canadian Club*.

This one for example is plotted on the axes mild v strong and value v prestige and we can see that Chivas comes out on the mild but prestigious side whilst Jack Daniels is considered strong and good value.

Looking at these other axis or attributes we can see that distinctive positions are occupied by these two brands. Such maps are useful for identifying gaps which can be occupied by new products and/or for repositioning tired or outdated existing products.

3.2 **Brand repositioning**

However well a brand is positioned in a market, the company may have to reposition it later. This is because a competitor may launch a brand close to the company's brand and cut into its market share or perhaps consumer preferences will shift, leaving the brand with less demand.

In the process of repositioning, the marketer wants to move from the current brand image and it requires research/analysis to determine the desired brand image and the points of differentiation with respect to competitors. The process also involves decisions to add new associations, strengthen existing ones and eliminate undesirable ones in the minds of consumers. In order to achieve the ideal positioning for the brand, the marketer strives to achieve congruence among what customers will value in the brand, what the company is currently saying about the brand and where the firm would like to take the brand (*Keller*).

For example, Lucozade was originally positioning as a vitamin supplement for people convalescing after illness, the sort of product seen by hospital beds along with the flowers and get-well cards, particularly where older people were concerned. Faced with seriously declining sales, Lucozade was successfully repositioning as a young sport person's aid to increased energy so as to **get better** at sports. This had associations with the previous image and also appealed to older people's aspirations/self image as well as young ones.

3.3 **Services**

One of the most prolific areas for new service development in recent years has been that of credit cards and it is a fairly safe bet that some of you in the audience have a wallet full of these. Certainly between us we could muster a great variety of each of which tries to occupy a distinctive position. Let me show you some on slides (show slides). Now then which famous one is missing? Yes, you're right, it's American Express the best known pioneer. Looking now at its positioning statement we can see words such as style, success, global, quality people etc which set it apart from the others and make us proud as well as confident when using it.

3.4 **Not-for-profit organisations**

Yes, these too seek to position their brands in a competitive marketplace although perhaps in a less ostentatious way than their consumer goods and services counterparts. For example, here is a positioning statement for the Royal Society for the Protection of Birds (RSPB):

'The RSPB promotes the conservation of birds and other wildlife, in the UK and worldwide, in the interests of wildlife, the natural environment, and the people who share it.'

The inclusion of other wildlife recognises the dependence of birds on this and at the same time appeals to a wider audience than if it was omitted.

And as a final example the Ramblers' Association with its excellent positioning strap line 'The right to roam' and its associated emphases on health and sociability.

The short videos that follow illustrate the brand positionings of these two not-for-profit organisations in greater depth and are contrasted with one on *Coca Cola* (show videos).

4 **Conclusions and discussion**

In summary it can clearly be seen that brand positioning is a key ingredient of brand management, the full process for which extends into market/brand situation analysis, brand strategy, the marketing mix and testing, evaluation and control. This is a fascinating area in which I know many of you are involved. In this modern world we market brands not products and the more we know about branding and brand positioning the better it will be for our career development. May I suggest some CPD in the form of further reading and invite you to take a handout detailing some good references.

23 Managing the brand

Examiner's comments. Good answers discussed types of brand strategy as well as outlining the criteria for stretching a brand. Poorer answers merely discussed brand strategies in general without identifying the criteria used in making brand stretching decisions.

REPORT

To: The Marketing Manager – Top Value Supermarkets Ltd
From: Jim Smith – Ace Consultants
Date: 10 August 200X
Subject: Entering the financial services market

Situation

Top Value Stores (TVS) is planning to enter the area of financial services. A key question to be asked is whether the TVS brand will stretch into financial services. The UK currently has several successful examples of retailers moving into financial services. These include Marks and Spencer, Tesco, Safeway and Sainsburys. This report will identify the key elements of a brand strategy and put forward the criteria that TVS should use to make the brand stretching decision.

Key elements of a brand strategy

A brand strategy must be linked to the overall marketing strategy. This means that the brand strategy must have clear objectives which are wholly integrated with other parts of the marketing mix. Most important of all is the need for the brand values to be accepted by the target markets.

As TVS has developed and grown, its brand will also have developed a personality and a set of values. Parts of the brand are highly visible (eg the logo) whilst other parts are invisible (eg the research and development and the quality control). *Davidson* calls the concept of invisible and visible brand features, the **Brand Iceberg**:

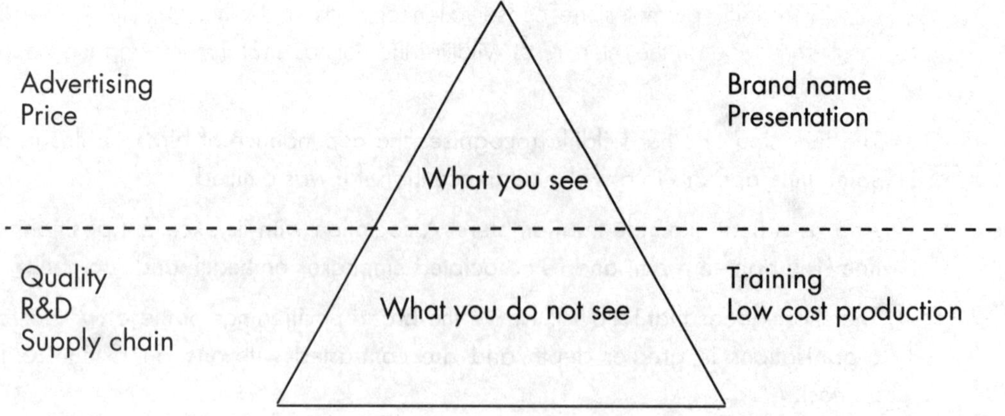

Another key element of a brand strategy is to analyse the brand by dividing the brand into five component parts – functional features, rational benefits, emotional rewards, values and personality, and to place this in a brand triangle. For TVS this could be as follows:

Personality	Modern, Risk-Taking, Dynamic
Values	Integrity, Secure, Professional
Emotional Rewards	Fulfilling lifestyle aspirations
Rational Benefits	Good value, convenient
Functional features	Friendly staff, car park, history

It is important to ensure that an evaluation of the brand as above will enable the business to both position itself effectively against the competition and also enable it to move into other market areas such as financial services. Often, ongoing market research with customers, employees and suppliers is needed to ensure that the brand remains fresh and appealing.

Basic brand strategies

TVS can follow anyone of four basic strategies.

(1) A company brand strategy: here the dominant brand identity is given by the corporate brand (eg Marks and Spencer, Top Value Supermarkets.) The main advantage is that both corporate and individual product brands can be integrated and this also leads to economies of scale resulting in the more efficient use of the marketing expenditure budget. Most retailers use this strategy in order to maximise brand identify and to build up customer loyalty.

(2) Individual brand strategy: here each product is given a separate brand name. This is unlikely to be applicable to a supermarket because of the wide range of products offered.

(3) Range branding strategy: this is more likely to be used by a supermarket such as TVS. Here groups of products are given separate brand names. For example, Frozen Foods, Canned Food, Drinks and Pharmaceutical product ranges could be given separate brand names. The advantage of this approach is that separate characteristics can be given to each brand but of course this is also quite a costly approach.

(4) Company and individual brand strategy: this is used a lot by companies such as Kelloggs and Heinz. This strategy attempts to use the strengths of both the corporate and product brands to build up separate and strong brand identifies. Different companies place varying amounts of emphasis on the two brand areas. Most retailers will treat the corporate brand as the most powerful brand. However, increasingly retailers are introducing ranges backed up by other brands and personalities (eg the George range at Asda or ranges in Tesco using the chef Jamie Oliver.)

Brand stretching criteria

Brand stretching refers to the process of taking a brand into an unrelated market. In this case, TVS are considering stretching a brand associated with supermarket retailing into the financial services sector.

A starting point is to examine the current core values of the brand. The brand should only be stretched if:

(a) The core values of the brand have relevance to the new market. In this example, if the core values are the cheapest and a minimum no frills approach to customer service then it may not be possible to stretch the brand. Whereas values of honesty and reliability will be able to be transferred.

(b) The new market area will not affect the value of the brand in its core market. If TVS was to experience problems in the financial services sector then this may well have repercussions on the core supermarket business. Virgin have experienced problems with Virgin Rail and to some extent the problems of delayed train services have also affected other Virgin businesses such as airlines, music and drinks.

Other criteria to be considered in stretching the brand are:

(c) Resources available: money to launch the brand and trained people to carry the strategy out.

(d) The nature of the financial services market: growth rate, new entrants, profitability and market size.

(e) The basic mission of TVS and the corporate objectives: are these in line with the new market? Are the values and aims consistent with the new market?

(f) Stakeholder expectations: are shareholders, employees and people connected with the business likely to support the new venture?

(g) The nature of the existing core market: in this case the supermarket industry. What are the future prospects and to what extent is it appropriate for efforts to be directed in other directions?

Conclusions

The success of any brand stretching decision is dependent on a clear understanding of the current brand's position. This will involve talking to customers, suppliers and competitors. Once a clear picture has been obtained, then an investigation into the intended market is needed. What are the brand values held by potential competitors in the new market? Will customers switch to a supermarket bank? Can TVS attract customers from other banks? What types of financial services products should be offered? Only when these questions have been fully answered can a positive decision be made to stretch the brand, which will hopefully lead to success in the new market.

24 Branding strategies and the communications mix

Examiner's comments: This question covers the role of product and corporate branding for a retail bank. It develops the use of the marketing communications mix in developing a new product branding strategy and explains how pricing contributes to the extended marketing mix. Crucial is the evaluation of the subject material with regard to a retail bank.

From: Brand Manager
To: Managing Director, The Retail Bank
Date: December 200X

Introduction

(a) **Report on the role of branding**

Introduction

A brand is a name, term or symbol which is used to identify the goods or services from one seller and to differentiate them from those of competitors. For The Retail Bank defining the role of branding as a strategy to differentiate products is important and should be incorporated into their mission statement. There are four key areas where decisions must be taken; Branding options, New brands, Brand extensions and Line extensions that relate to product and corporate brands.

Role of Corporate branding

The firm makes its company name the dominant brand across all of its products, such as with Vodaphone, Philips and Bentley motor cars. The main advantage is economies of scale in marketing investments and wider recognition of the brand name. It is also linked to reputation in the marketplace where corporate image and identity are central to the brand. It also facilitates the introduction of new products when the corporate name is well established. More importantly in recent times is the importance of stakeholder perceptions of the company and its stock market reputation. Consequently the company's internal communications is linked to corporate branding and constantly portraying a positive message to its publics. For The Retail Bank trust is very important component of the relationship with their customers and this is directly related to the perceived behaviour by the bank and reflected in its branding.

Role of Product Branding

Companies have used individual product brands within the marketplace. Each product has a distinct label with minimal reference to the corporate name. Managing a stable of brand names within the same product category permits finer segmentation of the market, with each brand name suggesting different functions or benefits for different customer segments. Another advantage is that the firm can differentiate its new products more effectively with individual brand names, whilst reducing the risk of individual brand failures harming the company's overall reputation. For The Retail Bank an increasingly more sophisticated and knowledgeable customer requires a more targeted and tailored range of products to suit their diverse range of needs.

Use of brand extension strategies deploys a successful brand name to launch new or modified products in a new category. A number of methods can be used such as licensing, product launches and gentle stretching. The benefits that can be gained include differentiation of the product and increased emotional link to customer. There can be a reduction of risk for intermediaries, it can allow premium pricing, helps targeting, increases power over retailers and defends against competition. It serves to offer a brand as a personality and added value. Brands have become a major point of strategic focus in companies and the concept of the brand has been widely applied: brands have a balance sheet and income value and have become recognised as tradable assets with a market value.

(b) **Marketing Communications Mix and brand launches**

For all new brands, the key objective is to generate awareness and for consumer products purchase or trial. Targeting issues should be considered. Thus the communications mix needs to achieve such objectives. This includes advertising, sales promotion, direct marketing and public relations.

Advertising - Major investment in advertising is normally required to generate rapid awareness. Advertising is usually seen as the most widespread form of promotion and is used to increase awareness of the product in the marketplace. It is also a medium to communicate in simple terms products that can be quite complex in composition. It is a method to get across a simple message to the intended customer segment. This is important for The Retail Bank that has a range of financially technical products.

Sales promotion - usually sales promotion for product trial is required. The use of publicity for a new brand is crucial as it is more credible than advertising. It includes a wide assortment of tools – coupons, contests, competitions, premium offers and price reductions. They attract customer attention and provide information that may lead to a purchase. Sales promotions invite and reward quick response, which is of benefit to The Retail Bank.

Direct marketing - is the most effective tool at certain stages of the buying process, particularly in building buyer's preferences, convictions and actions. However for The Retail Bank this tool is probably less relevant except for significant investment purchases such as mortgages.

Public relations - this includes all those activities that the organisation does to communicate with target audiences and which are not directly paid for. It can also reach many prospects who avoid salespeople and advertisements since the message gets to the buyers as news rather than as a sales directed communication. Again for The Retail Bank this will have limited appeal as banks rarely make good news and are often portrayed in a poor light to most publics.

The use of new technology to support the marketing communication mix is important. It will help The Retail Bank to develop and inform a new product branding strategy.

(c) **Development of pricing as an integrated part of the marketing mix**

It is through pricing that a company covers the cost of separate elements of its various activities: research and development, raw materials, labour and administrative costs must all be recovered through the price charged to the customer. Marketing costs must be covered by the final price of the product, including those costs incurred in promoting, selling and distributing the product. Consideration of the pricing element of the marketing mix and its link to the positioning and segments targeted is necessary. This is considered from a marketing perspective, with some consideration of the accountant or financial approach.

Pricing should be made in the context of overall marketing objectives and strategy. To this end, pricing decisions should be related to and be consistent with the other elements of the marketing mix. Consequentially pricing should not become a matter of routine for the accountant nor should they place too much emphasis on cost inputs alone. The economist and accountant use demand and costs respectively. The marketer however considers a wider range of inputs that include the competition, the market structure, legal and social considerations and distribution and trade influences. These considerations for The Retail Bank would be linked to market segmentation, customer targeting and the resultant product positioning.

Conclusion

The role of brands is very important in terms of both product and corporate branding to differentiate offerings in the market place. The communications mix needs to be adapted appropriately to achieve very specific objectives for new product/brand launches.

25 Product/Service portfolio's role in achieving marketing objectives

> *Examiner's comments.* Good answers fully described each model, addressed their weaknesses and outlined the ability of the models to complement each other in the planning process. Poor answers tended to describe the models but only spent limited time comparing and contrasting these alternative approaches.

Background

A **business portfolio** is the collection of businesses, divisions or products/services that a company manages on a day to day basis. These businesses are identified in portfolio analysis as **Strategic Business Units** (SBUs). Ideally they should be separately managed businesses with individual objectives and financial targets.

Portfolio analysis refers to the process of evaluating the various SBUs in an organisation. This needs to be done on a regular basis in order that decisions can be made regarding each SBU, such as whether to invest and grow, or whether to divest and develop a new SBU.

Boston Consulting Group (BCG) matrix

The BCG matrix is a model that is concerned about the generation and use of cash in a business. It is used by management to identify which SBUs need financial support, which SBUs can be left alone to generate cash and which SBUs need to be divested since they have no future.

The BCG matrix uses measures to evaluate each SBU-relative **market share** and **market growth**. Relative market growth refers to the market share position when compared to competitors. This is seen as a good indicator as to whether an SBU needs investment or not. If it has a dominant position then it should not need as much help as an SBU with low market share relative to the competition.

Market growth refers to the **growth rate of the market or industry**. In this case it is the chemical industry. The reason for this measure is that high growth markets (eg pharmaceuticals) may need more support than low growth markets (eg textiles.)

To construct a BCG matrix for the chemical company two sets of data are needed.

(a) The market growth rates of each SBU are plotted on the vertical axis.

(b) The market shares of each SBU in relation to the main competitor are plotted on the horizontal axis.

Relative market share is calculated using a log scale. At the mid-point there is a value of 1X. If plotted here the SBU has a market share equal to the largest competitor. At the extreme left-hand side there is a value of 10X meaning that this SBU has a market share ten times the market share of the nearest competitor. At the extreme right-hand side if plotted here the SBU only has a value of 0.1X, which means the SBU has a market share of 0.1 or 10% of the largest competitor. (See Figure 1)

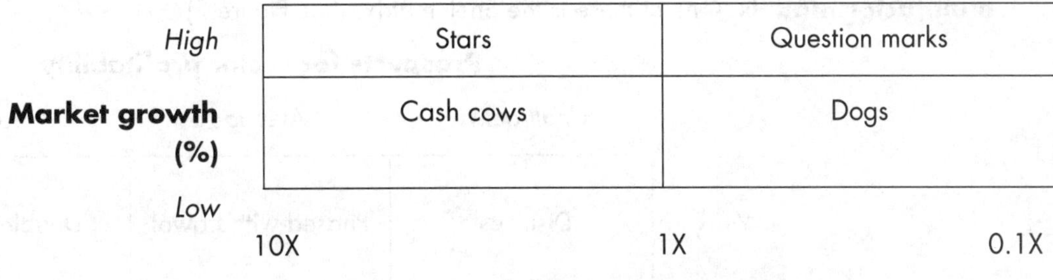

Figure 1: The Boston Consulting Group Matrix

The SBUs are plotted in the grid and represented by circles. The size of the circle indicates the sales of the SBU or product in relation to the whole organisation or product range.

Each cell is given a name and they each require different decisions.

(a) **Cash cows**. These products are cash generators. The cash may be used to support question marks and stars. The basic strategy here is maintain.

(b) **Stars**. These businesses are market leaders and require investment from the cash cows to enable them to grow in a growing market. The basic strategy is to grow this until the market slows and it may then become a cash cow to support other stars.

(c) **Question marks** – sometimes called problem children or wildcats. They are in high growth markets but may need money to enable them to become leaders. Management has to decide whether to support them, or direct investment at other SBUs.

(d) **Dogs**. These businesses are in low growth markets. They have low relative market share but they still may generate cash if they are in a niche, and they require little maintenance. Decisions have to be made whether to harvest, maintain or divest.

The basic objective is to have a balanced portfolio and to move the SBUs to products in an anticlockwise direction. Problems will occur if there is not sufficient cash to support high growth market SBUs. Also it is not sufficient to only seek to generate cash if one is looking to grow in the long term.

Weaknesses of the BCG matrix

(a) **Market growth** is not a good measure. A low growth market can be positive, if for example barriers to entry are high. This may well be the case in the chemical industry.

(b) **Relative market share** is inadequate as a measure. High market share, shared with a competitor, may still be a useful situation. For example, the UK chemical industry is dominated by one or two market leaders.

(c) **Market share** is not always a reliable measure. A niche position with low share may still be profitable.

(d) The emphasis of the matrix is on **growth** and ignores issues such as sustainable **competitive advantage**.

(e) **Cash flow in order to fund investment** is only one factor that can be looked at. Other factors such as return on investment, profitability, competences, assets, cost and competition are equally valid when assessing whether to invest in a SBU or not.

The Shell Directional Policy matrix

The problems of having just two measures in the BCG matrix led to the development of other portfolio models using a greater range of criteria to assess SBUs. These are known as **multifactor models**. One of these is the Shell matrix. (See Figure 2)

		Prospects for sector profitability		
		Unattractive	*Average*	*Attractive*
Competitive capabilities	*Weak*	Disinvest	Phased withdrawal	Double or quit
	Average	Phased withdrawal	Custodial growth	Try harder
	Strong	Cash generation	Growth leader	Leader

Figure 2: Shell Directional Policy Matrix (Shell Chemical Company 1975)

In this model, the measures used (competitive capabilities and prospects for sector profitability) are based on managers' weighting of a range of criteria.

Prospects for sector profitability include:

- Market size
- Market growth rate
- Competition
- Profit potential
- Technological, social, economic and political factors

The enterprise's **competitive capabilities** include:

- Market share
- Potential to develop a competitive advantage
- Opportunities to develop cost advantages
- Channel relationships
- Brand image/reputation

Once these factors are weighted and evaluated, SBUs can be plotted. The cell in which they are placed then gives some indication as to the strategy needed.

The main criticism of multifactor models is that they are based on managers' **subjective judgements** in weighting and assessing the various criteria. However such models do at least take into account a variety of factors, rather than just the two of the BCG model.

Conclusions

All portfolio models, whether multifactor or not, have basic weaknesses.

(a) They only consider **existing businesses** and are not concerned with new business development.

(b) They involve the **collection of information** that can be difficult to find.

(c) They involve the **interpretation of information** which can vary from day to day and from manager to manager.

(d) They place too high an **emphasis on growth** and fail to acknowledge the benefits of niching and maintaining profitable competitive positions.

(e) They can be quite **time consuming** to complete and may become **out of date** very quickly.

However, the main aim of such models is to **aid decision-making** rather than to give definitive courses of action. Also, ideally they should be used in conjunction with other models and analytical techniques. In this regard, they are useful tools in helping to develop strategic decisions. They can be applied to products and services as well as businesses/SBUs.

26 The new product development process

1 The NPD Process

The way to ensure that money is not wasted developing new product failures, is to do the job properly in the first place and this means adopting the following process.

1.1 Idea generation

My recommendation is that the company adopts a systematic procedure to generate new product ideas based on scanning its marketing environment to identify new opportunities. This should be supported by a programme of marketing research which is integrated with R&D. New ideas can also be generated from employee suggestions, the R&D function or simply by observing competitive activity and listening to customers. Techniques include the monitoring of patent applications, brainstorming, need/problem analysis, morphological analysis and attributive listing.

1.2 Screening of new ideas

This process should analyse each idea in terms of prescribed criteria including its potential development, the market potential, its likely PLC, financial and other resources required, its contribution and fit relative to overall company strategy, the company's capability to market the product effectively, and last but by no means least, the likely return on investment.

1.3 Concept development and testing

Having got through the initial screening process, we need to develop the ideas into conceptual products which meet identified customer needs and can be packaged to sell to market segments in viable quantities. Concept boards and positioning maps can be drawn up for use in conjunction with focus groups to gauge reactions from prospective customers.

1.4 Marketing strategy

A draft marketing plan then needs to be produced to indicate short and long-term sales, profit and market share objectives, together with details of the marketing mix.

1.5 Business analysis

Subject to favourable reactions to concept testing, the next step is to undertake more detailed evaluation. This would involve more comprehensive marketing research, a detailed competitor analysis and a full analysis of the resources required to launch successfully and achieve the sales targets. The market analysis should determine the degree of market attractiveness, the level of competitiveness, growth rates and the longer-term potential. Sales forecasts are needed of initial uptakes and the level of replacement sales, to facilitate more accurate operational plans.

1.6 **Product development and finalisation**

Prototypes of the new products need to be produced, tested and modified as necessary. This requires a substantial increase in commitment and investment.

1.7 **Test marketing**

This is strongly recommended as a standard procedure although there may be circumstances when this may not be possible. The product can be tested with a selected customer or customers and/or in a particular geographic region. It can involve simple trial or be supported by testing various marketing mixes to see which has the most effect on sales. This stage may require considerable investment and may need to run for some months before a decision can be made to launch the product.

1.8 **Commercialisation**

Essentially these are decisions taken after successful test marketing on when to launch, where to launch, which initial groups should be targeted and how it should be launched.

1.9 **Post-launch evaluation**

The launch itself needs to be tracked and performance against targets evaluated, together with competitors' reactions. Modifications to the marketing mix may be required and decisions will need to be made as to which further groups/regions the new product should be marketed.

2 The role of innovation and degrees of innovation

New product development is a risky business. Viewed against alternative growth strategies in *Ansoff's* matrix, it is judged by most writers to be several times more risky than market penetration or new market development. A majority of new products launched are thought to be failures.

So why do it? Well, mainly because of competition, and the product life cycle (PLC) which holds that all products follow the stages of introduction, growth, maturity and decline. Inevitably therefore, if a number of existing products are at the mature/decline stage and we do nothing, the company's sales turnover and profits will decline. Quite apart from this, there is the danger inherent in being seen as a 'stuck in the mud' company as opposed to 'go ahead' by the stakeholders and the market.

Some of the risk involved in NPD could be lessened in relation to the degree of innovation. This can vary widely.

2.1 Relatively small cosmetic modifications to the product and/or packaging

2.2 Adding useful but small features

2.3 Complete re-design of the existing product

2.4 New to the world products that create an entirely new market as was the case with the launch of the Sony Walkman.

Over time, companies will be forced into some degree of innovation in order to survive. Some companies will deliberately opt to be followers whilst others will prefer to lead the market in this respect.

27 New product development: innovation and branding

Report to: Cosmetics Organisation
From: A N Other
Date: 7 December 200X
Subject: The role of innovation; approaches and branding

(a) **The role of innovation**

Companies that fail to innovate will inevitably go out of business in the longer term as shown in the concept of the product life cycle below:

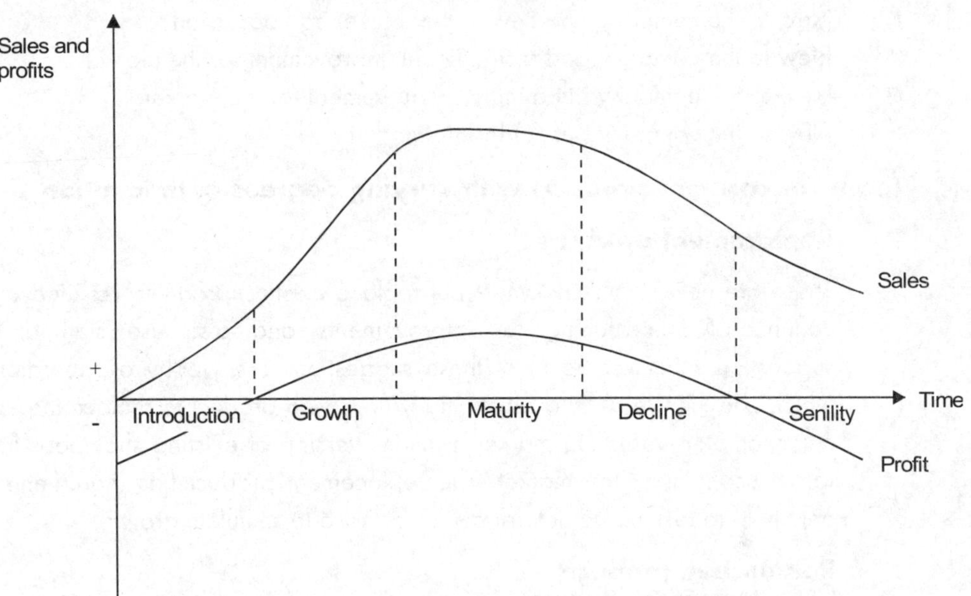

Obviously some products have a longer life cycle than others. However, who would have agreed thirty years ago that such a thing as coal had no long-term future? Today we have better ways of heating our homes and fuelling our power stations.

Another reason for existing products to decline is because most people want change, sometimes for its own sake but more often if something netter becomes available. So innovation is vital to survival of organisations.

Innovation is particularly important in the cosmetic industry where fashion dictates very short life cycles and competition is fierce. Societal factors impacting include the ageing population, blurring of male-female differences and increased importance of appearance.

As sales of older products decline, some become obsolete and new products are needed to maintain a balanced portfolio and the continued growth of our organisation.

Being innovative keeps us in front of our competitors and enhances our image in the market as a go-ahead enterprise. Customers are always looking for something new.

Some markets such as ours are characterised by **continuous innovation**: there is always something new going on and it is expected. **Discontinuous innovation** exists when otherwise stable markets are occasionally disrupted by technological breakthroughs.

(b) **Proactive and reactive approaches to new product development (NPD)**

A **proactive** approach exists when the company leads the market in introducing new products. Obviously, this entails heavy expenditure on NPD and a higher risk. NPD is a time-consuming process with no guarantee of success. However, a well managed technological breakthrough can bring much greater rewards. Quite apart from increased profits, proactive approach makes for a more exciting business environment and generally attracts a higher calibre personnel.

A **reactive** approach is one where an organisation is content to be a follower rather than a leader in innovation. This requires less expenditure on NPD and is generally safer than the proactive approach. There is also the danger of being seen as somewhat 'stuck in the mud'.

The decision on whether an approach is proactive or reactive is influenced by the **degree of newness** of the product.

- New to the company and new to the market eg liposuction
- New to the company and a significant improvement for the market
- New to the company but a minor improvement for the market
- New to the company but not for the market

(c) **Terms for cosmetic products with varying degrees of innovation**

1 **Replacement products**

These are new to our customers but replace existing products. As innovators we are continuously researching for improvements and also use staff and customer suggestion schemes. Some of these suggestions are worthy of laboratory research which can then result in a substantially improved product to replace the existing one. For example, we use to market a milder version of existing shampoos for the older (grey) segment of the market. The replacement product has ingredients which not only help to restore the natural colour but also to stimulate growth.

2 **Relaunched products**

As indicated, products reaching the decline stage of the PLC have reduced profits. Instead of making these obsolete and withdrawing them from sale, a more positive approach is to relaunch those with a 'makeover'. This could be simply a repackaging, new strapline, or some more substantive renovation of the actual product or both.

Again looking at our burgeoning 'grey' market, we have relaunched some of our skin creams with added moisturising and wrinkle-reducing ingredients.

3 **Imitative products**

These are simply 'copycat' or 'me-too' products launched by followers in the market. Their strategy is to wait until a market leader has undergone the expense and risk involved in a new product launch and when they see it becoming established and successful – to launch their own imitative version. This can of course be done at a lower price since the imitator has lower development costs. Eventually the innovator is forced out by price competition, having to develop further new products and so the cycle starts again. A good example here would be that of the anti-dandruff shampoos, a myriad of which appeared on the market some years ago.

(d) **The role of branding in NPD and its impact on marketing mix decisions**

We no longer have consumer products as such, we have brands. The American Marketing Association defines a brand as 'a name, term, sign, symbol, or design, or a combination of them, intended to identify the goods of one seller or group of sellers and to differentiate them from those of competitors'. This lengthy and complex definition arises partly because of the amount of legislation surrounding the ownership of brands. This is not surprising considering the huge equity of global brands such as Coca-Cola and McDonald's.

When we launch a new product, we have to decide whether it should have its own brand name or the company brand or a combination of both. There are benefits and risks involved here.

The benefit of launching under a tried and trusted company brand name is that it enhances the probability of success but it dilutes the brand essence and in the event of failure can damage the brand image. There are limits to how far the corporate or 'umbrella' brand can be stretched. A good example of a very successful hybrid approach in the form of corporate brand – product brand was Wall's Cornetto.

With regard to the brand's impact on the marketing mix, we have seen that positioning involves adjustments in the marketing mix to differentiate a new product from those of competitors in the target market segment. Branding's job is to communicate this positioning of the new product ie to achieve a favourable image in the mind of the potential customer of the brand value. Branding symbolises the essential features of the new product – its unique attributes, its packaging, pricing, distribution and promotion. They must all integrate so as to leave no confusion or doubts in the target customers' minds.

28 International new product development and innovation

> *Examiner's comments:* This question covers the role of innovation and new product development in an international context. It develops the role of innovation within organisations and uses the launch of a cereal snack bar in European countries as an example of new product development.

From: Marketing Manager
Date: December 20X3

(a) **Introduction**

Report: New product Development and the Role of Innovation
From: International Marketing Manager – Cereal snacks

Introduction

Companies need to introduce new products/services to their line to support the notion of breadwinners. It is vitally important for companies to possess a balanced portfolio within their product range that will have an impact on the development of new products. Innovation is the source of new ideas that will lead to different approaches of bringing new products to the market. International markets will demand this same new product development approach in order to sustain competitiveness, but also sensitivity to national requirements.

Role of Innovation within organisations

There are a number of strategic factors that span managerial attitude and organisational style. These include the following:

Top management support for innovation - there is sufficient supply of resources, incentive and motivation from senior management to service the needs of innovative activity in the organisation.

Long-term strategy with an innovative focus - it is implied in the planning process that the adoption of a long-term view is accepted. New products are planned to fit into the corporate strategic planning process.

Long-term commitment to major projects - through understanding the target market potential in detail the organisation is able to pursue a long-term approach and allocate sufficient funding to support the necessary activity.

Flexibility and responsive to change - the organisation is able to add variety and speed to quality and reliability.

Top management acceptance of risk - avoid low potential, low risk 'me-too' products; apply tight screening criteria and conserve resources for more worthwhile projects.

Support for an Entrepreneurial culture - actively manage the culture and management style in response to the market.

For an international market cereal snack products there is a need to understand the different requirements from different markets. This will inevitably mean understanding different national consumption trends and identifying likes and dislikes of each targeted market segment.

(b) **Approach to new product development:**

Idea Generation - the role of research and development, understanding market trends and competitor activity and customers' preferences are all important activities to be undertaken. Ideas can come from a number of sources including staff and other industry participants. Idea generating techniques such as brainstorming and scenario building need to focus on a cereal bar product launch planned for European coverage.

Screening Ideas - consideration of the synergy with existing products utilising conventional technology should assist in the screen process. A robust set of criteria should be established to help this process. Also consideration of the suitability of existing distribution channels and existing skills and assets is required. The fit with corporate strategic goals, combined with marketing goals including market growth targets, size of segmented market need to be assessed.

Concept Testing - this activity starts to describe, profile and visualise the product for the different segments of the European market. It will probably be based on national boundaries with a profile established for each country.

Business Analysis - the marketing strategy, production and financial analysis will need to be considered. Future business planning will need to consider the likely impact of exchange rate fluctuations. The outcome of this phase is to establish a competitive response to the market.

Product Development - the brand identity, packaging, labelling, promotion, pricing and launch strategy will all need to be considered for each international targeted market. The detailed requirements will need to be incorporated into the product development activity.

Test Marketing - test area selection, competitive response, timing and duration – simulated test market or controlled distribution mini-markets

Commercialisation - the launch and roll out activity will need to be established. Actual resource implications will need to be planned on a country-by-country basis.

Monitoring and Evaluation - accurate and reliable data will need to be fed back to the marketing function to gauge the performance within each of the targeted market segments to assess partial failure, outright failure or success. This will allow for responsive actions to be taken to maximise possible sales and minimise potential waste.

Conclusion

Innovation is lifeblood of all organisations with a constant need to bring new products to market. However, it is a risky and expensive process fraught with possible pitfalls. The challenge is to mange the process of getting innovation to market in order to exploit all potential opportunities.

29 Pricing frameworks

1 Introduction

The factors that influence pricing decisions in the case of an international airline company like BA, are extremely complex. They are not only influenced by tensions between short-term and long-term objectives but also by increasing, intense, global competition.

Some years ago,, BA had positioned themselves as *The* British airline – reliable, safe, comfortable, caring – and well worth a premium price. This unambiguous stance has since been overtaken by circumstances, not the least of which is the need to compete with no frills, low-cost, niche players, a host of which have entered the market.

2 Basic pricing approaches

2.1 *A cost approach*

No business can trade indefinitely below costs. BA needs to know its fixed and variable costs so as to be able to calculate break-even points. In the final analysis, BA needs to maximise profits, but this does not exclude operating occasionally on a marginal cost basis as part of overall strategy. Clearly an approach where BA always add a fixed margin to total costs has become outdated and unworkable.

2.2 *Demand orientated pricing*

The market segments into the low cost, no frills offer at one end of the spectrum and the high cost, luxury service at the other. What matters to BA is customer perceived value. How big is the premium price segment; how loyal are its customers and is this segment growing? Can BA convince more people that its service is what they want and good value? How important is safety and comfort to its target market?

3 Other factors influencing pricing decisions for BA

3.1 Demand has been seen to be highly price elastic. As cheaper prices have become available, so have more people taken to flying – particularly on holiday. This elasticity is set to continue. With ever more congested roads and high current rail fares (eg £174 return Manchester to London) demand for internal flights looks certain to continue to rise. Can BA afford to ignore these growth segments?

3.2 *Channels to market*

Quite a high proportion of flights are purchased through booking and travel agents, who receive a commission of around 10% on a small transaction. Obviously, this cost has to be absorbed in the prices charged. However, the direct channel to market is growing: already we see discounts for booking on the Internet being offered to the general public. Large corporations with heavy bookings for business travel are also increasingly likely to want to deal direct with BA.

3.3 *Stage of the PLC*

Kotler and others suggest that pricing should be varied according to stages in the product/industry life cycle. This is in effect a reaction to supply and demand. However, the airline industry is clearly still in the growth stage and although economies of scale operate to reduce prices, demand grows apace. The market naturally segments by price as well as by other variables.

3.4 *Off-peak/promotional pricing*

Unlike products, services cannot be stored. Empty seats represent irrevocably lost sales. A seat sold at a reduced price is better than no sale at all so long as the marginal cost is covered. For this reason BA along with other airlines will offer reduced priced during off-peak periods or times and to boost sales for new route launches or sometimes as a tactical measure to meet competition.

3.5 *Deliberate overbooking*

This practice appears to be spreading and in as much as it temporarily boosts profits, it also affects prices. It also results in airlines buying off or attempting to buy off passengers. In the long-term, this practice will simply drive business away to other airlines who guarantee seats.

3.6 *The PESTLE factors*

Political factors affect pricing in as much as some countries subsidise their national airlines and/or add taxes for entry.

Economic factors – particularly net disposable incomes directly affect demand and prices.

Sociological factors can have a devastating effect upon airline income and therefore prices. Attitudes to safety, dangers of viruses, thromboses and so on can all adversely influence demand. Counter measures taken by airlines drive up costs and therefore prices.

Technological factors can operate both to drive up prices and to bring these down. Technological improvements to aircraft/airports/air traffic control and so on usually result in higher costs in the short-term but offer compensating benefits in the longer term (eg increased passenger loads.

Legal factors are impacting ever more heavily upon pricing. Passengers are increasingly likely to seek substantial compensation for accidents, illnesses or traumas suffered as a result of flying, urged on by high-fee earning lawyers.

Environmental (Green) factors tie up with sociological/technological factors in increasing costs/prices. An environmentally conscious public will (with the help of various institutions) demand reductions in pollution and noise that substantially affect costs/prices.

4 Conclusion

This brief examination highlights just how complex pricing decisions for a major airline can be. BA can however position itself in the market so as to negate or even exploit some of the factors explored above. It could for example take the stance that safety, comfort and care are well worth paying more for. It could even make a virtue out of a high price that guarantees as seat; that provides more body room than any of its competitors; that can demonstrate the best figures with regard to take-off and arrival times; and so on.

30 Pricing and the integrated marketing mix

Examiner's comments. Better students, addressed the main factors affecting pricing (costs, competition and consumer demand) and applied these factors to the restaurant context. Those who failed seemed to forget that the restaurant existed at all, and gave no applied examples or recommended approach.

To: Partners
From: Entrepreneur
Subject: Marketing plan for restaurant – Pricing

1 **Introduction**

This part of the marketing plan outlines the factors that we need to take into consideration when **setting prices** and my recommended pricing approach. Since prices will inevitably affect **demand** and the restaurant's **profit**, this is a very important decision that will need continuous review.

2 **Factors to take into consideration**

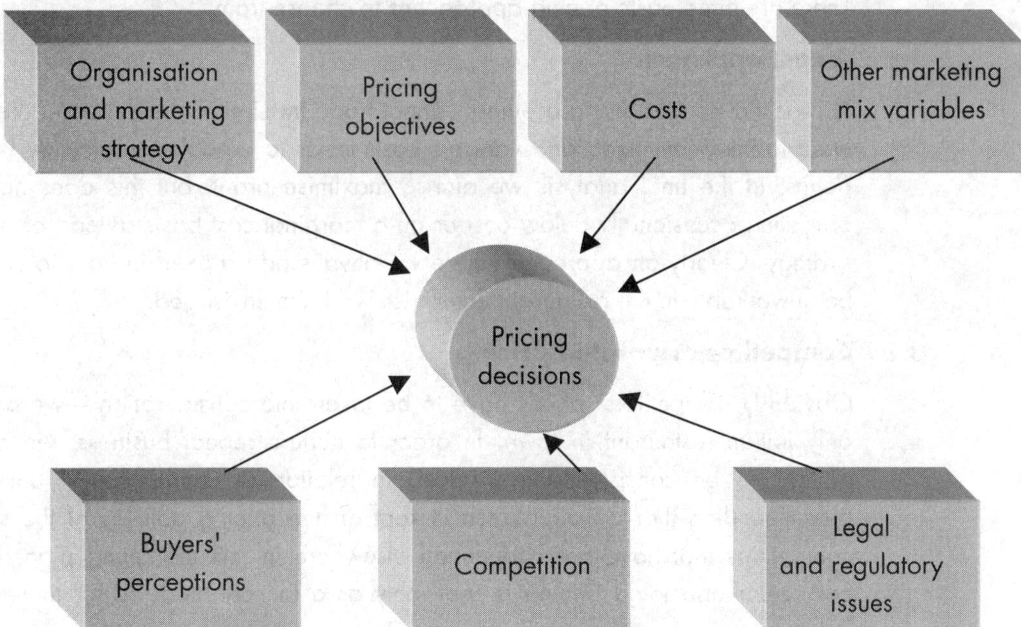

2.1 **Marketing strategy**

We have already agreed to position the restaurant as being up-market, offering *haute cuisine* and a highly distinctive ambience.

2.2 **Pricing objective**

To maximise profit whilst providing value and striving for repeat business/recommendations

2.3 **Costs**

Our city centre location is expensive. This combined with our up-market positioning means relatively high costs.

2.4 Other marketing mix variables

Products and services will be high quality. Place/physical evidence/ambience in keeping with an up-market positioning. People professional and trained – attracted from competitors and needing above-average remuneration. Promotion in quality media.

2.5 Buyers' perceptions

We want our prospective guests to see our premises, décor and menus as being impressive: a restaurant in which they will be proud to entertain business acquaintances and friends alike. A venue which discourages rowdiness, and where background music and interior decoration is quiet and tasteful.

2.6 Competition

There is of course strong competition around our city centre location, but at lunchtime and on Friday/Saturday evenings demand exceeds supply. At other times when demand is low, competitors tend to offer price incentives.

2.7 Legal and regulatory issues

We are of course bound by the national minimum wage and by the requirements of the Trade Descriptions Act when making special offers.

3 Pricing approaches and recommendations

There are three basic pricing approaches to choose from:

3.1 A cost approach

This acknowledges that a business cannot trade indefinitely below cost. We certainly need to know our fixed and variable costs so as to be able to calculate break-even points. In the final analysis we aim to maximise profit, but this does not exclude operating occasionally below cost or on a marginal cost basis as part of our overall strategy. Clearly an approach where we always add a fixed margin to costs would be unworkable in the restaurant enterprise we have envisaged.

3.2 Competitor orientated pricing

Obviously competitors' prices have to be taken into consideration – we are not the only Italian restaurant in town. In order to nurture repeat business, we cannot be thought to be consistently over-priced in relation to competition. I am therefore recommending that a daily watch is kept on the pricing policies of the six closest competitors that have been identified elsewhere in this marketing plan. However, competitor orientated pricing is seen only as a tactical measure for limited *ad hoc* use.

3.3 Demand orientated pricing

This is my recommended approach. Other parts of this marketing plan emphasise that our overall strategy is one of differentiation. Our positioning will be such as to justify a premium price. We are not appealing to bargain hunters but rather people to seeking a unique experience, able and willing to pay for it. Our research has shown that there is adequate demand for this experience at the peak business and social times.

4 **Conclusion**

Demand orientated pricing represents the best fit approach for our enterprise. It is in line with our sales/profit objectives, our differentiation strategy, our strengths and our distinctive competition advantage – all as outlined in other parts of the overall marketing plan.

31 Price planning

Report to: Low Cost Air Travel Company
From: Marketing Manager
Date: 7 December 200X
Subject: Forecasting techniques and pricing strategies for next year

(a) **Forecasting techniques**

This is a particularly important issue for our company since our pricing strategy is based upon achieving the forecast sales volumes. Wide variations from forecast will affect all components of the marketing plan from objectives down to the tactical elements of the marketing mix.

There are two main groups of methods which can be categorised as:

Qualitative techniques

Management judgement – asking managers for their opinions on next year's sales. The problem with this method is that its accuracy varies with the experience of individuals and whether they are pessimistic or optimistic in nature.

The Delphi technique or jury method – both of these involve assembling a panel of experts from outside the company. Such experts are few and may possibly be competitors.

Salesforce and or dealer surveys – these are perhaps viable but sales people are by nature optimistic, whilst dealers may deliberately under-forecast so as to get lower quotas for quantity discounts.

Scenario planning – the essence of successful scenario planning is a clear understanding of the external environment and the factors which impact upon our market. Some of our senior managers have this understanding and other people outside could be consulted.

Qualitative methods

There are a variety of statistical techniques which can be applied ranging from the simple extension of previous years' sales in the form of a moving annual total, through time series analysis/correlations/indicators and market testing, to so-called 'black box' techniques.

I would recommend a hybrid approach of trend extrapolation modified by scenario planning, that is, a combination of objective and subjective techniques. With regard to the main factors from the external environment impacting upon our business, we can not only identify them but also score them for their degrees of impact. Some outside consultancy is needed to act as a further moderator.

(b) **Main external factors affecting our pricing strategy**

The accepted framework covering external macro environmental factors affecting business is PESTLE, standing for **P**olitical, **E**conomic, **S**ociological, **T**echnological, **L**egal, (green) **E**nvironmental.

A framework for analysing external micro environmental factors is Competitors, Customers, Suppliers, Distributors.

These two basic sets of factors often interact: for example the economy affects competition and customers; sociological factors also affect customers' buying behaviour.

Pricing is affected by the basic economic law of supply and demand. This law is in turn affected by the PESTLE factors. Demand for air travel is currently relatively low following a boom period, due largely to the political factors of war with Iraq and terrorist activities worldwide. Shortfalls in demand result in increased competition and pressure on prices. International conflict also tends to result in higher oil prices and increased costs of aviation fuel, putting pressure on margins and prices. Here, we have conflicting pressures from similar sources – one placing downward pressure on our pricing strategy, the other exerting upward pressure on prices.

Changes in the economy clearly affect our pricing strategy and lower disposable incomes next year would mean customers seeking lower prices.

Technological factors such as video conferencing combine with safety fears to reduce business travel by air. Those airlines catering for business travel are likely to look enviously at our market and possibly compete in the short-term with special low-price offers.

Taking all the above factors into account we can expect increased demand for low cost air travel next year, but also greatly increased competition. I am therefore recommending that we maintain our existing prices, keeping a reserve to enable us to respond to aggressive price moves by competitors, where necessary.

(c) **Critical analysis of marginal costing and breakeven analysis in setting prices**

These two approaches are based on costs and are aimed at determining a profitable price. Before critically analysing these approaches, we need to understand how they work. Firstly, there are two basic types of costs – fixed and variable, defined as those that don't vary (in the short-term) with the amount of units produced or sold (eg rates) and those that do (eg labour and materials entering into the product/service).

Marginal analysis

Marginal analysis is the examination of what happens to a firm's costs and revenues when production or sales volume is changed by one unit. Marginal cost (MC) is the extra cost incurred when producing or selling one more unit. Marginal revenue (MR) is the additional revenue generated when the firm sells one more unit. Clearly MR minus MC = profit or loss. The firm should produce at the point where MR = MC because this is the most profitable level of production.

Breakeven analysis

Breakeven analysis is similarly concerned with costs and revenues but works on a total rather than a marginal basis.

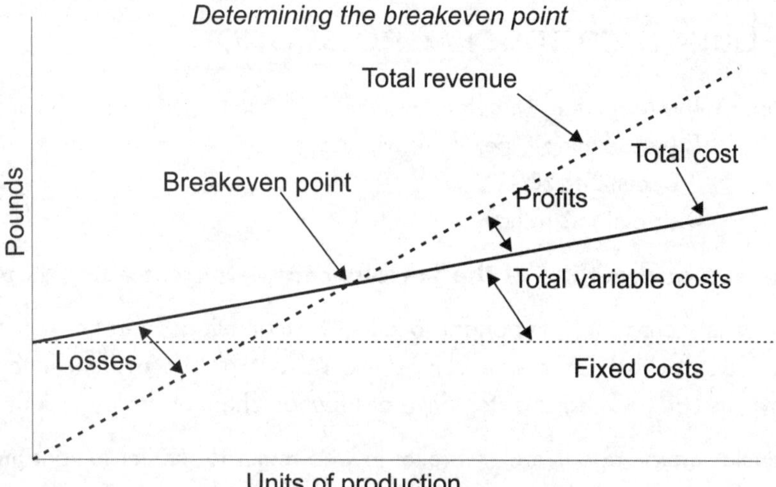

The breakeven point is where total revenue exactly equals total cost.

To calculate the breakeven sales revenue multiply the breakeven point in units by the price per unit. Marketers should determine the breakeven point for a number of alternative prices so as to establish the effects on total revenue/costs and thus avoid setting prices at undesirable levels.

Critique

Both the above approaches have a similar aim, that is to help us to determine the best prices to maximise sales and profits. The essential difference is that the marginal approach is based on one additional unit, whereas the breakeven approach is based on total volume.

Marginal analysis can give a false impression that pricing can be highly precise but as can be seen above, competitors or government action can quickly decrease a company's revenue and profits.

Breakeven analysis has the benefit of being simple. It does not however tell us exactly what price to charge or how to achieve a pricing objective of increased return on investment or improved market share.

Both approaches are bedded in cost plus principles, whereas a marketer will point out that there is no point in arriving at a price based on cost plus desired profit, if it is then too high to result in a sale.

For these reasons, we need to consider other approaches such as:

- Demand or customer related – what will the market bear, what will our customers pay?
- Competitor related – what are the competitors charging and what effect does it have on our sales?
- Company related – what are our financial objectives?
- Strategic/tactical pricing – what are our long-term pricing objectives and can these be reconciled with flexible/promotional pricing in response to short-term fluctuations in the market?

32 Distribution channels and support

Review to: The Marketing Director
From: The Marketing Operations Manager
Date: 7 December 200X
Subject: Distribution strategy

Introduction and outline of the various channels available to our company

Distribution is increasingly important to effective marketing operations in the modern context. Innovative distribution can create competitive advantage, as evidenced by the Amazon book company's use of the Internet. Alternative distribution channels today include the following.

- Manufacturer to agent/factor/broker to wholesaler to retailer to consumer/user
- Manufacturer to wholesaler to retailer to consumer/user
- Manufacturer to retailer to consumer/user
- Manufacturer to franchiser to consumer/user
- Manufacturer to consumer/user

In the latter case, manufacturers can use mail order or a call centre, perhaps outsourced. Increasingly companies use a multiplicity of channels to reach different target market segments.

In our company's case there are two alternative channels.

- Wholesaler (Tour Operator) to retailer ()Travel Agents) to consumer/user
- Tour Operator to consumer/user

the use of Travel Agents does of course entail the payment of a commission, which raises the question of whether we should market direct to consumers via the Internet or direct mail brochures, as in the case of Portland Holidays, or via telemarketing, or all three. Another option would be to vertically integrate downwards by setting up our own travel agencies. Furthermore, we could offer exclusive distribution to retail chains (Co-op Travel), voluntary groups etc, perhaps in the form of own-brand or label. We have to recognise that distribution channels are changing and look for opportunities to increase business b seeking new outlets.

Criteria for the evaluation of alternative channels

Overall distribution strategy, whether intensive, selective or exclusive, needs to be consistent with brand strategy ie if we want to develop an up-market brand image, then we should pursue an exclusive distribution strategy.

Equally there should be strategic fit between distribution and company objectives/overall strategy. The right channel mix is also dependent on market size, market dispersion/remoteness, buying behaviour and complexity, product characteristics, technology, competition and regulations. This is essentially a complex and fluid situation.

When evaluating individual channel choices, the following evaluation criteria apply.

- Access to and coverage of target market segments
- Cost of operation and margins
- Expected return
- Amount of control over brand
- Reputation/image
- Compatibility of culture
- Creditworthiness
- Degree of promotional support needed
- Staff knowledge/expertise

- Power-dependency relationships

The acid test when deciding whether to market direct to consumer is – can we do a better job than the travel agents at an equivalent cost or can we do an equivalent job at a lower cost?

Recommendation of an appropriate strategy for our target market

Since we address a number of target markets with a range of products, a multiplicity of channels is appropriate.

For our exclusive luxury cruises, a direct channel is the most appropriate since this affords us maximum control over the quality of the service. Advertising the cruises can be targeted more accurately by choosing media used by people with particular characteristics, who would not appreciate having to consult a busy down-market travel agent catering for the mass market, without the necessary staff knowledge and expertise.

Equally, our new range of special interest tours is best suited to a direct channel using the Internet, which can be backed up by a dedicated chat-room and help-line.

For our standard packages, we should continue to use the travel agents who generally provide a good service meeting the needs of our target customers for these packages and have the necessary physical presence in the population conurbations ie access and coverage of this particular market segment.

Channel support

The travel agents (TAs) will of course receive the normal trade discount when booking our standard packages. However, additional bonuses will be available based on the total bookings received pa

Brochures and posters will be supplied to support the TAs and prize incentives will be offered for the best displays of these.

Videos will be produced and supplied to support selected holidays to those TA chains willing to co-operate in special promotions as well as making staff training and holiday sampling available.

An annual survey of TAs will be conducted to ascertain levels of satisfaction and to solicit suggestion for future joint initiatives.

33 Tutorial question: Co-ordinating the communications and marketing mixes

The interdependency of elements of the marketing mix

One of the major problems involved in gaining a proper understanding of the nature of the marketing mix lies in its treatment in the literature, since authors typically tend to devote discrete chapters or sections to each of the individual elements of the marketing mix, focusing initially on the product and then moving successively through price, promotion and place.

This sequential treatment can be justified by the decision-taking process adopted in many organisations, in that the product is often the starting point in a series of decisions that embrace price, promotion and distribution.

The reader should recognise, however, that decisions made with regard to one element of the marketing mix inevitably affect other elements of the mix. For example, product, promotion and place all have cost implications which can affect price. Furthermore, where goods are placed (ie distribution) will affect both promotion (in the media used, need for branding and so on) and product (in its packaging).

The true nature of the marketing mix is therefore that of a set of interdependent variables as indicates in the figure below.

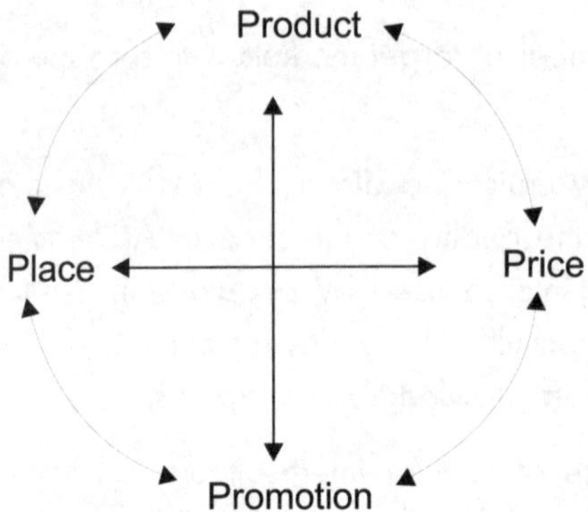

Integrating the elements of the marketing mix (Wilson, Gilligan, Pearson)

Recognition of the interdependency that exists among the elements of the mix highlights the need for these elements to be integrated in a harmonious way so that the greatest possible attractiveness of the total mix to its target market segment can be achieved.

It would, for example, be fatuous to advertise Rolls Royce cars in a children's comic or to endeavour to sell such cars door-to-door with an incentive of free balloons. A high-priced, high-status product such as a Rolls Royce car is aimed to meet the needs of particular types of adults – usually in particular occupations. Its promotion would be made in quality media and its distribution would be effected via exclusive dealers to the highest service standards.

By integrating the elements of the mix, dissonance and confusion in the messages being sent to the target audiences can be avoided.

The need for harmonious integration of the elements of the marketing mix applies equally to the marketing of services, as shown in Illustration 1.

Illustration 1: An Unnamed Local Authority's Bus Service in a Major City

The situation is one where the buses are clean and modern. Fare prices are among the lowest in the country and the frequency of service is excellent. Information of all the bus services is available in easy-to-read pamphlets placed in dispensers on each bus.

It would seem that all the ingredients in the mix are harmoniously integrated.

However, there is one problem in this otherwise happy situation and that is the drivers. They stop short or pass the bus stop to the irritation and inconvenience of the passengers. They also drive the buses in a series of jerks which makes the ride extremely uncomfortable as well as dangerous when passengers are leaving/occupying their seats.

As a consequence of this treatment an increasing number of previous passengers are using other forms of transport.

Expanding the four Ps and maintaining integration

In practice the framework of the four Ps is, as we suggested earlier, an over-simplification of a more complex reality. For instance, we can expand the element of product to include services, as shown in Illustration 1. Similarly we can expand the elements of promotion into at least four constituents, namely personal selling, advertising, sales promotion and PR. Further breakdowns of these sub-elements can be made, eg sales promotion into sales incentives, literature, point-of-sale display materials etc.

Each of these sub-elements also needs to be harmoniously integrated for maximum marketing effectiveness.

Co-ordinating the communications mix

Promotions here refers to the major forms of marketing communications, namely advertising, personal selling, sales promotion and PR, which we call the promotional mix. Some writers (eg Kotler, 1986) use the term 'communications mix' rather than promotional mix, in the same context, while others (eg Jefkins, 1990) use the term 'communications' to represent company-wide communications rather than just marketing communications.

Just as the elements of the marketing mix need to be integrated and tailored to the needs of particular market segments – so the elements of the promotional mix should be harmonized in order to avoid conflict and confusion in messages being sent to the target audience and to achieve maximum communication effectiveness.

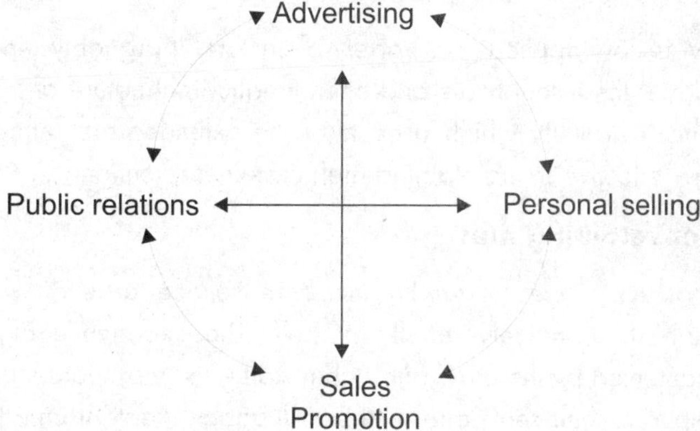

The role of the promotional mix is essential to make the target audience favourably aware of the availability of products and services in the market-place. Each element of the promotional mix can play a distinctive part in this role.

Marketing research and the marketing mix

In a marketing-led organisation we would expect decisions on the elements of the marketing mix (and their sub-elements) to be influenced by information inputs drawn from marketing research. That is to say product/service features would reflect identified customer needs and wants; advertising might be pre-tested to ensure impact and retention of desire-arousing messages; products would be placed in prime, attention-getting in store positions and perhaps accompanied by point-of-sale display materials again researched for cost effectiveness.

34 Customer relations: the contribution of the marketing mix

Report to: The Marketing Director
From: Relationship Marketing Manager, Provincial Airlines
Subject: Relationship Marketing Mix
Date: 15 June 200X

1 **Introduction**

Relationship marketing (RM) has been variously defined, one often quoted from *Grönroos* being that it 'is to establish, maintain and enhance relationships with customers and other parties at a profit so that the objectives of the parties involved are met. This is done by a mutual exchange and fulfilment of promises'. However, I much prefer the earlier approach by *Christopher, Payne and Ballantyne* when they say that 'Traditionally marketing has been about getting customers. Relationship Marketing addresses the twin concerns-getting customers and keeping customers'.

While RM is now applied in a variety of sectors, it arguably emerged in the service sector on account of the inseparable and often longitudinal nature of the exchange. The following report aims to identify which aspects of the extended marketing mix for services may be particularly effective in maintaining high customer retention rates for Provincial Airlines.

2 **Customer retaining mix**

2.1 **Product** – we start with the core service around which relationships can be established, namely the flight itself. The experience of this core service can be augmented by the crew and cabin staff – the way passengers are welcomed aboard, helped to their seats and with their luggage, kept informed, entertained and served – all offer opportunities to get closer to our customers and increase satisfaction. Relatively little things like something free to read and captain's announcements help to create a favourable and caring impression, so that customers will prefer to travel with us again on a future occasion. We can and should also do our utmost to influence other parties, particularly the airports and the authorities responsible for the provision of transport, to play a part in the retention of our customers, which are also theirs.

2.2 **Price** – there are a number of ways in which price can be used to maintain high customer retention rates. American Airlines was one of the first companies to pioneer Frequency Marketing Programmes which provide a financial reward for repeated custom. It is quite possible for Provincial Airlines to offer increasing discounts against the number of flights booked with us by ordinary passengers and indeed we already operate schemes of this nature for large companies. We could also offer free upgrades to business class and first class seats on a priority basis to repeat customers. This is in addition to a whole plethora of promotional price incentives such as Airmiles, early booking discounts, large group discounts and multiple product purchase offers.

2.3 **Promotion** – literally all elements of the promotional mix can be used to reinforce customer retention; advertising can remind people of the pleasurable experience of flying with us as can fliers (forgive the pun), direct mail shots, club magazines, cross selling and other forms of sales promotion. Personal selling extends to call centres, airport desk enquiries and of course the airline staff who have personal contact with passengers and their influences. PR in the form of favourable editorials is a very powerful influence on gaining and retaining customers, particularly corporate ones. Crises Management within PR is also an important issue in this respect: it is acknowledged that Michael Bishop of East Midlands played a crucial role in retaining customers, following a disastrous crash at that airport, through his handling of the media.

2.4 **Place** – our USP is that our flights are available from more provincial airports than our competitors and it is important that we expand our lead in this respect. After all it is no use promoting customer loyalty if prospects cannot fly with us from their airport of choice. Other aspects of distribution include good relationships with travel agents and other ticket sellers as well as telephone, fax and internet ordering systems (see Process below).

2.5 **People** – this is the most important element of the customer retaining mix for the simple reason that our airline services are provided to people by people. It is the interaction of customers and potential customers with our staff which makes or breaks the relationship. Each interaction in the process offers an opportunity to improve customer relationships and it is essential that all our staff are trained and updated in interactive skills. We need to maintain a continuous programme of internal marketing to ensure all staff recognise that customer satisfaction is key to repeat business and how best to recover a poor relationship.

2.6 **Physical evidence** – most services are intangible so that efforts need to be made to 'tangibilise' these favourably. In our case, we can do this via smart modern uniforms, clean aircraft exteriors and interiors designed with passenger comfort in mind and to allay fears.

2.7 **Process** – next to People with which it is allied, this element of the mix offers us real opportunities to improve customer retention. We need to visualise and chart the entire process by which a prospect first recognises the need to book a flight>through favourable recall of a preferred airport/airline>to actually making the booking>then beyond to the task of packing>getting to the airport>proceeding through embarkation to boarding>take-off and flight> disembarking>customs>transport from airport>and the return journey in its entirely. Each of these stages offers a chance for Provincial Airlines to play a part in making the process as seamless and hassle-free as possible and to do it better than anyone else. We want not only to please but to delight our customers to maximise repeat business (*Parasuraman et al*).

3 Conclusion

This report would not be complete without pointing out the need for market segmentation, target markets, research to assess reasons for customer churn, and a focus on internal marketing – to complement and support the customer retaining mix.

Payne's Loyalty Ladder suggest that we should proceed from customer catching = Prospect>Customer – to customer keeping = Client>Supporter>Advocate, through an emphasis on developing and enhancing relationships.

What we need now is an action plan with your endorsement to make this happen.

35 Planning the service encounter

Presentation: Characteristics of services marketing

To: Marketing recruits
From: Marketing managers, commercial cleaners

Equipment: slide projector, video and handouts

1 **Introduction**

Good morning and thank you for coming. This presentation will last for about an hour including a final video of our service staff in action and around half an hour has been allowed for following questions and discussion. A synopsis of my presentation is being passed round for reference purposes.

The aims of this presentation are:

To outline the distinctive characteristics of marketing a commercial cleaning service

To consider ways in which the marketing mix can be extended in this type of market

I will start with ...

2 **The characteristics of service**

2.1 **Intangibility**

You can't touch, feel or smell a service. 'A service is an intangible product involving deed, a performance or an effort that cannot be physically possessed' (*Berry*). However, our cleaning company can endeavour to tangibilise our services. For example, the tidy appearance of a room, the aroma of an air freshener and the demeanour of staff all offer opportunities for service tangibilisation and favourable impressions. It is very important that our services are provided pleasantly and cheerfully because if our commercial clients don't like our staff, they won't come back for more.

We can and do also tangibilise our services by providing cleaning aids which can be used by our clients themselves, in the event of an emergency.

2.2 **Inseparability**

As I have intimated, the service cannot normally be separated from the provider in the same way as a product. Services are usually provided for people, by people.

2.3 **Heterogeneity**

Most services are subject to inconsistencies. It is not like a production process which delivers more or less identical products continuously. It is difficult if not impossible to provide the same service, by the same person, to the same person, at the same time and in exactly the same environmental conditions. Nevertheless, we do try to provide a consistent service by selection and training standards, by allocating cleaning staff to service contracts and by inspections as well as feedbacks from our customers.

2.4 **Ownership**

Whereas the title to a physical good is transferred from seller to buyer, purchasing a service only confers the right of access or use. This can put our customers at a disadvantage and make them feel much more apprehensive than when buying a product. We address this by 'money back if not satisfied' guarantees and by providing third party references.

2.5 **Perishability**

Goods can be stocked but services cannot be stored. A clean office cannot be taken from a cupboard whenever wanted. Getting the time right is therefore very important to our clients and process times are often a condition of contract. For our hotel clients, an uncleaned room is a room not let and means irretrievably lost revenue. For this reason we have to have emergency systems so that our clients are not let down.

2.6 **The extended marketing mix**

You will already be familiar with the 4Ps approach to the marketing of products. *Booms and Binter* recommend the addition of three more Ps for the marketing of services, namely Physical evidence, Process and People – in the attempt to address the above five special characteristics.

2.6.1 **Physical evidence**

When trying to tangibilise our services in the ways previously discussed, we need to consider the image conveyed to clients and what we can do to improve this. One way we use is the provision of clean uniforms on a daily basis which are in our house colour and carry out company logo. Another no less important aspect is that of body hygiene which is emphasised on our initial training and enforced on our inspections. You will also find that all our cleaning staff wear company gloves and headgear.

2.6.2 **People**

Quite a lot has already been said about this aspect, but we do train and enforce refresher courses aimed at maximising customer contacts. This can be as simple as a smile or the common courtesies but it can make the world of difference to the way our business is perceived. We particularly encourage our staff to look for opportunities to do something extra or special for our clients without having to be asked.

2.6.3 **Process**

Although you may not have thought about it, cleaning is very much a process and one which is tailored to the individual and immediate need.

When a cleaner enters a client's premises, he/she has to make an inspection to establish the state of the rooms. These may be more dirty/untidy than usual or less. Next the cleaner has to make a plan, eg start by tidying up, then dust before vacuuming etc. Sometimes there will be spillages to attend to first, changing the usual sequence of the process. Accessing the necessary equipment and materials needed is part of this process and may call for pre-planning, stocking considerations etc.

This process starts with an environmental condition which is unsatisfactory and ends with one that hopefully will delight the client. It has to be managed for the process to take place efficiently and effectively. Opportunities to achieve competitive differentials/ advantages arise during and as a result of this process.

3 **Conclusion**

Well, time is almost up but I want to finally point out that it is part of our company mission to deliver a high quality cleaning service which is second to none. 'Service quality, differentiation and productivity are key' (*Bateson*).

You can play a vital role in maintaining and improving our existing cleaning services and who knows in developing new services and markets.

Please now give your attention to the video which shows some of our staff executing some of our cleaning services. This is where our marketing efforts fail or succeed and on which continual research and analysis needs to take place. There will be time for your questions and comments after the video …

36 Physical evidence in the integrated marketing mix

Physical Evidence (PE) is an element of the extended marketing mix for services (the 7Ps):

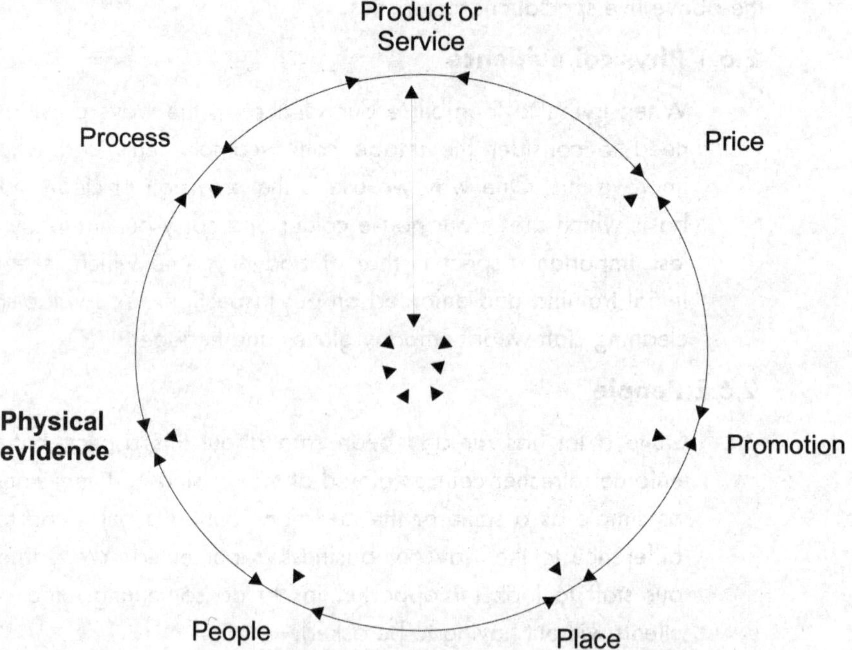

The need for PE arises essentially because of the lack of tangibility inherent in most services to some degree, which tends to cause unwelcome apprehension in users.

As services have become more important in the economy and as more organisations become marketing orientated, so the potential contribution PE can make to the efficacy of the marketing mix is increasingly recognised and applied.

Some of the constituents of PE and its partner elements of the extended marketing mix are shown in the following figure:

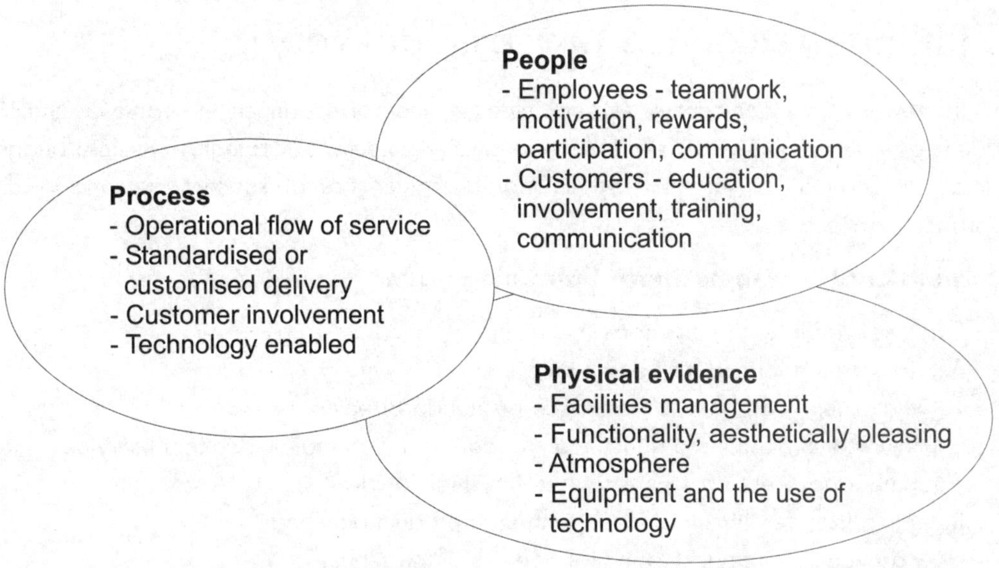

PE cannot be divorced from the people element since services are provided for people by people and people are therefore part of PE – for example, the appearance of staff providing a service can increase or decrease customer apprehensions.

Equally, PE cannot be divorced from any other element of the extended marketing mix: it adds cost and therefore influences price; it conveys messages and is therefore part of promotion; it has a physical presence in the place where the service is provided.

How PE can be developed in conjunction with people and process can be illustrated in the case of the UK's National Health Service:

Upon suffering symptoms of ill health, a person is likely to seek an appointment from the local doctor and may choose to do this by telephone or in person. Either way the person's natural anxiety can be lessened or increased by the method and manner of the receptionist's handling of the patient's request for an appointment. Upon arrival to see the doctor, the patient's apprehension will not be lessened by the PE of untidy appearance, time taken to find a scruffy file, delays in seeing the doctor at the time appointed, ancient magazines on the table, dirty toilets and so on.

Similarly unhelpful PE can confront the hapless patient upon entering the doctor's private surgery where instruments may be used to test the patient's condition and make a diagnosis.

It may be that the patient is referred to a specialist or a consultant when this process will be repeated to some degree. This time however, patient tensions will be increased and expectations enhanced. Even more dread can be present if the patient has to go to hospital by ambulance for emergency treatment when PE becomes paramount in regulating the patient's fear.

So much can be done through the use of PE to manage these situations and reduce tensions: friendly understanding by professionally trained staff; clean and tidy facilities, soothing background music; up-to-date technology; adequate signage; illustrations of the treatment processes; helpful literature; keeping the patient informer – are only some of the possibilities here.

Fortunately, the importance of developing appropriate PE is becoming more recognised in the public services as well as the private sector. More analysis of the inter-dependency of the elements of the extended marketing mix (and their sub-mixes) is however desirable in order to make further progress.

37 Planning the service process/delivery

The framework for planning the delivery of a service can be much the same as that for the marketing of a product, that is: situation analysis, objectives, strategies, tactics, budget and controls. It is in the detail that the special characteristics of services demand a different approach.

Situation analysis: some special planning issues

- Services are difficult if not impossible to store.
- Services are performed for people by people.
- To what extend can/should the service be standardised?
- Communications are more difficult to manage for an intangible-dominant service.
- Customer apprehensions/expectations vary individually.
- Sampling is more difficult to manage than in product planning.
- How do you plan capacity and manage use of the service?
- To what extent can the quality of the service delivery be consistent?

Objectives for services

Marketers of services like those of products share common interest in profitability, market share and sales. SMART objectives can be set accordingly. Since services are more difficult to mass-market, objectives for service providers are likely to be more modest in terms of sales and market share.

Strategies for service delivery

When developing strategies for the delivery of services, planners have to bear in mind customer expectations. These are influenced by previous experiences, friends/family, relevant media and personal needs. When experiencing the service, customers will consciously or unconsciously compare perceptions of service performance with their expectations.

In general terms, marketers of services will pursue a strategy of sustainable competitive advantage (Porter). They want not only to satisfy customers but to delight them, so as to gain repeat business and new customers through word-of-mouth recommendations. There are five main strategic imperatives to service/process delivery here:

1 **Empathy** – the skill of thinking and feeling as a customer; putting yourself in the customers' place, understanding their needs and organising the process around these needs.

2 **Responsiveness** – following on from the above, the system needs to respond quickly and effectively to enquiries, complaints and suggestions.

3 **Reassurance** – purchasers of services tend to be nervous of services especially on their first experience. The process needs to recognise this and attempt to alleviate this so as to put people at their ease and increase customer satisfaction.

4 **Tangibleness** – there are relatively few service processes which do not involve some material equipment or aids. These must be chosen carefully in the knowledge that their design and quality will affect customer perceptions. Intangibility can also be reduced by adding builders/atmosphere creators – see tactics below.

5 **Reliability** – this is the acid test of good service and determines whether the customer will continue to use the service. The process needs to keep promises made and be dependable.

Tactics for service delivery

Empathy can be developed through management testing of the service either personally or through the use of 'mystery shoppers'. Simple observation is a useful tactic as are watching customers' body language, listening to conversations and so on. Customer satisfaction surveys should be regularly conducted.

Responsiveness of the process can be improved by having staff available to handle queries, training and empowering these as regards actions. Complaint logging systems and analyses are essential features of the service process.

Reassurance: staff providing the service need to be trained to be considerate and polite in dealing with customers' anxieties as well as in techniques for reducing these.

Tangibleness: the atmosphere/ambience in which the service is being provided can be used to reduce customer tensions and enhance enjoyment. This can be done by adding suitable background music, air conditioning, perfume, flowers and so on. Where tangible aids are used in providing the service, these can be designed to impress customers and their benefits pointed out by the service provider.

Reliability: standards of service need to be laid down and internally marketed to all staff. Any let-downs should be addressed with apologies and compensation and the system modified, where appropriate.

Budgets and controls

Costs and revenues will need budgeting in the normal way. The highest cost is likely to be that of staff wages and salaries, but can also be that of providing suitable premises in which the service can be experienced. Insurance can also be unusually high as, for example, that covering renovating services for valuable paintings. There will be the usual marketing expenses covering communications and so on, with perhaps greater emphasis on continuous marketing research and training.

Controls will need imposing on performance against budgets, the quality and consistency of the service and on the systems/process involved.

38 Tutorial question: Non-business marketing

> *Tutorial note.* Charity, non-profit and non-business organisations are every bit as engaged in marketing as businesses seeking profit. They certainly need money in order to survive and a bit more than sufficient to cover operating costs, even if they do not call it profit. Employees will expect salary increases, new furniture/equipment when the old wears out and improved equipment. They will also need to research and to communicate with their target audiences like any other organisation. So what are these special types of organisations and what sorts of marketing strategies do they adopt?

Non-business marketing

This term can be used generally to cover all marketing activities entered into by organisations or individuals with a purpose other than the normal business objectives of achieving profit, return on investment, growth in market. The term covers both non-profit organisations and charities.

Dibb, Simkin, Pride and Ferrell suggest that non-business marketing can conveniently be split into two sub-categories.

Non-profit organisation marketing examples cited are hospitals and colleges but the differences here are becoming somewhat blurred as both these types of organisations are beginning to adopt more businesslike stances in a freer market. Nevertheless the basic objective of a hospital could be said to continue to be to provide high quality health care and for a college to provide higher quality education.

Social marketing seeks to shape or grow perceived beneficial social attitudes such as protecting the environment, saving scarce resources, contributing towards good causes and so on.

Kotler clarifies non-business marketing objectives by considering the idea of exchange rather than profit. Thus the police try to serve the public's need for protection with objectives of law enforcement and receive in return funding (through taxes) and a certain degree of support from the public. A charity offers satisfaction and an outlet for compassion and, for some people, a means of reduction of guilt, receiving in return financial contributions from donors and support from voluntary helpers.

Charity marketing

A good current example of the marketing strategies adopted by charities is the BBC's Children in Need campaign. This raises millions of pounds by organising, or rather persuading other people to organise, mammoth showbusiness events. The famous Terry Wogan fronts it all on an extended television programme which co-ordinates all the fund-raising activities entered into by other showbusiness people and the general public.

Non-profit marketing

To illustrate the types of marketing strategies adopted by a non-business organisation other than a charity, I would cite the example of a new university (formerly a polytechnic). Its objective could be said to raise the standard of higher education. It seeks to meet this objective by the marketing strategies of developing better courses, covering a wider variety of subjects and promoting to a wider target market. Such a university would be in competition with other universities and higher educational providers nationally and internationally. It would therefore develop competitive strategies, one of which might be to develop a competitive differential advantage. In the case of Nottingham this might be the attractions of a city claimed to be 'Queen of the Midlands', or its track record. It could also adopt a strategy of seeking new market segments abroad, perhaps offering high quality distance learning packages.

Non-profit organisations would normally seek growth (though not in profit terms) like any other organisation. In order to achieve growth they will endeavour to develop distinctive and effective marketing strategies.

39 International context's impact on marketing strategy and mix

Briefing Paper

To: Managing Director, Creative Consultants
From: John Royal, Marketing Executive, Creative Consultants
Subject: Globalisation and marketing strategy

Background

Globalisation is the process whereby the world is shrinking from hundreds of separate domestic markets to one global market. This has come about due to the lessening of geographical and cultural distances as a result of the wide availability of jet plane travel, satellite technology including the development of the world wide web and the consequent communications technology accompanying it. All companies now have a worldwide market that is more accessible than ever before. This world market opens up new customer groups to sell to but also opens up new suppliers and distributor to trade with.

A lot of the changes are happening so quickly that many companies are unclear as to how to respond. 'Marketing managers in countries around the world are now asking: what is global marketing? How does it differ from domestic marketing? How do global competitors and forces affect our business? To what extend should we go global?' (*Kotler, Saunders, Armstrong, Wong*). This paper will consider the drivers of globalisation and then discuss the impact of globalisation on an organisation's marketing strategy.

Key drivers towards globalisation

(a) **Cultural and economic convergence**. Customer needs are converging in many markets. The impact of television and other means of mass communications has meant that consumers across the globe are now demanding similar products and brands. McDonalds, BMW, Coca-Cola are but a few of an increasingly large number of brands available in virtually all countries. From an economic point of view, the breaking down of trade barriers and the opening up of previously closed parts of the world such as China and Eastern Europe has meant that there is a convergence across countries such that there is a global demand for most products and brands.

(b) **High production development costs**. The cost of getting products to market is high and often the domestic market is not sufficient in demand terms to give an adequate return on the investment involved. This the opportunity to sell globally can help to spread the costs and produce good returns. As the same time, actual production costs can be reduced by switching production overseas where costs such as labour costs can be lower. It is likely in the future that development costs will be lower overseas due to cheaper set-up costs such as building costs, research and development costs and so on.

(c) **Government policies** leading to low trade barriers. Most countries are now looking to lower tariffs and taxes on imports provided reciprocal arrangements can be made for corresponding exports. The increased size of the EU and the growth of other reground trade blocs such as North American Free Trade agreement has improved opportunities to enter international markets by reducing the number of countries one has to negotiate with.

(d) **Rapid technological change**. The increase in mass communications on a global level has enabled organisations to seek out and talk to overseas customers. This, coupled with the political changes in Eastern Europe, the Far East and other regions, has led to vast investment in the infrastructure of the regions concerned, which again has helped to drive globalisation forward.

(e) **Compatible technical standards**. Because of the availability of mass communications and the increasing number of trade agreements between countries and companies, technical specifications and standards are tending to be standardised right across the globe. This high technical specifications for products can be achieved in most regions of the world. This again has helped to increase the availability of products globally, whether it is Nike shoes or McDonald's burgers.

(f) **Economies of scale**. The high costs of bringing a product to the domestic market can be spread once overseas markets are entered. The demand potential is so great in some areas that production costs can be massively reduced. Raw materials can be bought in sufficient quantities to reduce variable costs whilst plant utilisation is thus reducing fixed costs.

(g) **Low transport costs**. These are being reduced as organisations enter into agreements and alliances with countries and companies. Rather than distributing to overseas markets, many firms now set up production facilities overseas. Due to modern communications, standards and controls can be maintained on issues such as quality and strategy. The availability of modern fleets of ships and aircraft is also contributing to lower transport costs.

The impact on an organisation's marketing strategy

All companies are potentially operating in a global market. The world wide web now gives overseas competitors direct entry in to domestic markets. Firms must be aware of this particularly where barriers to entry to their markets are low. What are the implications of this?

(a) Firms need to identify who these overseas competitors are. This means that firms mist now take a global perspective of their business rather then a purely domestic point of view.

(b) The forces of globalisation may force some companies to compete on a world scale which may mean radical changes in the way they operate.

(c) The option of developing alliances and joint ventures is becoming a necessity. These alliances can be with both domestic and overseas partners. Such alliances are a relatively low risk method for acquiring the additional assets and competences necessary for an organisation to act on a world scale.

The impact on an organisation's marketing mix

Globalisation can of course affect the **product**. Whilst a company can choose to market existing products to new international markets, the likelihood is that at least some modifications will be needed to achieve success. Differences in electrical supply, climate and so on can materially affect the export of goods and appliances.

Transportation and infrastructure, particularly the lack of adequate facilities, will impact upon **place**, that is, distribution and logistics and also on costs and therefore **price**.

Possibly the greatest impact will be on **promotion** if a foreign language is involved. Literature will have to be re-written. Ownership of TV, access to the Internet and so on may be limited to the few, necessitating changes in the normal media used.

Looking now at the extended mix, changes will be needed in **people** as it is probable that the exporter will need to work with indigenous staff – some countries insist on this. The culture of the target market will of course be different to some degree and the organisation will have to respect different religion and practises.

Clearly **process** and systems will be affected by some of the above-named differences with **physical evidence** perhaps being more complicated.

Finally, treating **probe** or market research as another element, sophisticated data may not be available on the market or indeed on the population at large. Such data may be difficult or even impossible to originate.

Conclusions

Overall globalisation is going to have an impact in most market and industry sectors. Although some companies may still opt to concentrate on the domestic market, dangers may still occur as overseas competitors start to compete. Such competitors may be totally radical in their marketing strategy and they may well have advantages such as a lower cost base to compete on. Therefore it would seem prudent for most businesses to start looking at their market on a global basis and to take advantage of the opportunities a global market offers.

40 Marketing planning context: business-to-business

1 Introduction

Business-to-business marketing (B2B) plays an important part in commerce generally and in the UK in particular a large proportion of its GNP, as well as contributing a great deal to exports and the balance of payments. B2B trade items includes raw materials, components and services as well as finished products; it also covers the sale of consumer goods to re-sellers.

Characteristics of industrial marketing, as opposed to marketing direct to consumers are: fewer customers, high value/risk transactions for credit, relatively infrequent purchases, rational/professional buyers and often, quite complex products. However, industrial demand derives from consumer demand eg consumer demand for canned goods drives the market for cans and with this, the canning machinery market.

As a consultant who specialises in advising in advising industrial marketers, my mainstream experience is of less than excellent cases but from time to time a company with a very high standard of marketing approaches me. Such a company is Hotits a company specialising in the provision of IT services to hotel chains, whose name has been disguised for reasons of confidentiality.

2 Target market and buying behaviour

The market is defined as hotel groups above a specified minimum size, which can be regional, national or global. Sub-segments are luxury, first class, mid-scale, economy and budget. The market involves three main players: the owner, the operator and the franchisor. For example, in the case of Marriott Grand Hotel Moscow, Marriott is the franchisor, the City of Moscow is the owner and the Interstate is the operator. The owner of a hotel group owns the real estate and may own the furniture and the equipment including the IT system. In short, the owner bears the capital expenditure. The operators pay fixed leases, rents and operating expenses and keep the operating profit (ie bear the business risk). The franchisor provides the brand name, sets the standards and markets the hotel, in return for a fee from the owner or the operator.

The composition of the DMU is thus:

Buyer – the buyer selects suppliers and negotiates the acquisition process. This could be the owner or a person authorised by the owner eg a technical expert. The selection process is driven by the needs of the operator and/or franchisor.

Decision taker – this is the money spender, who can be a private person, a funder or an institutional owner. The decision takers are strongly influenced by buyers, gatekeepers and influencers.

Influencers – these can be the operator and/or the franchisor. Influencers normally specify the technical requirements and recommend preferred suppliers.

Users – the immediate users are the hotel employees as well as the potential hotel customers. The purchase decision on say, room equipment, is often determined *via* field trials. In this scenario, guest feedback is a critical factor.

Gatekeepers – within the hotel environment these consist largely of consultants, operators' employees (general managers, receptionists, secretaries and so on) and technical specialists.

The most important power is wielded by the influencer. Influencers are almost always located within the headquarters of large hotel chains. A professional customer relationship management strategy is critical to winning over the influencers.

To enhance the relationship between Hotits and hotel chains, dedicated key account managers have been assigned. These provide customers with a single point of entry to Hotits. All projects can therefore be developed and managed centrally so as to ensure seamless communications and services on a global basis.

3 Objectives, strategies and marketing mix

Hotits' overall aim is to be the single-source turnkey provider of best-in-class IT solutions and systems to its hotel chain partners, with an objective of achieving a 25% global market share by 2007.

Overall strategy is essentially one of differentiation combined with product development. Differentiation/NPD will be achieved by migrating customers to Application Service Providing (ASP) with Hotits taking some of the risk as a partner. ASPs for the hotel industry could include shared service centres for IT, communications, video, warehousing and professional services.

Products/Services – the essential features and service benefits

- The perceived risk must be low
- Relatively low complexity, easy to use and train
- High degrees of compatibility and customisation
- Trials and handholding
- Turnkey approach

The hotel market is international and service-orientated. The intangible service packages have to meet customer expectations of excellence. This necessitates a focus on workflows, processes and IT consulting.

Pricing – Hotits intend to enhance market share, not by reducing prices but by changing conditions of payment. A balance will be struck between value enhancement and payment conditions, which takes into account local conditions and circumstances.

- Offer risk-sharing models
- Offer price bundles rather than single product pricing
- Offer success-related contracts for turnkey projects

Distribution – Hotits has direct channels to more than 150 countries. The company's distribution strategy has two main features.

- Empowerment of local companies to provide the entire product range and to act as a knowledge broker for smaller regional companies.
- Selective with alliances and indirect channels.

Promotion – Hotits believe that the following issues must be addressed within all communication channels:

- Customer satisfaction
- Customer retention
- Brand awareness
- Cost cutting

A full communications programme takes in personal selling, sales promotion, PR, advertising in hotel media, special articles and success stories. However, it is in other communication domains that Hotits demonstrates its B2B marketing excellence.

(a) **Internet**

Hotits is to have its own branded portal for specific hotel information open to all suppliers. There is to be no requirement to be a certified partner and no restrictions on competitors. The idea is to allow customers to benchmark the products online. Within this portal, visitors should have the ability to access a specialised, multilingual agent via a call-back button.

(b) **Shared knowledge database**

This would include information on various types of projects, success/failure stories, community chat forums, events and so on. Every subscriber would be required to contribute upon pain of losing their access rights, with attractive incentives for outstanding contributions.

(c) **Extranet**

This provides a dedicated information platform for special customers for non-public data on planned new products, developing technology and presentations and so on, with the facility for customers to submit suggestions for service features, complaints and so on. The chat forum provides opportunities for interaction with existing users.

(d) **Key account management and customer relationship building**

This is another area in which Hotits excel with tailor-made systems – see 2 above. Key account managers are selected on the basis of a well proven set of suitable characteristics, in consultation with hotel group partners and are continuously trained and assessed.

4 Controls and Contingencies

In addition to the usual quantitative and qualitative control systems recommended by Kotler, Hotits conduct the following surveys, benchmarked against previous years and other organisations:

(a) **Customer surveys**

Satisfaction; loyalty; responsiveness; accessibility, use of above platforms; ratings v competitors; complaints/suggestions

(b) **Employee surveys**

Satisfaction; loyalty; responsiveness; use of CRM platforms

(c) **Partner surveys**

Satisfaction; loyalty; initiatives; use of IT facilities; growth

5 Conclusion

Not only can Hotits be seen to be excellent exponents of customer centred marketing, but it can also demonstrate success in terms of above average industry growth in sales, profit and market share. Furthermore it has been cited as a caring, green company by a number of special interest groups. Furthermore it has been cited a caring, green company by a number of special interest groups.

41 Marketing planning context: not-for-profit

> *Examiner's comments.* An unpopular and poorly answered question with the major weakness being lack of structure. The examiners give notice that this type of question will come up in future and candidates are advised to have at least one detailed case study prepared in each of the context areas of the syllabus.

Case history: Excellence in not-for-profit marketing
The Royal Society for the Protection of Birds

(a) **Background**

The Royal Society for the Protection of Birds (RSPB) is the largest wildlife conservation charity organisation in Europe, with over a million members and a strong interest in the maintenance of environment and biodiversity generally. It owns or manages about 150 nature reserves in the UK and employs around 1,000 staff.

(b) **Objectives**

In common with most not-for-profit organisations, objectives are not primarily concerned with sales and profits, although the RSPB necessarily has to raise income and increase membership in order to realise its broader objectives.

- Supporting conservation
- Informing and educating
- Managing nature reserves

(c) **Strategies**

(i) **Working internationally**. The RSPB works with Birdlife International Partners on major conservation projects in Europe, Africa and Asia.

(ii) **Leading research**. In the last financial year that RSPB invested over £2m in biological and economic research.

(iii) **Influencing policy**. The RSPB campaigns and advises key decision-makers, publishing policy reports and commenting on topics from protecting the marine environment to forestry.

It regularly briefs MPs, MEPs, officials and political advisors, in promoting changes to UK and EU legislation.

The RSPB deals with as many as 350 planning cases each year in its efforts to influence local authority policies and decisions.

(d) **Target markets/market segmentation**

In not-for-profit marketing these are audiences rather than buyers. Whilst the total potential market comprises most people/organisations, this naturally segments into people/businesses more environmentally concerned than others, and those with very little interest in conservation. The latter may be due to a lack of knowledge which RSPB attempts to redress through its information and education programme.

Segments targeted are many and varied. They include:

- Influencers and decision takers
- Young people
- Children
- Members
- Community groups
- Schools
- Charitable trusts
- Businesses

- Non-members
- Volunteers
- The Lottery

The above list is by no means exhaustive and differs from the profit sector in its diversity.

Whilst the same basic messages are used to emphasise the importance of bird and wildlife conservation, sub-contents have to be tailored to the particular audiences being addressed and the sub-objectives. For example these can vary from asking existing members to contribute more, to getting children interested in joining.

(e) **The marketing mix**

(i) **Products**

Whereas other businesses may make widgets, the RSPB provides a service which was originally that of protecting birdlife in the UK but has now extended to the conservation of biodiversity and the environment generally.

Other ancillary services include advice, information, education, research, management and partnership.

The RSBP strives to maintain the highest quality and ethical standards in all its services, in keeping with its Royal Charter.

(ii) **Pricing**

Clearly, the RSPB membership charges tend to rise under inflationary pressures and the charity strives to increase contributions from its sponsors. In this sense the charity operates like any other business. It is also businesslike in its continual endeavours to improve efficiency and effectiveness and thereby provide more value for money to its members/sponsors.

(iii) **Place**

Distribution has both widened and deepened over the years. National headquarters exist in England, Scotland, Wales and Northern Ireland, supported by nine regional offices.

An RSPB presence in various forms can be found in Europe, Africa, Asia and the Middle East.

(iv) **Promotion**

The RSPB advertises for new members in the national media from time to time and maintains a database for direct mail shots. It does, however, increasingly use PR, publicity and word of mouth in its promotional mix. When a wildlife conservation issue arises in the media a spokesperson from the RSPB is invariably available and indeed called upon to comment.

Literature also plays an important part in the promotion of the RSPB with a variety of leaflets, cards and information packs, some of which are specially designed for individual market segments eg children.

Point of sale material features in nature reserves and regional offices and at special events.

The personal approach provides a valuable contribution to promotion both on a face to face and telephone basis. Obviously, great care is taken not to cause any offence.

A direct mail catalogue order service exists for various promotional items. The internet is being looked at as a potential new promotion medium and a website has recently been established.

(v) **People**

People are particularly important in a charity which relies greatly on volunteers and which offers considerably less than marketing-for-profit organisations in terms of salaries and perks. In practice the RSPB is able to attract people of high calibre who work extremely well as a team. This is in addition to a membership which includes many celebrities, politicians and other notables with an interest in wildlife conservation.

(vi) **Process**

The RSPB is very much involved in the AIDA communication process, namely in gaining favourable Attention; stimulating Interest; arousing Desire to join or support and achieving Action the form of an application or donation or the volunteering of services.

In this process, the part played by the written and spoken word is most important.

(vii) **Physical evidence/ambience**

In the case of the RSPB, people, process and physical evidence are very much integrated. Premises, literature and staff are all part of the tangibilisation of the services. The approach in the first part of the process has to tread a fine line between being too laid back or too confrontational. Timing is also important. Physical evidence/ambience cannot be garish or overbearing. it needs to convey an air of niceness combined with an image of conviction.

(f) **Conclusion**

That the RSPB constitutes a case of marketing operations excellence in the practice of not-for-profit marketing is evidenced in its systems, literature, second-to-none reputation, and its measure of public goodwill.

As a direct result of this excellence its continues to grow successfully n very measure: membership, income, staff, physical presence, influence and results.

42 Planning and the mix in a virtual marketplace (1)

Outline: Direct Marketing leaflet
Date: 15 June 200X

1 **Illustration – The expanding universe**

2 **Headline – Expand your business universe to increase sales via the net – it's easy and very cost-effective**

3 **Follow up text to headline**

Yes, the benefits of the Internet have been over-hyped, but many thousands of companies have increased their profits by developing an effective website and Internet strategy.

We specialise in Internet site development; we specialise in helping the smaller organisations, AND we have a portfolio of delighted customers to prove that what we offer really does work. The even better news is that it need not cost you more than £XXX to get started. You have nothing to lose, so please read on!

4 **How you can use the Internet**

- To send messages via email wherever, whenever, cheaply and without paperwork
- To transfer files between staff, customers and suppliers as and when needed

- To click into news and opinion so as to aid and improve decision taking
- To search and browse so as to improve product knowledge
- To post and present information to facilitate brand building and generate sales
- To make it easier for potential customers to do business with you

5 **Effects on marketing strategy and the marketing mix**

You can build databases enabling you to segment your market much more accurately and keep this bang up to date. Over time this not only improves efficiency but also helps to create better, more lasting customer relationships.

Markets – can be exploited that are not geographically near or physically contactable – the net literally expands your universe

Brands – the net liberalises your customers and competitors' customers to access service providers anywhere in the world, where previously these customers have been limited to local providers. This leads to the globalisation of service brands – the world is your oyster.

Products – you can generate a new range of information based products/services which can be tailored to (and by) individual customers.

Promotion – the Internet allows a new approach to promotion. It creates a new mass communication medium for marketers to use – one which promotes far greater two-way discourse. It allows customers to 'enter' an advertisement, providing involvement and direct response, and it's cheap!

Distribution – the Internet allows you to operate anywhere in the world market from a small and centralised base. It makes service delivery instant. For products, interlinking systems of physical distribution are already developed to allow, for example, next day delivery of groceries for Internet orders.

Price – by dealing direct with your customers you save the reseller's margin allowing you to increase profits AND to reduce prices, thus boosting demand.

Service – your services are available 24 hours a day, 7 days a week without prohibitive cost implications.

Participation – this is the new kid on the block as far as the marketing mix is concerned because the Internet allows your customers to participate in the ordering process at the design stage. You can virtually walk your customers through the range and the design/finishing options. This gives your customers the feeling that they are in charge, that they are telling you, rather than you telling them.

SO HESITATE NO LONGER, SIMPLY TELEPHONE 1231234 NOW FOR MORE DETAILS AND/OR TO ARRANGE A QUOTATION FROM OUR FRIENDLY STAFF. THEY WILL NOT TRY TO PRESSURE YOU AND THEY WILL NOT BLIND YOU WITH SCIENCE

43 Planning and the mix in a virtual marketplace (2)

> *Examiner's comments*. Good answers discussed how Internet and e-commerce developments were likely to have an impact at a strategic level. Poorer answers tended to concentrate on the impact of the Internet and e-commerce on the communications mix in general. Weak answers merely discussed Internet developments generally from a technical perspective.

Business-to-business (B2B) marketing is more widespread than business to consumer marketing because many business purchases are involved in just one consumer purchase. The

B2B market incorporate manufacturers, intermediaries such as retailers, as well as many other businesses such as designers, carriers and banks. *Kotler et al* suggest that the B2B market consists of four types of business:

(a) **Firms that buy goods and services** in order to produce goods and services to sell to others

(b) **Wholesalers and retailers** that buy goods to resell at a profit

(c) The **institutional market** comprising schools, universities and hospitals

(d) The **government market** comprising both central and local government

Because of the diverse nature of the B2B market it is not surprising that the bulk of the predicted European Internet sales of $64 billion for the year 2001 are likely to be business to business transactions.

The internet will affect the B2B sector in two main areas.

- Customer management
- Marketing strategy

With regard to **customer management** the Internet provides many opportunities.

(a) A website is available 24 hours a day, 365 days a year. It can provide a **continual dialogue** between customer and company. In the B2B sector this continual availability is essential. Technical data or new product information can be accessed and downloaded. Different customers can be given access to different types of information using access passwords.

(b) The **interactivity** of the Internet allows problems to be overcome quickly. Information can be exchanged. Thus customer relationships can be enhanced and developed.

(c) The **Intranet**, where public access is denied, can help to develop relationships between the customer and the business. Often in B2B markets customers know each other and meet regularly at, for example, trade fairs and conferences. The Intranet can provide a constant open channel of communication.

(d) The Internet can also be used to develop a **total relationship strategy** with other related groups. For example, the six-market model (*Christopher et al*) of relationship marketing identifies internal influence, referral, employee, supplier and customer markets. The Internet can be used to recruit employees, set up meetings between suppliers and customers and distribute press releases for the media.

(e) Face to face contact is largely not needed and the opportunity to develop **on-line relationships** instead is evident. The need for businesses to develop **databases** is therefore apparent. Such databases will need to hold considerable amounts of up to date information which can also be accessed by customers. Such availability and exchange of information will enable customers to be managed far more effectively.

The areas of **marketing strategy** likely to be affected by the Internet are:

(a) **Products** – a large number of information based products/services can be developed to be easily accessed by both existing and potential customers. These could include product technical data, latest trends for the industry, product availability schedules and discussion forums for customers.

(b) **Markets** – physical nearness is no longer a problem. Worldwide markets can be developed and those nearer home can be serviced without costly sales teams making face to face contact.

(c) **Services** – the Internet will speed up the move from transaction based marketing to relationship marketing. All businesses will need to invest in the new technology to provide the services that will be demanded. The investment needed will include training for both management and employees as well as the purchase of 'state of the art' systems.

(d) **Communications** – the Internet is a mass communications medium which must be integrated into existing communication strategies. The constant availability of the medium along with its potential for interactivity means that new promotional strategies will have to be developed.

(e) **Brands** – the worldwide nature of the Internet means that businesses are not restricted to using local providers. This is particularly so in the services area eg consultancy, design, market information. New global service brands may start emerging.

(f) **Distribution channels** – an organisation can now supply a world market from a small centralised base. Expensive market entry strategies may not be needed as the Internet becomes sophisticated in terms of access and the use of technology.

In conclusion, the Internet will contribute greatly to the way firms interact with customers in the B2B sector. Customers will be managed more effectively but only by those companies who fully embrace the new opportunities. This will involve investment in training and hardware. It will also involve a change of marketing philosophy for businesses as they become far more customer focused.

44 Service encounters and the extended mix (SERVQUAL)

A service encounter can be viewed as the experiencing of a mixture of tangible and intangible elements and benefits as illustrated in the 'servuction' model below adapted for a hotel service situation. Here customer A sees the visible elements of the hotel reception, part of which can be active and part passive. These can influence A's perspective of the service benefits about to be received. Customer B sees the visible elements but also has the opportunity to observe the way A is being treated and may alter his intended behaviour as a result. Neither A nor B can see the office behind reception where most of the operations are managed and co-ordinated.

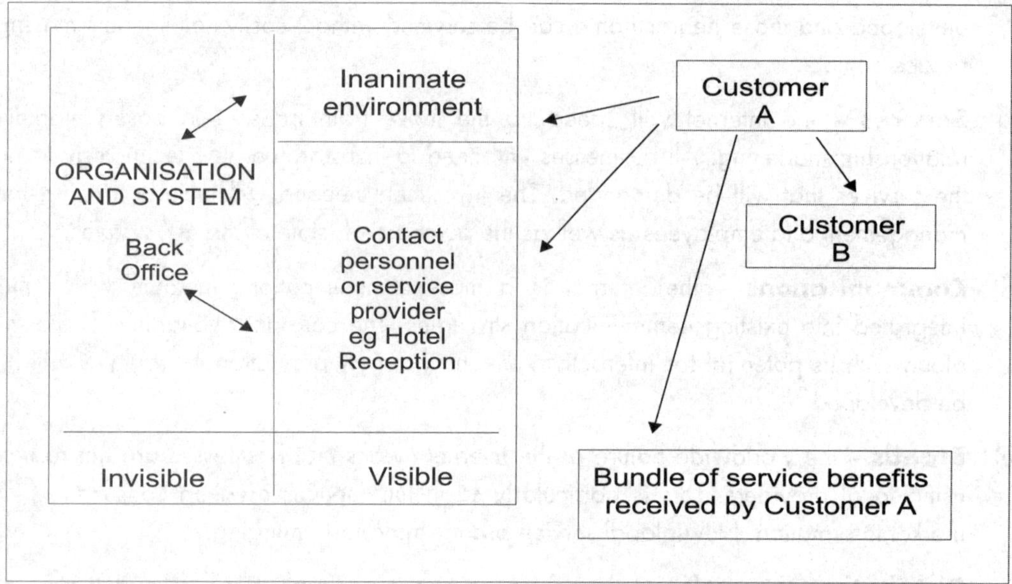

Source: Adapted from Langeard *et al* (1981)

The inanimate environment

In the absence of more tangible elements, customers may look for other clues with which to evaluate the service. The attention and care given by the hotel to the foyer can influence customer perceptions of the service, positively or negatively.

The contact personnel

Services are provided by people for people and customers are likely to judge the hotel service by their interactions with reception staff, which can vary with individual members of staff.

Part of the extended marketing mix will be to train staff to deliver a consistent high standard of service.

Organisation and system

The benefits received by customers visiting the hotel's reception will be determined to a large extent by the back office, in the form of policies and procedures and the design of the systems used.

The **servuction** model provides a basis for understanding and applying the extended marketing mix to optimise customer satisfaction.

Another valuable model in service marketing is the so called 'Gaps Model' or SERVQUAL as illustrated below which asks what can be done to deliver a quality service.

Service quality ("Gaps Model")

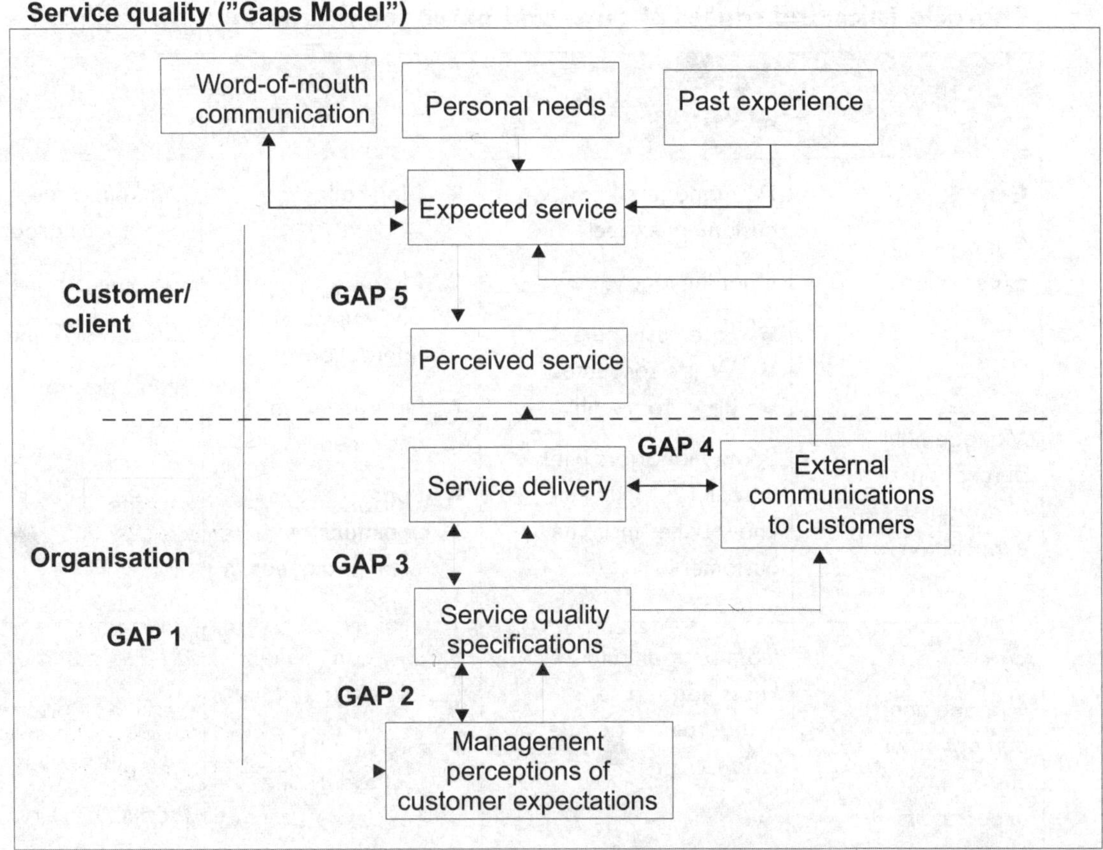

Source: Parasuraman, Zeithaml and Berry (1985)

Step 1 is to understand needs and expectations through marketing research and close customer relations.

Step 2 is to use this information for service process design and development.

Step 3 is to implement the service to the standards expected by the customer and organisation.

Step 4 is to ensure consistency in service delivery and to communicate *realistic* promises to customers and potential customers.

Gaps in any of these areas will create a gap between customer expectations and perceptions of performance which is often referred to as 'Gap 5' or SERVQUAL. *Overall* quality depends on the size of gap 5, but gap 5 is a function of gaps 1 - 4.

An attempt has been made in the following table to determine how the extended marketing mix can be applied to close gaps 1 – 4.

Characteristics and causes of gaps and extended marketing mix implications.

Gaps	Characteristics	Causes	Marketing mix implications
Gap 1 Customer expectations ↓ Management perception of customer expectation	Do managers know what customers expect? If not they may: ■ Lose customers ■ Waste resources ■ Be uncompetitive Some managers think they know better than the customer!	■ Non-collection of data ■ No management and customer interaction ■ Distance from customer ■ Poor communication with employees in contact	Marketing research – focus groups Consumer panels Direct marketing Staff training
Gap 2 Management perception of customer expectation ↓ Service quality standards and specifications	Do management use knowledge to set standards for people to follow? If a gap exists here then it tends to be significant.	■ Low commitment to service quality ■ Are goals set focused on the customer? ■ Inadequate rewards ■ Task standardisation + procedures ■ Management believe it is infeasible	Quality control Service standards Sales incentives Product development Market testing
Gap 3 Service quality standards and specifications ↓ Service delivery	Service gap – gaps emerge when employees are unable or unwilling to deliver. However, these should be easy to: ■ Identify ■ Rectify ■ Manage. These gaps tend to occur in organisations with a high degree of direct contact with customer.	■ Lack of sequence of work ■ Poor employee to job fit ■ Poor technology job fit ■ Role conflict: Customer Supervisor Organisation Role ambiguity	Process development Staff selection and training IT investment Resolution of conflicts: Customer supremacy Relationship marketing Internal marketing

Gaps	Characteristics	Causes	Marketing mix implications
Gap 4 Service delivery ↓ External communication	The gap between what organisations promise in marketing messages, advertisements etc. and what they actually deliver	■ Inaccurate communication ■ Over promising ■ Lack of co-ordination between marketing and service delivery	Harmonisation of communications mix Advertising agency briefing Staff de-briefings Suggestion box/brainstorming

Source: Adapted from Parasuraman, Zeithami and Berry (1985)

45 Service quality

Report to: Richard Adams, Marketing Director, Browse Bookstores (BBL)
From: James Gill, Gill Associates Consultancy
Date: 7 December 200X
Subject: Response to a price-based attack

(a) **Criteria affective student perceptions of service quality**

Services are different from products in being intangible, inseparable from the provider, 'unstockable' and heterogeneous. Perceptions are therefore more important, a fact that has been recognised in the following model:

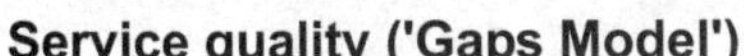
Service quality ('Gaps Model')

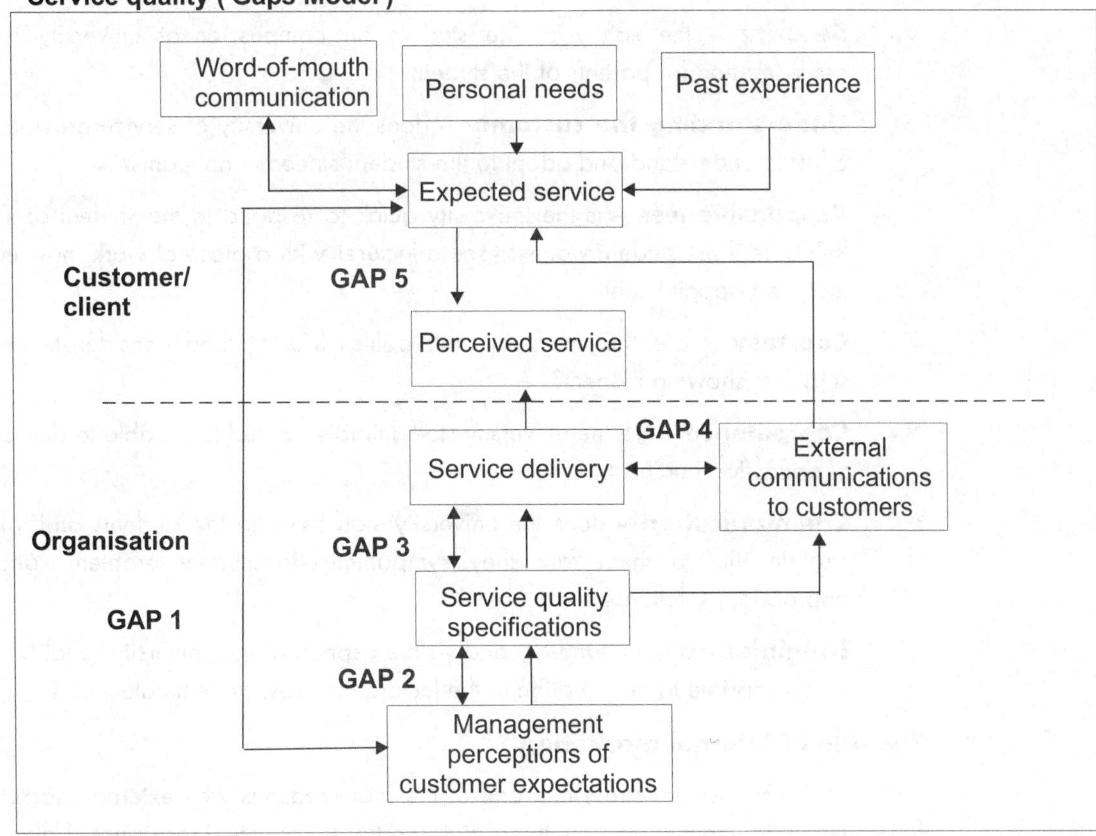

Source: Parasuraman, Zeithaml and Berry (1985)

It is important to understand that gap 5 is a function of the other four gaps, ie gap 5 cannot be completely closed until the other four have been closed.

Gap 1 – that between management perception and customer expectations could indicate that the management does not fully appreciate students' needs or possibly that student expectations have been raised too high during open days and by other recruitment promotions

Gap 2 – that between management perceptions of student expectations and service quality specifications might be due to lack of suitably high service standards

Gap 3 – that between service quality specifications and service delivery could be caused by poor selection and training of university staff

Gap 4 – that between service delivery and external communications could mean that the university's communications to recruitment centres (schools, colleges etc) and parents are misleading

Gap 5 – the above gaps add up to a gulf between the expected quality of service and the perceived services to the dissatisfaction of the student customers.

Parasuraman *et al* (1990) researched the ten main criteria that influence students' perceptions of service quality to find these were:

1 **Access** – consideration of ease of access to the service for the student ie 24 hour access to computer lab or libraries.

2 **Reliability** – consideration of the service reliability in terms of the expected standard.

3 **Credibility** – is the service provider (lecturer or admin staff) trustworthy and believable?

4 **Security** – the safety of the student on campus or at university is a major consideration for parents of the student.

5 **Understanding the customer** – does the university of service provider make an effort to understand and adapt to the student's needs and wants?

6 **Responsiveness** – is the university quick to respond to the student and willing to help – ie if the student wants to see a lecturer with a piece of work, how easy is it to make an appointment?

7 **Courtesy** – are the university staff polite, friendly and considerate towards the students, showing respect?

8 **Competence** – are the university staff suitably trained to be able to deliver the level of education purchased?

9 **Communication** – does the university staff listen to the students and take time to explain this to them, are they sympathetic to student problems and suggest appropriate solutions?

10 **Tangibles** – are the tangible and visible aspects of the university suitably impressive or appropriate to the situation ie the lecture theatres, student cafes, etc?

(b) **The role of internal marketing**

Piercy and other writers stress that one of the main reasons why external marketing plans fail to live up to expectations is internal staff inertia, if not actual resistance. Unless staff fully buy in to the external plan it will not realise its full potential. Closing customer service gaps as discussed above will often demand changes in university staff attitudes and behaviours and some people are naturally resistant to change.

So the role of internal marketing in this context is:

1 To gain the support of key decision makers for our external plan in terms of resources needed: the right staff, the necessary finances, training sand so on

2 To change the attitudes and behaviour of university managers and staff working at the interfaces with students and influencers

3 To win commitment to making the marketing plan work and acceptance of the premise that marketing is too important to be left to the marketers

4 To manage incremental changes in the culture so as to continuously improve the quality and consistency of services for our students

Internal marketing research will be needed to establish the size of the service gaps and subsequently to check regularly that these gaps stay closed.

(c) **Marketing mix for international students**

Our external marketing plan embodies an objective of 19,000 students of the academic year 2006, 10% of which are to be full-time international students. In order to succeed in the international market segment, we need to adapt our existing marketing mix.

Service

All aspects of our service need to be modified to take into account the different cultures and potential language difficulties of our international students. Staff training will help and a series of seminars is recommended to discuss how best to handle these special customers' needs/wants in terms of lectures, tutorials, care, accommodation, catering and so on.

Price

Certain countries offer government sponsorships and also some students will have access to company funding schemes and/or family financial support. We can premium price in these circumstances. Students from other countries may require a degree of subsidy. We shall have to make provision for fluctuations in exchange rates for foreign currencies.

Promotion

Personal visits are the best form of promotion, particularly for some of our far-eastern target markets. Small teams comprising international marketing lecturers and support staff will need to travel out to the countries concerned and interpreters will have to be hired as necessary. This will of course add considerable cost and impact upon price. The promotional objective will be to establish contacts with the 'movers and shakers' in education, government and related agencies. Reciprocal visits will be encouraged. The promotional and media mix will be tailored to the country concerned, following data gathering by the visiting team. An international promotional co-ordinator will be appointed to ensure that our university brand image is both favourable and consistent.

Place

Although this will remain largely the same, some adaptation will be desirable. For example some tailoring in the furnishing of on-site accommodation could be considered together with educational visits to international events and talks, outside the campus. Another possible adaptation in distribution would be the establishment of 'branches' overseas.

People

Mention has already been made of having the right people, properly trained to provide our normal services and this tenet will be of ever greater importance when dealing with international students. A special Liaison Officer could be allocated to interface with the international students and university staff on particular matters of concern, empowered with directorate support.

Process

One of the most useful responsibilities of the proposed Liaison Officer would be to ease the administrative burden of application and registration processes on international students.

Physical evidence

A degree of adaptation of this element for international students is appropriate but not so much as to mar their learning of English and British custom, which are two of the most attractive features of coming to our university for the students and indeed their sponsors.

46 The Lens Shop Ltd

Examiner's comments. 'Good answers referred to Porter or Davidson and used one of these models as a framework and applied it to TLS directly. They then went on to discuss the factors that might influence the sustainability of TLS's position. Poorer papers merely listed factors, that may be giving TLS competitive advantage, without any discussion of theory.'

(a) Subject: Sources of competitive advantage
To: The Managing Director
Prepared by: The Marketing Manager

Introduction

(i) **Competitive advantage** is anything which gives an organisation an edge over its competitors – the reason why a customer would select TLS's products or services over other competitive offerings. Once an advantage has been gained, competitors will try to copy or supersede it, so continuous improvements in offerings are needed unless the advantage can be protected.

(ii) **Competitive strategy** is the search for a favourable competitive position in an industry. The aim is to establish a profitable and sustainable position. Porter suggests three generic routes to achieving competitive advantage.

(1) Overall cost leadership
(2) Overall differentiation
(3) Focus (segmentation based on costs or differentiation)

Sources of competitive advantage for TLS

(i) **Cost leadership**

This strategy seeks to achieve the position of **lowest cost producer** in the industry. This enables the company to compete on price and earn the highest unit profits. *Porter* has identified several major factors that affect costs which he terms 'cost drivers'. Not all of these apply.

(1) **Economies of scale** are not possible. TLS is a **specialist** retail store, as opposed to Dixons with many more locations.

(2) **Experience and learning effects** can bring efficiencies through repetition of tasks. Experience can be gained through hiring experienced staff and through training. The concept was derived from the manufacturing sector so its application to retail services may be questionable.

(3) **Capacity utilisation** is important to profits, especially for smaller firms. Our smaller, secondary sites with small stock holdings will be a source of cost advantages.

(4) **Linkages** between quality control and stock return, for example, can drive costs up or down. External linkages with suppliers can also reduce costs. Our access to discounted products of old product lines will provide a cost advantage.

(5) **Interrelationships** with other SBUs in a corporate portfolio can help to share costs but this is not possible for our smaller, single business unit organisation.

(6) **Integration** such as contracting out delivery and/or service can affect costs. As we are not vertically or horizontally integrated this is not an option for competitive advantage.

(7) **Timing**. Being first to the market can provide access to low cost products, ensure prime locations and gain us technological leadership. As we operate in an established market with a number of general and specialist camera retailers, this is not a route to competitive advantage for us.

(8) **Policy choices** such as product line, service, warranties and so on all affect costs. They also affect the perceived uniqueness of the offer to customers and hence if the competitive strategy is not clear this can create a dilemma. If cost advantage is the strategy then the general rule is to reduce costs on factors which will not significantly affect valued uniqueness.

(9) **Location and institutional factors** can also reduce costs, such as sites near raw material and government regulations. This is not viable for TLS.

From this analysis, discounted old products, small stores in secondary locations and low stock holding all create a cost advantage for TLS. This enables the company to offer lower prices with a price guarantee of being £10 below other local retailers for a similar brand of camera.

(ii) **Differentiation**

This is a competitive strategy based on raising the quality of the product and thus its costs and sale price. Loyalty is built up and, because customers are not so price sensitive, profits can be increased through higher prices. Organisations following this strategy must continually innovate in order to stay ahead of competitors in quality, thus necessitating larger R&D and promotional budgets. Competitive advantage can be achieved through what Porter calls 'uniqueness drivers'.

(1) **Product differentiation** seeks to increase the value of the good or service on offer to the customer. Products are made up of four components. The **generic product** which is photography, the **expected product** which is a retail site with a range of products and prices with reasonable customer service, the **augmented product** which constitutes all the extra features and services that go beyond what the normal camera consumer expects and the **potential product** which is anything that could be offered. TLS offer an augmented

product in the form of the buy-back service for upgrades, selection of recent reviews from Camera magazines and sales staff are also knowledgeable and helpful.

(2) **Brand differentiation** is related to the product offer and moves companies from thinking about **tangible product** benefits to **emotional image** benefits. TLS may be able to establish this in the future, through owning the value and service position in the camera market.

(3) **Distribution differentiation** comes from using different outlets, networks or coverage of the market. The less formal, friendly atmosphere of the shops may be a potential source of differentiation from the large, formal multiples.

(4) **Promotional differentiation** involves using different types of promotions at different intensity or content. The TLS colour catalogue is a 'fun' brochure distributed in an innovative way, especially through direct mail to existing customers. This should be a loyalty builder.

(5) **Pricing differentiation** can be successful if TLS enjoys a cost advantage. This is TLS's major point of differentiation with its £10 lower price guarantee, discounted price old stock products, cheap three year extended warranty and buy-back service.

(iii) **Sustainability of current situation**

(1) TLS operate on a **differentiation strategy based on price differentiation** with elements of **product differentiation** based on information and customer service. This is financed through their low cost sources of 'old' product lines from distributors and their location and store size policy. (This is similar to Richer Sounds approach in the hi-fi sector.)

(2) The **risks** of this strategy are the **threat of competition** from lower cost specialist retailers and the vulnerability of a price-based attack by larger competitors such as John Lewis and Dixons, should they go for an aggressive strategy in this product category. Perhaps the greatest risk which needs to be protected is the relationship they have with distributors to clear their shelves of old product lines. If this supply ceased, TLS would lose a significant advantage.

The most useful ways of creating a defensible position lie in exploiting the following.

(1) Unique and valued products
(2) Clear, tight definition of target markets
(3) Enhanced customer linkages
(4) Established brand and company credibility

In the future, creating closer bonds with customers through interactive communications and enhanced service through internal marketing initiatives (see question 1(b)) should strength TLS's position. The buy-back service should help build in switching costs and should be retained together with building the awareness of the brand from specialist camera consumers to the general public. Public relations should help, following the lead of **Richer Sounds** with innovative employee relations policies and incentives together with shouting about their buy-back service.

(b)

> *Examiner's comment.* 'This was a relatively straightforward question. Good answers were in report format and discussed fully the benefits of internal marketing, implementation and the potential problems. Poorer answers failed to tackle the issue of implementation effectively. There was very little mention of internal target markets and the internal marketing mix.'

To: The Managing Director
Prepared by: The Marketing Manager

Report on the development of an **Internal Marketing Programme**

Please find outlined below an overview of an internal marketing programme as requested.

(i) **What is internal marketing?**

'Treating with equal importance the needs of the internal market – the employees – and the external market through proactive programmes and planning to bring about desired organisational objectives by delivering both employee and customer satisfaction'.

Originally, the scope of **internal marketing** was considered to be the motivation, training and development of employees involved at the customer interface, with the aim of delivering a better service to the end customer. This is obviously important in a service industry like camera retailing. However, internal marketing also includes non-contact employees as well. In fact, internal marketing covers any planned effort to overcome any resistance to change in an organisation and to ensure through proper communication, motivation and training that employees effectively implement corporate and functional strategies/plans.

This concept is obviously important in the retail sector where customers' expectations of the service encounter are rising. The head office staff who support the shops are also critical in terms of delivering customer satisfaction.

(ii) **Development and implementation**

People inside the organisation, to whom the plan must be marketed, are considered internal customers. The first stage is to group these internal customers into three segments.

(1) **Supporters**: those likely to gain from improving service levels.

(2) **Neutrals**: those whose gains and losses are in balance.

(3) **Opposers**: those who are likely to lose from the change or are long term opponents.

An internal marketing mix has to be developed for each of these target groups.

(1) **Product**. This is the plan/strategy itself together with the attitudes, values and actions that are needed to successfully carry it out.

(2) **Price**. The price is what internal customers have to pay as a result of accepting the plan/strategy. This could be changes in work patterns and greater effort to achieve high levels of customer satisfaction.

(3) **Promotion**. This is a critical area in the mix, and involves any communication medium that can be used to effect the attitudes of key groups. The promotional mix includes: presentations, training workshops, discussion groups, written

reports etc. This communication has to be a two way process. At times, it may be necessary to adapt the plan in order to gain support.

(4) **Distribution**. This categorises the places where the product and communications are delivered to internal customers, such as in-store, meetings, seminars, informal conversations, away days and so on.

Although an internal marketing programme gives a framework within which to work, successful implementation is reliant on three key skills.

(1) **Persuasion**

- Present a shared vision for the group through a customer service charter.
- Communicate and train.
- Eliminate misconceptions through two-way dialogue.
- Sell the benefits through success stories in the company newsletter, employee of the month awards, incentives for the best store etc.
- Gain acceptance by association, perhaps with Richer Sounds retail success and employee benefits.
- Support words with action, for example the MD rewarding best practice and reviewing the customer feedback comments.

(2) **Negotiation**

- Make the opening proposition high – leave room for negotiation.
- Trade concessions.

(3) **Politics**

- Build coalitions.
- Display support.
- Invite the opposition to contribute.
- Warn opposition.
- Control the agenda.
- Take incremental steps.

Benefits of internal marketing

For TLS, improved **employee satisfaction** and **customer responsiveness** will lead to improved **customer satisfaction**. The higher the relative service quality of any business the higher the return on investment (PIMS research). A clear customer service charter should lead to greater clarity in the purpose and objectives for each store. Customer complaints should reduce thereby saving time dealing with them. Employee turnover should reduce as well. As indicated in the first part of this report, excellence in customer service combined with a competitive pricing strategy should help achieve a sustainable competitive advantage for the business in the highly competitive market in which we operate.

Potential problems to overcome

To achieve the stated benefits, a number of implementation barriers need to be considered. Time is important and potential problems can arise by not taking enough time to allow people to adjust to the changes implied by the plan. Persistence is required in the face of opposition; modifications to the strategy may be necessary on the way. Key detractors and recalcitrant players may exist and if negotiation and persuasion are not successful these people can be removed or if this is not possible, you have to wait till that person leaves or changes job. A final potential problem is lack of resources, both human and financial. Internal marketing programmes require a budget for training, communications and staff time. If this is not available the likely chances of success are greatly reduced.

47 The wet shave market

(a) From: Marketing Manager
To: Marketing Director
Briefing Paper: Gillette's Spend on NPD and Promotion

Introduction

In looking at the new product development literature, there is a focus on the new product development (NPD) process and the factors which differentiate between new product successes and failures (for example Cooper and Kleinschmidt, 1986; Johne and Snelson, 1990).

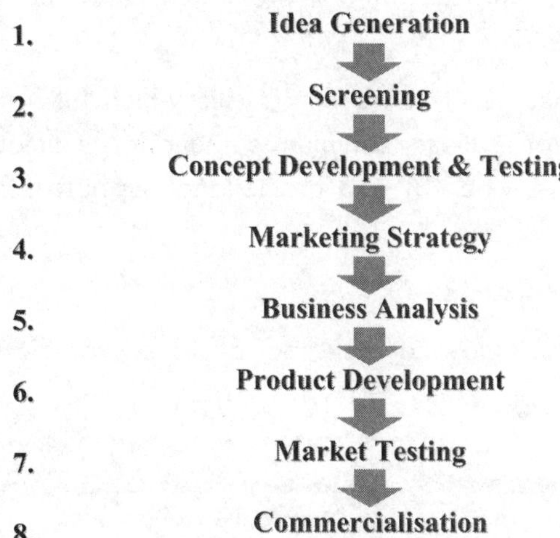

Storey and Easingwood suggest that there has been little consideration of the product beyond the core benefits offered. An area that has been neglected is the potential contribution that the marketing of the product and the support given to the product can make to new product performance. Yet most new products are not radically different from existing products (Booz, Allen & Hamilton):

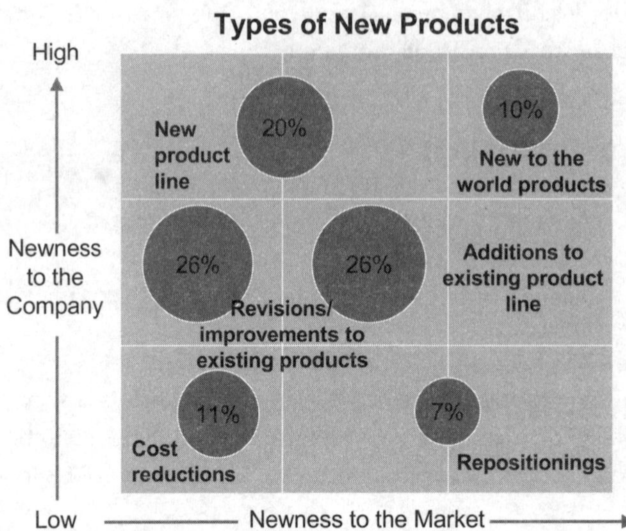

Source: New Product Management for the 1980's (New York: Booz, Allen & Hamilton, 1982)

and thus the marketing support in the form of promotion, may be one area where competitive advantage can be gained.

This briefing paper therefore focuses on the strategic role which NPD can play and the reasons why our major competitor, Gillette, continue to spend large amounts of money on the NPD process (£460m on the Mach 3) and promotional support (£215m on product launch).

The strategic role of new products

Based on the work by *Wong* the following table indicates the strategic roles which NPD can play.

Strategic Role (Rationale) of NPD	New Product Type
Maintain technological leadership	New to the world New product line
Enter future/new markets	New to the world
Pre-empt competition or	New to the world
Segment of the market	New product Line Repositioning
Maintain market share	New product line Repositioning Additions to existing lines
Defend market share position/ Prevent decline	Repositioning Cost reductions Revisions/improvements to existing lines
Exploit technology in a new way	New to the world New product line
Capitalise on distribution strength	Additions to existing line

Analysing Gillette's approach to NPD, we can surmise that the Mach 3 is likely to maintain technological leadership for Gillette which pre-empts us and other competitors and thereby maintains their market share. In light of their aggressive approach to the market, it is vital that we respond by maintaining product parity with Gillette and, through our own innovation process, continue to seek new innovations which may give us an edge in the future.

Why £215m on global launch (majority promotional spend)

Referring back to the research conducted by Storey and Easingwood (1996), the potential contribution that the marketing of the product and the support given to the product can make to new product performance is great. In general, marketing efficiency and effectiveness have been cited as contributing to success. More specifically, a misdirected sales/distribution effort can affect success adversely and an effective communication strategy ideally should educate users about the value of the product (for example Cooper, 1980). The launch strategy is the link between the development process and the marketplace. A strong launch effort, with appropriate targeting and pricing strategies, is linked to success (Storey & Easingwood, 1996). In addition, advertising and promotion have been found to work best when geared to the creation of a strong brand image, which Gillette has certainly cultivated (*Berry and Hensal, Easingwood and Storey*).

In Storey and Easingwood's study of financial service product launches they found that promotion played an important role in NPD success and that it should:

- Be effective in raising awareness
- Be effective in explaining/convincing
- Result in more effective advertising/promotion
- Be responsible for creating the 'brand' image
- Be consistent with marketing strategy

Gillette spends £215m on launch promotion because it is important to any product's success to raise awareness of that product with the target customers. Both these goals can be aided by the creation of a strong brand image for the product and by attractively positioning the product in the market. Consistency with the rest of the marketing strategy helps ensure that a uniform image is presented to the consumer. A strong corporate advertising campaign, as run by Gillette prior to the Mach 3 launch, in general will also help in the selling of specific products.

Conclusions

It is clear that our main competitor, Gillette, will gain significant advantage through the launch of their innovative new product, the Mach 3. The second part of this briefing paper addresses the question of the options we have for response to this significant global product launch.

(b) **Strategic options available to Wilkinson Sword in the wet shave market**

The first key strategic option for us is to decide whether we are a market follower or market challenger (*Kotler and Singh*) in this sector. This part of the paper will therefore be divided into the options under each positioning decision.

(i) **Market follower strategic options**

Market followers accept the status quo and avoid risks of confrontation following a me-too strategy – product imitation, not product innovation. Our options include:

- Cloner: copies, in extreme a counterfeiter.
- Imitator: copies some things but maintains some differentiation.
- Adapter: takes leader's products and improves them growing into future challenger.

We should be aware that PIMS research shows low ROIs for followers (*Hooley, Saunders & Piercy*).

(ii) **Market challenger strategic options**

Kotler provides a number of possible market challenger, or attack, strategies for challengers trying to take share from market leaders such as Gillette, as illustrated below.

(1) **Frontal attack**

This is the direct, head-on attack meeting competitors with the same product line, price, promotion, and so on. In principle, to succeed the attacker needs three times the resources as the defender and, because you are attacking your enemy's strengths rather than weaknesses, it is generally considered the riskiest and least advised of strategies. A modified frontal attack tempts away select customers by shifting resources to a single marketing element (for example, via price or advertising) but this depends on no or slow competitor reaction. Direct attacks are risky but there are numerous indirect alternatives.

(2) **Flanking attack**

The aim is to engage competitors in those product markets where they are weak or have no presence at all. Its overriding goal is to build a position to launch an attack on the major battlefield later, without waking 'sleeping giants'. Porter refers to this as a niche or focus strategy. Segmental flanking is based on satisfying market needs not being met by competitors' different products or approaches to the market. Geographic flanking serves areas in a country or the world with similar products and approaches, but where opponents are weak or non-existent.

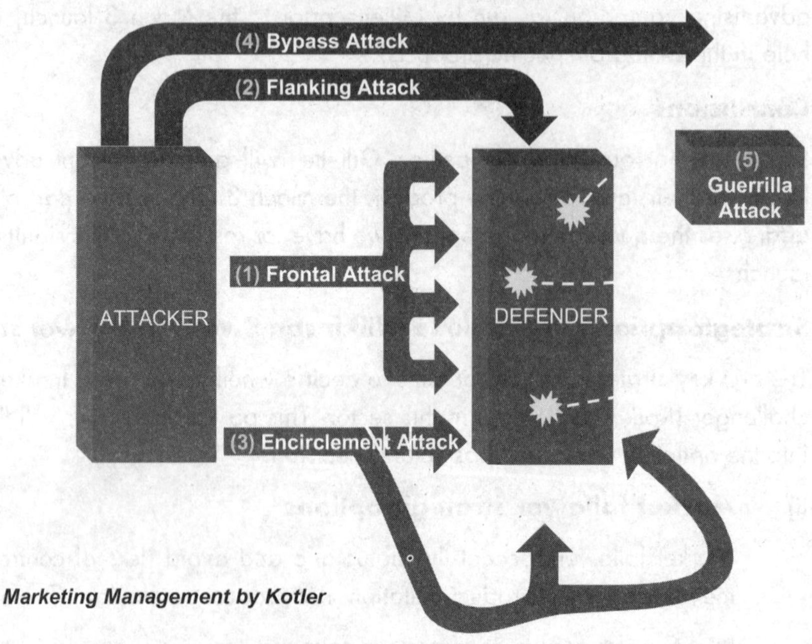

(3) **Encirclement attack**

Encirclement involves a multi-pronged attack aimed at diluting the defender's ability to retaliate in strength. The attacker stands ready to block the competitor no matter which way he turns in the product market. In business there are two conceptually distinct forms of encirclement: product and market. An attacker can encircle by product proliferation, or by expanding the products into all segments and distribution channels. Encirclement is feasible when the attacker has superior resources, is willing to commit these resources for a long time to achieve market dominance, has access to distribution channels and product development capacity.

(4) **Bypass attack**

This is the most indirect form of competitive strategy as it avoids confrontation by moving into new and uncontested fields. Three types of bypass are possible: develop new products, diversify into unrelated products or diversify into new geographical markets. Developing new products is referred to as 'leap frogging' where a business takes advantage of a technological development emphasising the next generation of products and becoming the pioneer of the new demand/technology life cycle.

(5) **Guerilla warfare**

Guerilla attack is less ambitious in scope and involves making small attacks in different locations whilst remaining mobile. They take several forms: law suits, poaching personnel, interfering with supply networks and so on. The overriding aim is to destabilise by pricks rather than blows. The risks are strong competitive retaliation if the threshold of tolerance is passed.

(6) **Strategic alliances**

Both a defender and attacker can benefit from alliances, which is where independent partners pool resources in order to achieve a limited objective and promote reliable superiority where none existed.

Suggested approach for Wilkinson Sword

We need to consider all the options listed and conduct cost/benefit analysis of each. Based on suitability, feasibility and acceptability criteria we will be able to make an informed strategic decision of our best response.

Due to our smaller size and resources, at this stage my gut reaction would be to favour a market follower approach in the shaving system sector:

- Adapter: takes leader's products and improves them growing into future challenger

  and

- Frontal attack against Bic in the disposable sector as they are much weaker

I look forward to your comments in due course.

48 Easyjet

> *Examiner's comments.* Good answers used a theoretical framework upon which they could build an answer. Weaker candidates failed to use the value chain in their analysis of the company. Models are a key area of the syllabus and students need to understand a wide range of models and be able to apply and criticise them.
>
> Good answers discussed branding strategies in part b and identified the factors that need to be considered when evaluating these choices. These answers were also applied specifically to EasyJet's situation. Weaker papers failed to demonstrate an understanding of branding strategy options...(some) failed to identify that the question was about branding.

(a) **Report**

Subject: EasyJet, core capabilities for use in family of companies
From: Tess Jessop, consultant.

Introduction

Identification of an organisation's current and potential capabilities requires assessment of the resources it possesses. In this particular case, a distinction is required between assets and competencies. Competencies are the abilities and skills available to the company to marshal the effective exploitation of the company's assets. The company's assets are:

- **Financial**. Working capital
- **Physical**. Ownership and control of the facilities
- **Operational**. Production and plant machinery
- **People**. Quality and quantity of human resources
- **Legal**. Ownership of copyrights and patents
- **Systems**. Management information systems and databases.
- **Marketing**. Marketing strategy

In contrast, the companies core **competencies** are:

- **Marketing**. Such as brand extension, business analysis and new product development
- **Selling**. Supply chain management, pricing and promotion
- **Operations**. Such as speed of response, total quality management, payment systems, cost management and health and safety

Value chain analysis

The value chain developed by Porter can be used to categorise the organisation of EasyJet into a series of processes. This will help identify EasyJet's key capabilities that generate value for their customers and stakeholders.

The Value Chain

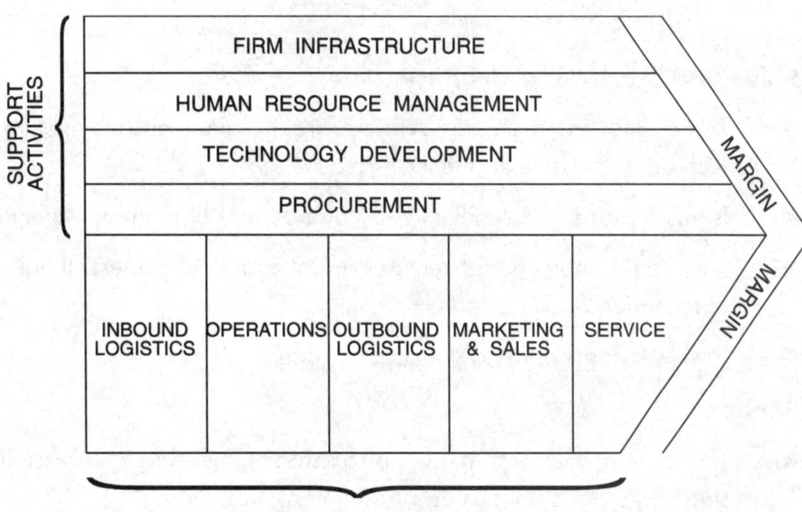

Firm Infrastructure

- Headquarters based in Luton
- Easy access to major transport routes
- Low airport costs
- High emphasis on Internet bookings
- Low administrative paperwork, for example, free allocation of seating
- Sole ownership of EasyJet by Haji-Ioannou

Human Resource Management

- 'Hands on' approach from entrepreneurial owner
- Active search for opportunities to stretch the brand
- Pro-active marketing team breaking traditional airline establishment practices

Technology development

- Heavy investment in technology has led to simplification of processes, for example, Internet bookings
- Reduction of staff costs
- Improved profit margins

Procurement

- Customer friendly, simplified booking system
- Low airport costs
- Informal approach adopted by airline staff

The **support activities** will now be analysed in relation to EasyJet's **primary activities** in order to identify the activities that will be used to benefit future growth.

Inbound logisitics

Customer friendly, simplified airline service (achieved by investment in technology) has led to less bureaucracy and has reduced labour and airline costs leading to easy payment, easy booking and easy seat allocation.

Operation and outbound logistics

- The use of secondary airports and fast turn around times together with simplified and efficient processes has resulted in lower fares.
- Space and increased seat allocation has been created by not offering business class and reducing catering facilities. This has also led to lower fares.

- The airline has a less formal appearance and approach to customers than some competitors.

Sales and marketing strategy

- The airline has a clearly defined target market and segmentation. It combines this with an aggressive marketing strategy.
- Is has a Branson style PR strategy and attracts high media attention at very little cost.
- It uses joint promotional ventures in national newspapers. It has also been the subject of television documentaries.
- EasyJet adopts a friendly, informal approach.

Service

- The company adopts a budget approach, offering only essentials, such as safety, single destination flights and fast turnarounds.
- It is also growing, providing increasing airport locations but maintaining reliability, flight frequency and low cost.

Conclusion

In conclusion, by using the value chain as a tool for analysis, it can be seen that EasyJet may be good at some of its primary activities (core capabilities). However, not all of these are transferable into other brands. This is because there is a unique interrelationship between EasyJet's assets and competencies. Those that can be transferred are:

- Low overheads
- Economies of scale
- An aggressive marketing approach
- Legal patents and copyrights
- A perceived high value of the brand

(b) To: Stelios Haji-Ioannou
From: Keith Reed
Subject: Branding Strategy

Introduction: the importance of branding

It is useful to consider the importance of branding before the individual branding options as this will impact on the choice of branding strategy.

Brands are designed to enable customers to identify products or services which promise specific benefits. In the case of EasyJet, these are no nonsense, easy to book, cheap flights. EasyJet have been able to differentiate their service from that of competitors based on these benefits.

EasyJet has a distinctive orange logo and has the booking telephone number painted clearly on the side of its aircraft. These have become good promotional tools which have motivated customers to choose EasyJet's service.

It is now necessary to evaluate the branding options open to EasyJet in terms of expansion into other business areas, primarily Easycafes.

Options available

Family branding

This can be divided into two components. Firstly, a blanket family brand name such as Heinz. This has the advantage of enabling a global organisation to introduce new products quickly and successfully as well as consolidating expensive promotional activity behind one message.

Secondly, separate family names, such as Volkswagen use. They now own Skoda and Seat and are able to adopt a family approach, particularly in style and parts. This is more costly in terms of promoting each brand. However, savings are made by the economies of scale in production by using up to 80% of existing Volkswagen parts in some models of Skoda and Seat.

Corporate umbrella branding

This is where the company name covers a wide variety of products which the name suggests. A good example is Virgin. They operate an airline, Virgin Airways, but also have Virgin cola, Virgin direct, Virgin mobile phones, Virgin trains and Virgin clothes under their corporate umbrella.

The important issue when using corporate umbrella branding is that all of the businesses must be seen to be successful so that they can add value to each other. Until recently it has been a successful strategy for Virgin, but the closure of the Virgin clothing operation in the UK and the failure to deliver good service on Virgin trains may have damaged consumer perception of the brand.

Multi-brand approach

This approach has been taken successfully by competitors Unilever and Procter and Gamble for a number of years. They each have a range of products under different brand names within the same product line. Examples are: Bold, Persil and Dreft (washing powder). There are many other examples. Each brand satisfies the needs of particular segments within that line. Also, if any brand fails, it doesn't adversely affect the parent company or other brands in that line.

Individual brands need separate marketing mixes which is costly. However, an additional benefit to those mentioned above is that a multi-brand approach stifles competition because other companies may have to launch several brands to successfully compete in that line.

Company and individual branding

This is when a company produces a range of similar products, targeted at a particular segment in the market. An example of this is Kellogg's, who target cereal eaters in the food market. Kellogg's have a range of products to cater for differing tastes within that segment. They range from Special K, for the health conscious, to Crunchy Nut Cornflakes.

The existence of the related products in the same market segment does not benefit the other products in the range. However, in the case of Kellogg's, the image of quality is transferable. It is costly to operate such a branding system, but the benefit lies in the fact that consumers are targeted precisely.

Key issues

In making a choice of branding strategy for the future, several key questions need to be answered. These questions are listed below.

- Can the existing brand values be extended to other products and services easily?
- Will the brand extension damage the core business or strengthen it?
- Are there sufficient resources available to carry out a systematic and planned expansion?
- How will the branding strategy be managed?

- Can similar marketing communications be used for all new products and services?
- Would EasyJet's current client base have similar needs for Easycafe services?
- What are the needs, wants and values of 'Joe Public' for Easycafe services?
- It will also be necessary to undertake an audit of any competitor's branding strategy.

Conclusions

Once the questions above have been successfully discussed a value judgement can be made. This will be aided by market research information on current and potential customer groups on their perception of the EasyJet brand and its extensions. The results of the competitor branding audit can also be used to make this judgement.

My preference would be an umbrella branding strategy such as Virgin uses. Easycafe could build on EasyJet's existing reputation and image which could be transferred to other services and products. The distinctive orange logo could be utilised. There would be no need to redesign separate names for each product and service, similar communications messages could be used and the website and other printed material would need little adaptation.

Another advantage is seeing Virgin's recent experience. EasyJet could learn from Virgin's setbacks in brand stretching by trying to make more judicious choices in the future, based on market analysis.

49 Weetabix

> *Examiner's comments.* Good answers outlined and evaluated the strategic options open to Weetabix. The emerging price war in the sector needed to be considered. Poorer answers failed to address the price war aspect and only discussed possible options at a tactical level.

(a) **Report**

To: Marketing Director
From: Consultant
Subject: Price Wars/Strategic Options open to Weetabix

Introduction

Piercy states 'Price wars are dangerous and highly contagious'. This results in reduced margins, the product or service becomes a commodity, sold on price alone, and the weakest companies go to the wall.

It is important to consider and try to understand why Kellogg's is initiating a price war. It is probably initially to respond to the growth of own label brands, but the repercussions will affect all the brands within the sector. If Kellogg's maintain the strategy of price war, over a significant time frame they hope to increase market share.

This will be mainly at the expense of own label brands but it will also result in reduced margins for any competitors who wish to compete. It will also seriously weaken smaller producers.

Kellogg's assumptions are based on:

- The fact that they are a low cost producer
- The fact that they have dominance in the sector
- The fact that customers are responsive to price cuts

For Kellogg's, trying to re-establish lost market share in a mature market will be costly as historical evidence shows it is rarely cost effective. However, their aim is to recover lost sales.

Response of Weetabix

Before considering any strategic response a complete competitor analysis of Kellogg's needs to be carried out. This should be based on the following:

- Size of the company
- Costs (own and competitors)
- Perception of the company
- Financial state
- Resources
- Company objectives
- Historical behaviour in other markets
- Demand elasticities
- Interrelationships within the product lines

Once this has been evaluated, Weetabix can respond.

The response to entering the price war should be based on the following criteria:

- Reduction of price is compatible with brand
- Costs can be reduced or fall to help maintain reasonable margins
- Company's marketing objectives are to maintain and increase market share
- Excess supply in the sector

Conversely, Weetabix should abstain from entering the price war if:

- Costs are rising
- There is excess demand for the product
- Price fall is incompatible with brand image
- Objective is to harvest
- Customers are price insensitive

Options available to Weetabix

Below are some of the options open to Weetabix

(i) **Respond to Kellogg's by entering the price war**. This may cause other players to react by also entering the war. This will squeeze margins throughout the market. Only those with the most resources, particularly cash, will survive the war.

(ii) **Focus on core strengths**. One way is to focus on Weetabix's core strengths, looking at other niches in the market, for example, the eat while you travel segment.

(iii) **Form a strategic partnership**. This is an ever increasing undertaking by companies to maintain a competitive advantage. This could take the form of collaboration with Jordan's to develop new products, thus adding to the product portfolio, an obvious current weakness in the company. Alternatively, Weetabix could launch a promotional alliance with Jordan's crunch bars, for example, giving one free with every large packet of Weetabix. Whatever the collaboration, a small company like Jordan's could be squeezed out in the cereal war and might welcome an alliance.

(iv) **Total withdrawal of the brand**. This must be the last resort, but in the baked beans price war when supermarkets sold own labelled beans as low as 6p, Crosse and Blackwell withdrew from the market with their own brand. Your company manufactures own label products and have a vested interest in the growth of this market as well as the survival of the Weetabix brand. The margins for Weetabix become too prohibitive and you are forced to withdraw, the shortfall in the UK may well be met by manufacturing more own label cereals. Promotional costs will drastically be reduced. However, returning to the market when it becomes more attractive could be prohibitive, as the re-launch costs could be enormous to recapture market share.

(v) **Increase promotional activity**. Conduct detailed research into your current and potential market segments, particularly attitudinal responses to price and preferences. From analysis of this research a schedule of promotional activities can be arranged to meet the outcomes of the analysis.

Conclusion

Generally, the only beneficiary of a price war in the short term is the consumer, not the business or the brand. Therefore, very careful consideration is needed before entering into any price war. The options highlighted may well be better alternatives than responding too quickly to Kellogg's stance.

(b) **Report**

> *Examiner's comments.* Good answers gave a wide definition of innovation and outlined the specific elements relevant to an innovation audit. Poorer answers discussed the audit merely in relation to the new product development process.

To: Board of directors, Weetabix
From: Consultant
Subject: Audit process for innovation

Introduction

Innovation and new product development is essential for companies' survival in the market place today. With core technologies widely available and shortening product life cycles, getting new products to the market place quickly is essential. It is essential for companies to remember that the key driving force behind new product ideas and innovation is the human resource.

Resistance to change

New methods of management thinking can experience some resistance from established managers. This lack of management enthusiasm may be due to lack of knowledge or concern to maintain the status quo. Management can tend to focus too heavily on methods and products that have been successful in the past and see budgets for innovation and product development as taking resources away from core business. Similarly there can be a tendency, especially in the West, towards short-term profits rather than long term growth and stability

Old planning systems

Often old planning systems have been downgraded and inputs can take over from outputs. Large organisations that have been split into functional areas which operate at different sites tend to develop their own goals without knowledge about the customers needs through an integrated marketing communications strategy.

Old structures/functional specialists

Individuals often have limited responsibilities and this inhibits new thinking and creativity. Product development itself is often slow with poor planning and lack of market research or even an allocated budget for innovation in the first place.

An innovation audit

Top management needs to create a priority for innovation by making it one of the organisation's goals. By assessing the company's innovation record all internal obstacles can be identified and steps started to incorporate 'innovation and learning' as part of the company culture. 3M expects each of its divisions to have a minimum of 25% of its profit from products introduced in the last five years. This goal demands that management and financial resources are devoted to innovation.

An audit to assess the company's position regarding innovation can take the following steps:

1 **Benchmarking**

Compare the company's innovation record with other leading businesses. What is achievable can be discovered by examining what others have achieved. Managers within the organisation will also be able to see that proposed goals are not unrealistic. Research into competitor activity can also teach much about allotted research time, allocated product development budgets and employee involvement, for example, and this can be compared with profit margins and market share.

2 **Assess creativity**

Management should undertake an attitude survey assessing the key areas of the organisation's climate of creativity. This should cover the following areas:

- Allocated resources for creativity and product development
- Supervisory support
- The degree of teamwork/taskforces working within a creativity infrastructure
- The personnel involved (Teams should consist of experienced people from R & D, marketing, engineering, production and sales sharing multifunctional skills.)
- Recognition, unity and co-operation
- Political problems and leadership styles of senior management, attitudes that might be blocking innovation and creativity

3 **Measurement of current performance in innovation**

This will involve analysis in the following areas:

(a) **Innovation/value portfolio analysis**. Are there regular review meetings focusing on opportunities in the market, analysis of innovation performance, and are objectives being met?

(b) **Customer satisfaction ratings.** What level of customer involvement and feedback exists in product development? To what extent is research identifying new target markets? Teams should be working together, talking to different customers, looking and listening

(c) **Rate of product development**. Many organisations fail to use profits on a continuous basis from current successes to develop more innovations. Processes should exist for idea generation, market testing and assessment of commercialisation. Effective planning and scheduled product development is essential as delay to the market place may result in loss of potential sales.

(d) **Staff turnover**. Are the staff motivated and rewarded for creativity? If a company is not investing in its people providing training and incentives a culture of creativity will be hard to achieve. A good communication structure is essential as is an understanding of the market environment and investment in technology help to develop the core capabilities for innovation.

Conclusion

As a company grows there is the danger that they lose the often close contact with customers that a small organisation can maintain. A vision and priority for innovation needs to be incorporated into the mission statement which should permeate throughout the culture of the organisation. Innovation and creativity should not be left to the research and development department.

With multi-skilled task forces from all functional departments from the organisation potential conflicts can be eliminated and time schedules co-ordinated thereby reducing some of the risks involved in encouraging innovation, and product development.

50 Freeplay energy

Examiner's comments. Good answers outlined the likely internal and external influences on Freeplay's mission, goals and objectives. In particular they discussed trade-offs. Strong answers went on to discuss the possible tensions between Freeplay's stated desire to improve the lives of individuals in the developing world and its current dependency for sales in the developed world. Poorer papers tended to be unable to distinguish clearly between mission, goals and objectives.

(a) REPORT

To: The Management Team – Freeplay Energy
From: John Smith – Star Consultancy Ltd
Subject: Issues involved in developing the mission, goals and objectives of Freeplay Energy

Background

Freeplay Energy (FE) has grown to a £30m business within the last twenty years. With the 1994 agreement signed with BayGen Power the company has moved from being a one man business to an international company. The basic values of the company – helping disadvantaged people and improving the lives of people in poor economies – are now under threat as the company considers its future. These values are an integral part of FE's mission, and they differentiate it from other businesses. They define FE's primary objectives and the way it develops its strategies.

Influences on the mission and objectives

Johnson and Scholes identify four major influences.

(i) **Corporate governance**. To whom are the managers of FE accountable? Does Trevor Bayliss still have an influence on managerial decisions? Who owns FE? These are some key questions that need to be addressed, because there needs to be some regulatory control on what the managers do. A big factor must be the influence of the local charities in South Africa. We are told they co-own the Cape Town factories but what influence do they have over decisions made by FE? For example, a switch of production to China to produce for the USA market could have a devastating effect.

(ii) **Stakeholders**. These groups will include customers, suppliers, shareholders, employees, financiers and the wider community. A lot here depends on the power and influence of the various groups. Whose finance is involved in the business? To what extent is the South African government involved? Are one or two suppliers providing raw material at a low price to support the business? These will have to be consulted before FE can start developing corporate and marketing objectives.

(iii) **Business ethics**. This relates to the social responsibility of FE. Certain groups, such as employees and disadvantaged groups depend a great deal on FE for their livelihood. If the business is to expand into other markets, eg UK and Germany, with more products, to what extent will the less powerful stakeholders be better off? Growth may actually be detrimental if prices are squeezed and wages have to be cut. An important aspect here is the expectation of individuals' ethical behaviour. This may vary between South Africa and the USA.

(iv) **Cultural context**. Where is the priority in the mission of FE? The business needs to assess where its priorities lie. The fact that BayGen Power is South-African based must have an influence on the mission and objectives in that its primary responsibility is to look after its employees and local charities. This may well be at odds with an expansion strategy. There will be various sub-cultures surrounding the business at various levels. These will have different influences and must be taken into account.

Specific internal influences

The above points can be taken into account if the specific influences on the mission and objectives are considered.

(i) **Management style**. How does the management team approach its business decisions? To what extent are risks taken? Who are the dominant personalities? Such influences will shape the nature of any objectives set for the short and long-term.

(ii) **Organisation culture**. This relates to the whole organisation (management and employees) and how it relates to suppliers and local community. Is FE likely to embrace change? This is an important point because the new product ideas will involve bit changes. If the organisation finds it difficult to change to new practices then the objectives must be set in accordance with this factor.

(iii) **Internal stakeholder expectations**. This relates to what employees, shareholders and trades unions want from FE. Expectations will vary but some common ground will exist and it is important that the expectations of all parties are considered.

(iv) **Internal resources**. What is the financial situation of FE? Particular factors such as cash flow, available funds and financing facilities must be evaluated and assessed before establishing a mission and objectives.

Specific external influences

(i) **The micro-environment**. This relates to the customers, competition and markets with which FE is concerned. The markets in the USA and Germany are very different to those in Africa. Competition is also likely to be more aggressive and numerous. FE needs to analyse this environment before deciding on the mission and objectives.

(ii) **The macro-environment**. How will economic, technological, social and political factors impact on FE's business in the future? Since a large part of FE's business is in developing countries then future political influences may have a major effect. Emerging technology may overtake some of FE's new product ideas.

(iii) **External stakeholders**. FE with its emphasis on social responsibility is perceived favourably by the general public, but this may change if they alter their mission and objectives. Pressure groups such as local charities could exert considerable influence on FE if they were unhappy about its future direction.

Trade-offs

In addition to the above, FE's future strategic direction will have an influence on its mission and objectives. Management will need to trade off various activities and opportunities in order to arrive at this direction.

Weinberg identified a number of trade-offs.

(i) **Short-term v long-term**. Does FE concentrate on the radio and the African continent or does it take a long-term view and consider new markets and products?

(ii) **Profit margins v competitive position**. Does FE concentrate on a few profitable niches or does it expand both globally and with its product range, on a volume market share basis?

(iii) **Market penetration effort v market development effort**. Does FE stay in Africa or does it look to expand around the world?

(iv) **Related v non-related growth opportunities**. Does FE stay with 'technology' products or does it move into other areas such as food retailing or education?

(v) **Profit v non-profit objectives**. Here FE must decide whether to prioritise profit or the social responsibility objective, primarily in Africa.

(vi) **Growth v stability**. FE must decide whether to stay in existing markets with their core radio product, or expand into other product areas and new markets.

(vii) **Risk avoidance v risk taking**. FE need to decide what risks need to be taken. With their responsibility to local charities, can they afford to take risks?

Conclusions

Freeplay Energy is a unique company. Founded on a unique product it must now decide how it can move forward without compromising this uniqueness and the central values and philosophy of improving communications across the world. Only by undertaking a full analysis of its situation and through consultation with all interested parties will it be able to establish its mission, objectives and goals.

(b)

> *Examiner's comments*. Good answers demonstrated a clear understanding of segmentation and related this specifically to Freeplay Energy's situation. Poorer answers tended to discuss the theory of segmentation but failed to relate this sufficiently to the situation faced specifically by Freeplay Energy. Weaker papers discussed segmentation variables in general but failed to outline the overall process or the specifics of the case.

REPORT

To: The Management Team – Freeplay Ltd
From: John Smith – Star Consultancy Ltd
Subject: Market segmentation, targeting and positioning

Background

Freeplay Energy (FE) is now marketing its products in a number of countries worldwide. It is also selling its products to various customer groups. Once the objectives have been established the markets must be identified. The segmentation, targeting, positioning (STP) model outlines the major steps involved in arriving at a planned target marketing strategy.

Segmentation

This is an area apparently neglected by FE as they have grown, but now it must be addressed. *Doyle* identifies a number of reasons why segmentation should be undertaken.

(i) To meet **consumer needs** more precisely – FE have already established that their products appeal in different ways to various customers.

(ii) To **increase profits**-segmentation will allow FE to price highly in certain segments in order to maximise profits.

(iii) To gain **segment leadership** – by identifying and dominating segments, FE will achieve economies of scale and develop brand loyalty for their 'technology' products.

(iv) To **retain customers** – providing products for specific segments will achieve loyalty not only to the original FPR1 but also to subsequent FE products.

(v) To focus **marketing communications** – segmentation identifies media channels which can reach target groups. For example, the 'outdoor segment' may well be reached through specific magazines and digital TV channels.

Segment requirements

To have real potential, segments should be identified using the following criteria.

(i) **Homogenous**. Each person within the segment should have similar needs regarding the product. For example, the outdoor segment will require durability from the flashlight whilst the innovator segment will require a smart design. Thus both segments will require clearly identifiable but different marketing mixes.

(ii) **Exclusive**. Ideally the segment should not be offered a similar product by the competition.

(iii) **Substantial**. The segment is large enough in sales and profit potential to justify a targeted strategy.

(iv) **Accessible.** The segment should be reasonably accessible in terms of distribution and communication channels.

A number of segmentation bases can be used to segment the market.

(i) **Geographic** by country or region – FE already know that their products are perceived differently around the world.

(ii) **Demographic** – by age, gender or ethnic group. It may well be that many of FE's products could be aimed at younger 'innovator' groups.

(iii) **Geo-demographic** – household addresses can be used to identify specific geographic areas. ACORN or MOSAIC groups could be identified who have the likely age and socio-economic profiles to be targeted by direct mail.

(iv) **Phsychographic** – lifestyle, social class and personality could be used to identify specific segments. Particularly in the UK and USA, FE's products can be seen as possessing lifestyle characteristics.

(v) **Behaviouristic** – to what extent are these products purchased for a particular occasion, or are they purchased for specific benefits?

Assessing attractiveness of segments

Once particular segments have been identified then FE need to match their particular assets and competences to the segments. If the segments do not match then decisions have to be made as to whether to enter those segments or not. Overall the segments need to match the long-term aims and objectives of FE.

Jobber gives examples of assets and competences.

(i) **Marketing assets** – does the segment allow the company to take advantage of its brand identity and current sales and distribution structure?

(ii) **Cost advantages** – does the segment allow the company to use its existing cost base or will it involve considerable investment?

(iii) **Technological strengths** – can existing technology be used to gain advantages in the segment?

(iv) **Managerial capabilities and commitment** – does the company have the necessary to skills succeed in the segment?

A matrix as below could be used to position potential segments.

Fit with company's assets and competences	**Segment attractiveness**		
	Weak	*Average*	*Strong*
Weak	USA		
Average		UK	
Strong		Africa	

Criteria can then be weighted and the segments plotted in the matrix. The figure above shows how countries might be positioned for FE.

Positioning

Once a segment has been identified then a definite positioning statement must be established. It is important that a position should have.

(i) **Credence** – it should be believable. For example can the 'underdeveloped countries' brand be transferred to the USA?

(ii) **Competitiveness** – will FE's products have similar competition? Can the uniqueness of FE be used to position them?

(iii) **Consistency** – will FE's products be positioned using the same values of social responsibility and helping less well-off countries?

(iv) **Clarity** – will any positioning undertaken be clearly understood and accepted in the segment?

Conclusions

It is vitally important that FE identify segments that will enable them to grow profitably. The identified segments must then be matched with FE's assets and competences. Then, only by careful targeting and effective positioning can this growth be achieved.

51 Marks & Spencer

(a) REPORT

To: The Marketing Director, Marks & Spencer plc
From: Jim Smith, Star Marketing Consultancy
Date: 17 March 200X
Subject: Current strategic position of M&S in the UK clothing market

Situation analysis

Marks & Spencer (M&S) has experienced a significant decline in fortunes over the last three years. From achieving a profit of £1,115m in 1998, there has been a decline of 63% to a figure of £418m in 2000. With the share price falling 70%, M&S is now valued considerably less than its value of £17 billion in 1998. A number of reasons can be identified from the case information, including aggressive competition from both new players (eg Matalan, Gap) and existing players (eg Next, Debenhams). Another reason would appear to be the lack of competitive advantage that M&S has over its rivals in the UK clothing market.

Competitive advantage

'The notions of competitive advantage and marketing strategy are intrinsically linked' (*Ensor and Drummond*). A basic for advantage is first of all identified and then delivered to the marketplace by the subsequent marketing strategy. The original advantage offered by M&S, as stated in the background information, was a good quality range of functional and fashionable clothes backed up by good customer service. However, increasingly, this advantage has been eroded by competitors. *Porter* identified three **generic or fundamental strategies** that can be used by an organisation to obtain competitive advantage.

- **Cost leadership** – maintaining a low cost base in order to price lower than competitors. This can be done by achieving low costs of production and distribution.
- **Differentiation** – concentrating on differentiating the product offer. This can be achieved by offering a better service or building up a significant brand image. Often the differentiation is perceived rather than actual and can be heightened through marketing communications.
- **Focus** – deciding to concentrate on a single or a few market segments. This can in itself create cost leadership and differentiation advantages by limiting marketing activities to one niche.

Competitive advantage and M&S

In the case of M&S, they have been pursuing a combination of the three generic strategies (see figure below).

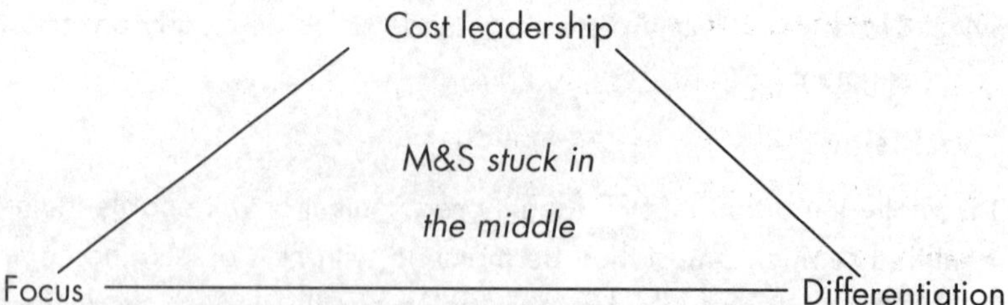

M&S have therefore tried to please a wide range of customer tastes and in doing so, have found their market eroding, as competitors have been able to specialise and concentrate on specific niches.

The stuck in the middle position is evident in that:

- M&S are operating in a broad rather than a niche market, eg M&S are trying to appeal to adults in the age range 25-55 year old across groups A, B and C1 whereas retailers such as Gap appeal to a specific type of 'lifestyle' shopper.
- M&S cannot achieve advantages as a cost leader due to the increased expansion of discount operators such as Matalan.
- M&S are perceived not to be differentiated attractively from their competitors. Debenhams and Next are perceived to offer particular shopping experiences of greater quality.

Competitive advantage and the UK clothing market

It is possible to position the different competitors in the matrix below.

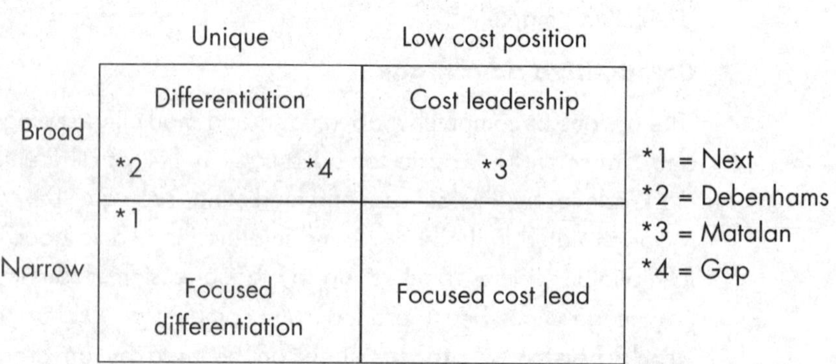

(Adapted from Porter 1980 – Drummond & Ensor, 2001)

M&S need to decide on a clear strategy for their clothing in terms of:

- Relevance – does the strategy meet current and future market needs? The poor performance of M&S would appear to show that previous loyal customers are shopping elsewhere.
- Defence possibilities – once a strategy has been decided, to what extent can it be imitated? M&S need to ensure that their product offer is unique and so established in consumers' minds that competitors are unable to offer something similar. Clearly M&S were in such a position a few years ago but now must try and build that position again.

Other strategic models

Depending on the availability and quality of the information available to M&S, a number of models could be used by the management team. These could include portfolio models, the value chain and positioning maps.

Conclusions

The current position of M&S in the market is that their once very strong product offering is now looking very tired and both new and revitalised competitors are claiming increased market share. Over the last few years, M&S have experienced strategic wear-out. They no longer meet customer needs and their strategy of quality products and service has been surpassed by competitors.

Davidson summarises the causes of strategic wear-out as follows.

- Changes in customer requirements – the M&S customer is looking for a more modern, fashionable range.
- Changes in distribution systems – new and existing competitors are now using the internet as well as traditional methods to market their products.
- Innovation by competitors – many competitors are now innovating in many areas, including the production of several ranges throughout the year to maintain interest and keep the image fresh.
- Poor control of company costs – many retailers are sourcing effectively from around the world as well as keeping a close control of their management and marketing costs.
- Lack of consistent investment – the most successful retailers need to invest in new stores, new technology and improvements in warehousing and distribution.
- Ill-advised changes in successful strategy – it can be dangerous to change suppliers, design new ranges and invest in new areas of the market.

It could be argued that the above factors have all contributed to M&S's demise. It will be interesting to see whether the initiatives taken by the new management team will turn their fortunes around.

(b) REPORT

To: The Marketing Director, Marks & Spencer plc
From: Jim Smith, Management Consultant
Date: 17 March 200X
Subject: Evaluation of options open to Marks & Spencer

Background

M&S have undertaken a number of measures to try and recapture their former dominant market position. These can be summarised by positioning them within the Ansoff Matrix.

Market \ Product	Current	New
Current	Market penetration *2 *7	Product development *1 *4 *3 *5
New	*6 Market development	Diversification

*1 = Fashionable clothing
*2 = Cost-cutting
*3 = Designer clothing
*4 = New financial services
*5 = Website business
*6 = Lingerie boutiques
*7 = Advertising campaign

The above positioning is assuming that most of the new initiatives are aimed at current customers, bearing in mind M&S's large customer base.

Evaluation of proposed options

- **More fashionable** lines of clothing – quite a high risk strategy.

  One could argue that M&S's strength was in non-fashion ranges and in clothing that was smart and classy, suitable for the office but not for a night out. Also, this option is perhaps aimed at attracting younger age ranges but may alienate the core group of older age groups. M&S need to ensure their loyal customer base is satisfied and looked after. Their main problem now is to win these customers back!

- **Cost cutting measures** – the question to be asked here is whether M&S are operating in a price sensitive market. Are the loyal M&S customers prepared to pay higher prices for quality products? To what extent will the brand suffer if lower priced merchandise is offered? Will lower costs mean a lowering of quality standards?

- **Designer collection** – the main question to be asked here is whether these new ranges will attract existing customers or new customers. Also the impact on price must be assessed assuming that such designers will involve additional costs in using their names. The impact on the M&S design image must also be considered.

- **Financial services** – although the financial services market is attractive with low barriers to entry and quite high growth, one must consider how this will affect the core product clothing range. The M&S reputation is in food and clothing retailing and the management team must be careful about neglecting their core product.

- **Confetti network** – on the surface a good initiative but as with the previous option, the core business could be neglected. Also this option does carry risks as the consumer still has to be convinced about shopping on-line.

- **Lingerie boutiques** – is the idea of trying to open up markets on the continent a good one. The M&S image on the continent, which good, is not as strong as in the UK. A lot will depend on the set-up costs and how the stores will be managed. A key question will be whether to franchise the 'msl' stores or not.

- £20 million **advertising campaign** – a new initiative by M&S having advertised very little in the past. At the end of the day, the advertising will only work if the merchandise meets customer expections. The slogan, 'exclusively for everyone' has to be questioned in that this is possibly underlining Porter's 'stuck in the middle' competitive position that M&S are in.

Overall, these proposals appear to be trying to meet the needs of all customer groups, both here and on the continent. This may be difficult to achieve with so many competitors specialising in each of these areas. However, a main problem M&S face is that a focus strategy would be difficult to achieve without downsizing its operations. Assuming a cost leadership position would both be difficult and unwise, then a differentiation approach may be the most appropriate. Some of the above proposals may achieve this but clear objectives for the entire M&S operation must be decided before the chosen strategy is adopted.

Alternative options

Alternative options could include:

- Modernising and updating the stores to improve the shopping experience.
- Alliances with other stores to compliment their existing ranges, eg having an M&S **shop within a shop** in Debenhams or having a Gap shop in M&S stores.
- Separating clothing from other areas as food and furnishings and having dedicated M&S clothing outlets.
- Improving the range of services associated with clothing retailing eg buying on-line, clothing advisers, home delivery etc.
- Using alternative marketing communications strategies rather than advertising eg sponsorship, database and direct marketing.

Conclusions

In deciding which options to pursue, M&S need to evaluate their assets and competences.

Assets are both intangible and tangible (*Hooley et al*) and include:

- Financial assets – finance, capital
- Physical assets – stores, warehouses
- People assets – management, staff
- Marketing assets – image, reputation, brands
- Internal assets – cost structure, information systems, culture
- Alliance-based assets – links with competitors, banks, suppliers
- 'Competences are the abilities and skills available to M&S to exploit their assets.' (*Ensor and Drummond*). They include:

  (i) Strategic competences – strategic direction, skills and vision

  (ii) Functional competences – the management of the various functions-marketing, human resources, finance and so on

  (iii) Operational competences – how the business is run on a day-to-day basis

  (iv) Individual and team competences – skill levels of individuals and their ability to work in teams

(v) Corporate-level competences – the skills available at a corporate level. How can this be transferred and communicated to the functional levels of the business?

M&S need to understand its core competences and its resource base. By exploiting their unique assets, particularly brand image and quality, they can achieve a more defensible competitive position. This is imperative in an increasingly more competitive marketplace.

52 Xbox

> *Examiner's comments.* The question proved problematic for many candidates. The majority of good answers analysed Sony's actions in the games market by discussing the defensive strategies open to a market leader. Weaker candidates merely restated the mini case details without using any relevant theory.

Part (a)

REPORT

To: The Marketing Director, Star Software Ltd
From: Paul Roberts, Games Consultancy Associates
Subject: The Appropriateness of Sony's Actions

Background

The games hardware market has grown considerably over the last few years up to being a $20 billion a year business. This in spite of the penetration in to most households of the personal computer and the consequent apparent maturing of this market. The games hardware market has managed to maintain massive consumer interest, in particular with the desire to up-grade and buy the latest console.

Alongside the hardware market has grown the games market, often linked to films, cartoons and TV programmes. The hardware producers have been profitable in this sector along with many independent games producers due to licensing arrangements. The introduction of the Microsoft *Xbox* will undoubtedly have an impact, since Microsoft is a new player in this market that has historically been dominated by Sony, Nintendo and Sega. The size of Microsoft with its significant resources, will have a real impact on the market. As a software producer dependent on the success of the hardware producers, we must monitor the situation closely.

Sony's market position and possible strategies

Sony is the market leader in this particular market. Sony, as a leader can adopt any of three major strategies.

(a) **Expand the total market**

(i) Targeting groups that are currently non-users: this could involve producing software games for girls rather than just for the mainstream market of boys.

(ii) Discover new uses for the product or service: this could involve giving internet access and opportunities for online gaming. Other uses could include e-mails, text messaging and playing CDs and DVDs.

(iii) Increase the rate of usage: this can involve targeting existing users and encouraging them to buy more than one console, maybe to play with friends or to use different consoles for different activities such as gaming and e-mailing.

(b) **Guard existing market share**

(i) Strong market positioning: this can be achieved through strong brand development, concentrated advertising and good point of sale material.

(ii) The development and refinement of an effective competitive advantage: this can involve developing the brand image through association with sports stars and celebrities.

(iii) Continual innovation in the organisation's products and processes: innovation in the design of the product as well as the availability of new types of software is important in maintaining market share.

(iv) A proactive approach: it is important for the leader to set the standard for the market rather than just reacting to competitive strategies.

(v) Substantial advertising: ensuring that the product's name is constantly on view to potential target markets.

(vi) Healthy customer relationships: this is extremely important in ensuring loyalty to the brand. It involves relationships with both distributors and consumers. It is often achieved through good channels of communication either through the telephone or on the Internet.

(vii) Strong distribution channels: this are channels that will support the product through good promotion, realistic pricing and excellent use of merchandising and point of sale skills.

(c) **Expand current market share**

(i) Developing new products: in the games market this is about producing a better console and introducing new games and accessories.

(ii) Expanding distribution channels: this can increase the availability of the product. It may also give access to new market segments; for example, selling through department stores may attract older customers.

(iii) Pricing: by reducing the price or by maintaining a price that is lower than competitors, then market share can be increased.

(iv) Expanding into new geographic markets: moving into other countries can be a more cost effective means of expanding market share rather than trying to get more share in a crowded market.

(v) Mergers, acquisitions or strategic alliances: this can be more cost effective than increasing market share through promotion or lower prices. It may involve merging with a competitor or it could involve entering into an agreement with a distributor.

Evaluation of Sony's actions

Sony has used all three approaches to maintain its leadership in the market.

It has expanded the market through targeting new users. This has mainly been achieved through up-grading the consoles and developing more games. This has attracted users of the Nintendo or Sega systems. The product has more uses than just playing games. The agreement with AOL created a significant competitive advantage. The rate of usage has also been increased as Sony users have bought extra consoles to play certain games.

Sony has also guarded existing market share by using the strong lifestyle characteristics of the Sony brand. A heavy promotional budget ($750 million) has helped to keep the Sony

Playstation product in demand. Product development such as access to video and being able to use Playstation 1 games has meant that their existing customer base has remained loyal.

Finally, Sony has expanded its market share through development of the product and through agreements with other parties such as AOL and RealNetworks. The price has been kept low and the product has entered many geographical markets, such that it is virtually a global product.

Conclusions

Sony has used a number of strategies to protect its leader status. A key priority has been to maintain hardware sales so that the demand for software can also be maintained. The withdrawal of Sega from the market may be an indication that this market is now maturing or even declining. However the demand for playing electronic games seems no sign of abating and the opportunity of online gaming may well boost the market to even greater heights. However perhaps the most crucial part of Microsoft's entry may be how loyal Sony's customers will be and to what extent they may switch to Xbox. At the same time, a key question is whether new users will buy Sony, Nintendo or Microsoft.

Part (b)

> *Examiner's comments.* Good answers outlined the attacking strategies available to Microsoft and evaluated these options in the context of the scenario described in the mini case. Poorer answers listed the different attacking strategies available without evaluating the appropriateness of such strategies.

REPORT

To: The Marketing Director, Star Software Ltd
From: Paul Roberts, Games Consultancy Associates
Subject: Actions to be taken by Microsoft

Background

Microsoft has an enviable reputation globally but is a new entrant in the games console market. Microsoft will have to make a decision as to what overall strategy it should pursue. Firstly, Microsoft can adopt a challenger strategy and attack the leader who is Sony. Alternatively, they can accept the status quo and current position of competitors and become a market follower. Both approaches require different marketing strategies as will be explained in the next two sections.

Market challenger approach

Here the basic idea is to attach the market leader and steal market share. At the same time, by using a combination of strategies, new users of games consoles will be attracted to the Xbox. Specifically, Microsoft can use the following strategies as highlighted by *Kotler and Singh*.

(a) **Price discounting**: either on the console or on the software from the information available, the Xbox at $299 will not be the cheapest console, but Microsoft may well offer cheaper software to encourage usage. They may also offer consoles at discounted prices for a limited period of time.

(b) **Cheaper product offering**: there is no evidence to suggest that Microsoft will offer a cheaper product but if sales do not meet early forecasts then this may become an option.

(c) **Product innovation**: Microsoft have a reputation for innovation and their proposed use of broadband technology together with the alliance with NTT Communications is certainly an innovatory move.

(d) **Intensive advertising**: this involves a massive commitment and the current budget of $500m will enable Microsoft to carry out much advertising. However Sony is spending $750m.

(e) **Market development**: this can involve developing new segments as well as broadening the usage of games consoles and software. There is always the danger that by developing the market, this will also benefit competitors such as Sony and Nintendo.

(f) **Prestige image**: in Microsoft's case, this will mean trying to transfer their image to this new market. This may be done through the use of endorsements, advertising and promotion at point of sale.

(g) **Product proliferation**: this can mean broadening the product range in to smaller consoles or related products such as mobile phones. It could also involve creating a big software range. In the short term it seems likely that Microsoft will offer one console and 15-20 games.

(h) **Reduce costs**: this option enables prices to be reduced and/or profit margins to be increased. Microsoft as a large global company can probably spread many of its costs across its operations but the initial investment costs will be high-manufacture, design, sales and advertising. In the medium term if sales have achieved forecasts then overheads will decrease and Microsoft may be able to also reduce promotional expenditure.

The above strategies can be combined to develop an attacking strategy. Various approaches can be used:

(i) **Frontal attack**: a direct attack on the leader which requires plenty of resources as the leader will defend determinedly.

(j) **Flank attack**: this is attacking the weakest part of the leader. It may be the actual product design or the software or even the after sales service.

(k) **Encirclement attack**: here the challenger develops a range of products which in combination may encroach on the leader's position. The main problem is the cost of developing the products and to what extent each product competes with each other.

(l) **Bypass attack**: here the challenger attacks areas where competitors are not active. For example, Microsoft could target the educational market or the small business market.

(m) **Guerrilla attack**: this involves short-term tactical initiatives such as price cuts, promotions or sales drives. The objective is to involve the competitor in plenty of time to counter such attacks. In the longer term a more sustained attack may be launched by the challenger.

It would appear from the current information available that Microsoft are pursuing a frontal attack. They do have the resources to carry out this type of attack but it is important for Microsoft to set targets and measure results rather than just blindly fund all activities.

Regardless of the strategy adopted, to be successful, three key conditions have to be present:

(n) The market challenger has a sustainable competitive advantage. In this case, it may be the actual Xbox.

(o) The challenger has to be able to negate the leader's advantage. Can Sony's Playstation 2 outweigh the advantages of the Xbox?

(p) There has to be an obstacle hindering the leader from retaliation. This could be monopoly legislation or limited resources. In this case it is not obvious if there is a hindrance but it may be that Sony are not prepared to commit themselves to the market as much as Microsoft.

An alternative strategy could be to use a flanking approach as adopted by Nintendo who have targeted younger users. Microsoft could possibly target the 'grey market' of over 50s who know the Microsoft name and want to own a games console as well as a PC.

Other approaches

Microsoft could adopt a different approach by attacking other challengers such as Nintendo or they could concentrate on more regional markets such as Europe or North America.

Alternatively, Microsoft could adopt a follower strategy. In this regard, they would not rock the boat but merely follow the leaders and challengers. In this way, they would not need to spend massive sums on advertising and promotion and would be unlikely to engage in a price war. They would rely on their good corporate name and the quality of their product. Both *Levitt* and *Kotler* have claimed that such a strategy can be as profitable as a strategy of innovation.

Conclusions

Microsoft undoubtedly feel that the games hardware and software market is going to grow. However, even with the withdrawal of *Dreamcast*, the market has powerful competitors in Sony and Nintendo. Microsoft can only be successful by pursuing a structured strategic marketing plan and by being prepared to be flexible in this extremely dynamic market.

53 Howden Joinery

Part (a)

REPORT

To: The Managing Director, MFI
From: The Marketing Director, MFI
Subject: Howden Joinery's competitive advantage and sustainability of their current position

Background

Howden Joinery, part of the MFI group, has shown remarkable growth in the last couple of years. The number of outlets have doubled to 200 depots and operating profits in 2001 were £15.3m out of total group profits of £63m. This was an increase of % over the previous year. International expansion of the operation is now being considered.

Howden Joinery's competitive advantage

One way of evaluating Howden Joinery's competitive position is to use *Porter's* generic strategy approach.

It could be argued that Howden Joinery are pursuing a focused differentiation strategy because they are operating in the specific market niche of small builders and they are concentrating on kitchens only.

However, one could also suggest that Howden Joinery is following a focused cost leadership strategy.

(a) The depots are located on low rental sites on industrial estates.

(b) Show room space is kept to a minimum in order to have plenty of room to hold stock and thus maximise revenue in each depot.

(c) The cost base is low because the kitchen units are produced by existing factories thus ensuring operating efficiencies by minimising the costs of labour intensive procedures such as kitchen assembly.

The strongest argument regarding Howden Joinery's competitive position is that they are following a focused differentiation strategy.

(a) The kitchens are of good design and quality.

(b) Many of the kitchen units are already assembled so that they can be easily installed by the builder.

(c) The depots are conveniently located on industrial estates, thus giving easy access for builders to carry out their purchasing.

(d) Howden Joinery staff help builders, using computers, to design kitchens for their customers.

(e) Many of the units are fully assembled thus saving time for the builders and also helping to maintain quality.

(f) Howden Joinery are able to offer trade prices and credit terms to builders.

(g) The builders are able to develop good relationships with Howden Joinery staff. This means that Howden Joinery have a loyal customer base who are happy to recommend them to other builders.

(h) The builders are supplied with colour brochures which they can show to their customers. This makes life easier for the builder and at the same time guarantees the repeat business for Howden Joinery.

All of the above points help to differentiate Howden Joinery from competitors.

Other sources of competitive advantage

(a) The fact that Howden Joinery use a focus strategy means that they are able to gain economies of scale through its factories and it is also beneficial to their staff who can rapidly gain specialist product knowledge which is an important part of building customer relationships.

(b) By focusing on business-to-business, Howden Joinery are able to avoid the high marketing costs associated with the retail consumer sector. These costs specifically are advertising and promotion expenses and costs incurred due to tactical marketing strategies such as promotional pricing.

(c) A final competitive advantage is that the Howden Joinery stores reach maturity later than if they were just retail stores for the consumer. This means that new initiatives do not have to be taken too soon and the business can be developed carefully without there being too much pressure to bring new ideas to market.

Is the current position sustainable?

There are dangers to the adoption of a focus strategy.

(a) Howden Joinery's costs may increase thus offsetting any cost or differentiation advantages. In this case, the raw material costs of the kitchen units could increase and the builders may buy from other operations even if they have to assemble the units themselves.

(b) The requirements of the target market and those of the market as a whole may converge. This would mean that existing competitors would imitate what Howden Joinery are doing. Howden Joinery would then have to concentrate on a differentiation strategy (eg brand development, more use of technology).

(c) Competitors may invade particularly lucrative sub markets within the strategic target: this may out focus the focuser. In this case, some competitors may target only large builders or they may target only those builders in the most lucrative regions such as London and the South-East.

Conclusions

Overall, Howden Joinery has considerable sources of competitive advantage. *Davidson* identifies ten main types of competitive advantage.

- Superior product or service
- Perceived advantage
- Global skills
- Low-cost operator
- Superior competences
- Superior assets
- Scale advantages
- Attitude advantages
- Legal advantages
- Superior relationships

Howden Joinery would appear to have most of these types of competitive advantage but they still need to be vigilant as their success will attract competitors who will want to imitate this success.

Part (b)

REPORT

To: The Managing Director, MFI
From: The Marketing Director, MFI
Subject: The criteria to be used in order to evaluate a new international market

Background

The success of Howden Joinery to date has obviously opened up the possibility of using the successful business format in other overseas markets. However, many of the market conditions in the UK which have led to the success of Howden Joinery may well not be present in overseas markets. It is important for Howden Joinery to fully evaluate very carefully any potential market.

Criteria for evaluating market attractiveness

- Market size
- Market rate of growth
- The market's profitability
- Consumer behaviour

- Cultural closeness
- Quality of potential franchise partners
- Customer's price sensitivity
- Predictability
- Pattern of demand
- Quality of competition
- Potential to create a differentiated position
- Likelihood of new entrants
- Power of suppliers
- Powers of customers
- Barriers to entry/exit

Since overseas markets are being considered than it is particularly important to consider cultural and buyer behaviour issues.

Cultural issues

Is the market home oriented? Do consumers spend a lot of money on kitchen furniture? What proportion of the population own their own homes? Do consumers renew their kitchen furniture and, if so, how often?

Buyer behavioural issues

Do consumers use builders to build kitchens? Who are the influencers of kitchen purchases? Is it the family, shops or the husband or wife? Do consumers like standardised furniture or do they like it to be individually made so that it is different and unique? Where do consumers buy kitchens from?

Criteria for evaluating Howden Joinery capabilities

It is also important to consider the criteria for evaluating Howden Joinery's capabilities for entering overseas markets.

Capabilities consist of assets and competences.

(a) **Assets, advantages of scale**: to what extent will Howden Joinery be able to use existing suppliers to obtain economies of scale?

(b) **Production processes**: is it possible for existing processes to be used overseas? Eg assembly of units in the factory.

(c) **Customer franchises**: can the existing brand names be used? Do they have any value? Can customer databases be obtained?

(d) **Working capital**: will there be sufficient to establish the business?

(e) **Sales/distribution network**: can a network be set up overseas? How similar or different will it be to the UK? How much training of staff will be needed?

(f) **Relationships with other organisation**: can strong relations be built with suppliers and financial institutions? What is the potential for joint-ventures?

(g) **Property**: what is the availability of suitable depots? Is it possible to expand?

Competences

(a) **Marketing**: new product development, brand management, market research and so on. Howden Joinery will need to find those markets where these assets can be most beneficially used.

(b) **Selling**: in supply chain management, customer service, relationships development etc can these competences, so strong in the UK, be developed overseas.

(c) **Operations**: stock control, motivation and control, industrial relations etc. These competences must be developed in a suitable overseas market.

Alignment of market attractiveness with organisational capabilities

Once the above areas have been researched it is then possible to develop a portfolio model such as the Shell directional policy matrix, to analysis market opportunities against corporate strengths.

Market segment attractiveness			
Unattractive	Average	Attractive	
Strongly avoid	Avoid	Possibilities	Weak
Avoid	Possibilities	Secondary targets	Average firm's capability
Possibilities	Secondary targets	Prime targets	Strong

Here particular overseas markets can be put in to the matrix and then given some sort of priority:

- Prime targets
- Secondary targets
- Possibilities

Conclusions

Because a franchising operation is being considered, Howden Joinery will be offering out their expertise in both selling and operations to potential franchisees. Therefore it is essential that Howden Joinery are able to appoint competent, trustworthy and motivated franchisees in the countries that they select. Therefore, an additional set of criteria need to be applied to each country, regarding the availability and acceptability of franchise operations in the country and the likelihood of suitably qualified franchisees being selected.

54 Guinness in China

REPORT

To: The Marketing Director, Guinness Worldwide
From: Advisor

(a) **Global marketing, information needed for market assessment**

> *Examiner's comments.* Poorer candidates failed to answer both parts of this question ie the types of information required *and* their sources.

(i) **Introduction**

Following the initial success of Irish-themed pubs in Asia, it is becoming increasingly important to detail the types and potential sources of information required to assess the relative attractiveness of the various emerging markets around the world.

This information is vital to the updating of our global marketing plan as well as to determining market entry sequence and advising marketing mix decisions. In specifying this information it needs to be pointed out that it will be difficult to standardise in practice, owing to differences in data availability, accuracy and modernity: generally speaking, the less developed the country the greater the difficulty in obtaining reliable data. Clearly differences in culture and social systems will also affect comparability.

(ii) **Types and sources of information** *(Dibb, Simkin, Pride, Ferrell)*

(1) **Preliminary screening**

A thorough investigation of the so-called macroenvironmental forces (PESTLE) is essential before Guinness enters a new foreign market. Political, Economic, Social/Cultural, Technological, Legal and Environmental (physical and green) factors affect every business. For example, there may be political instability in the relationship between China and Taiwan and economic weaknesses in Asia generally: different dialects/customs within the various provinces in China. Such factors not only weigh upon market entry decisions: they impinge upon marketing mix elements like pricing and promotion. Legal constraints with regard to the employment of indigenous people in management and/or the repatriation of profits may render a given country unattractive.

Secondary data can normally be obtained from foreign governments anxious to attract inward investment. In Russia this might be the Chamber of Commerce and Industry or the trade organisation Amtorg. International banks and embassies are other good sources. With regard to primary data, there are market research agencies which specialise in particular countries and have experience in consumer research where cultural influences make direct questioning difficult. Trade missions and international exhibitions offer opportunities for direct contact and observation, where ways of doing business vary considerably from the western world as in China and Japan.

(2) **Analysis of market potential**

A raft of information is ideally required under this heading which can be grouped into information concerned specifically with market access and information dealing with product potential.

- **Market access**
  - Tariff levels, quotas and other trade limitations
  - Documentation and import regulations
  - Local standards, practices and other non-tariff barriers
  - Patents and trademarks
  - Preferential treaties
  - Legal considerations: investment taxation, repatriation, employment, Codes of Practice

  Historically, developing countries with extremely adverse balance of payments seek to restrict imports using one or more of the above mechanisms. A preferential treaty with the country's government does however offer a short term guarantee to the would-be exporter.

- **Product potential**
  - Customer needs and wants

- Local production, imports, consumption
- Exposure to and acceptance of product
- Availability of linking products
- Specific key indicators of demand
- Attitudes towards foreign products
- Competitive offerings
- Availability of intermediaries
- Regional/local transport facilities
- Conditions for local manufacture
- Availability of manpower

Although conditions are favourable for Guinness in a given market as regards demand, there may be barriers to local production, not the least of which may be the quality of water.

- **Other determinants of profitability**

- Going price levels
- Competitive strengths and weaknesses
- Credit practices
- Current and projected exchange rates

The last item is particularly important and cross-relates to both sales forecasting and macroenvironmental scanning. The recent collapse of currencies in the Far East is a telling example of the need for continual vigilance and market intelligence.

(iii) **Conclusions**

There exist many sources for most of the individual information items listed above and these sources will vary according to the country under consideration. However, general sources include government statistics, banks, international Chambers of Commerce, foreign trade organisations, trade directories, market research reports, exporting agencies/consultants - and of course - primary research.

The extent and the complexity of the data required for effective global operations is such that in my opinion the services of an information specialist are needed. There are a growing number of specialist databases and the Internet is predicted to play an ever-increasing role in international marketing.

If, as seems clear, Guinness is going to continue to expand its international operations, then there is also a real need to establish a formal marketing information system, the details of which I would be pleased to advise you on separately.

(b) **Optional market entry methods: an evaluation of Guinness's current approach in Asia**

Examiner's comment. Most students were able to demonstrate a good knowledge of market entry methods and were also able to apply these satisfactorily to this specific case situation.

(i) **Introduction**

This part of the report necessarily reviews the various market entry methods open to companies wishing to operate internationally before proceeding to identify the advantages and disadvantages of Guinness's current approach (licensing and direct manufacturing) to market entry in Asia.

(ii) **Optional market entry methods**

(1) **Exporting**

Obviously, if an organisation is exporting by default it is simply responding to occasional unsolicited orders and very little structural change is required beyond having someone to handle the special shipment/payment arrangements which might result. No choice of country is consciously made. However, some organisations might be stimulated by such events to try to increase orders from a given country and even be prepared to modify its products/services to suit. Such an organisation may seek to appoint an export agent in the foreign market to represent its interests in return for a commission, or alternatively find an experienced export merchant in the home country which buys goods to export into the foreign country concerned (an export merchant specialises in finding sellers in say the UK whose products meet the needs of buyers in foreign countries).

Finally, there is the situation where buyers from foreign countries/government contact domestic organisations to buy direct without the need for an intermediary. However, this is only one step up from exporting by default.

(2) **Licensing**

As an alternative to simple exporting, a company may license an owner of a foreign operation to sell and/or produce its goods in return for royalties. A lump sum initial fee may be charged as a condition or act of good faith when the licensing agreement is effected. The licenser is likely to provide the licensee with any necessary manufacturing/marketing expertise in the interest of maximising sales and profits. The licensing operation is similar in many ways to the more modern system of franchising.

(3) **Joint ventures**

In international marketing terms, a joint venture is a partnership between two organisations, one indigenous and the other foreign. The organisations can be companies, government or other institutions. For example, the Chartered Institute of Marketing (CIM) branch in Singapore could be said to comprise a joint venture between the CIM and the Singaporean body. Joint ventures are a flexible way of co-operating with a foreign organisation in the interests of both parties. The type of bond varies from a loose 'gentlemen's agreement' to a detailed legal document clearly setting out each partners role and rights and binding both parties for a given term and this may involve some exchange of shares. This organisational structure has proved a very popular way of market entry for many firms within the EU. Many companies set up joint ventures in China, for example motor manufacturing.

(4) **Strategic alliances**

These are similar to joint ventures and can be defined as 'co-operation between two or more industrial corporations, belonging to different countries, whereby each partner seeks to add to its competencies by combing its resources with those of its partner' (*Jain*, in *Advances in International Marketing*, 1987).

Partners in an international strategic alliance are likely to have been former rivals competing in overseas markets with similar types of products or services. Each may bring a distinctive competence to the alliance, eg one a low cost, the other a high quality. The number of strategic alliances has been growing rapidly over the last decade.

(5) **Trading companies**

Trading companies are not engaged in manufacturing and simply provide a link between sellers in one country and buyers in another country. They will, for example, seek out and assist UK manufacturers to sell them products which meet the requirements of buyers in overseas markets. They will then buy these products direct from the UK manufacturer and in turn sell them to the buyers overseas. A trading company therefore acts as a middleman taking title and undertaking the arrangements for physical transfer of goods from one country to another. In many ways trading companies are similar to export merchants. No structural changes other than that involved in producing the right sort of products, are required.

(6) **Direct ownership**

This is where a company sets up a subsidiary in the overseas market to manufacture and/or market its products/services directly. Clearly both considerable investment and risk are involved but the rewards can be correspondingly high. A wholly owned subsidiary may be allowed to operate independently of its parent in the interest of maximising overseas market share. This form of structure, taken to its ultimate, leads to full multinational status where the parent headquarters are based in one country but production, marketing, distribution and finance are spread and moved globally to take full advantage of cheaper labour costs, locally available raw materials, easier finance etc.

(iii) **Evaluation of Guinness's current approach in Asia**

The current approach in Asia appears to be licensing and direct manufacturing. theses are evaluated in terms of their advantages and disadvantages as follows.

(1) **Licensing**

■ **Advantages**

- Lump sum and royalties received
- Less risky than direct ownership
- Suitable for markets subject to political instabilities
- Circumvents government restrictions on importing
- Avoids investment costs
- Reduces direct distribution and promotional costs
- Avoids restrictions on repatriation of profits

■ **Disadvantages**

- Signals a less than full commitment to the market
- Returns on investment may be sub-optimal
- Allows less control than direct ownership
- May restrict flexibility
- Less individual market knowledge/expertise is gained
- Learning curve rewards are forsaken

(2) **Direct manufacturing**

- **Advantages**
  - Leads to full multinational status
  - Spreads operations costs
  - Signals fuller commitment to the market than other options
  - Allows greater quality control than licensing
  - More manufacturing units lessens risk of supply disruptions
  - Allows shorter lead times
  - Reduces investments in stock
  - Gives direct control over production
- **Disadvantages**
  - Riskier than other options
  - Better to own marketing than manufacture
  - Need to employ indigenous staff/management
  - Local restrictions, labour laws etc
  - Potential lack of local production skills
  - Requires large capital investment

(iv) **Conclusions**

Whilst the current approach has the advantage of being cautious and prudent in the short term whilst market potential is being established, I do feel that a brand with the global potential of Guinness demands a move to direct ownership of both manufacturing and marketing as soon as possible.

55 Cafédirect

(a) **Strategic approaches taken by A Supermarket's competitors**

To: The CEO, A Supermarket
From: The Ethical Advisor
Date: 5 December 200X
Subject: Report on ethical trading

1 **Introduction**

A recent television documentary highlighted the vulnerability of major supermarket chains to allegations of unethical trading practices by the media. The case in point concerned a Zimbabwe supplier of peas to Tesco whose pickers received less than 1p for the contents of a pack of mangetout retailing at 99p.

By contrast, ethical practices represent an opportunity for favourably distinguishing A Supermarket from its competitors and for increased profit.

We have now reached the stage when ethical auditing by consumer representatives, the media and indeed the City is increasingly likely to identify and publicise unethical practices by the major chains. For example, Sainsbury has recently received adverse media publicity by its decision to open two stores on Christmas Day on a trial basis, which provoked outrage among traditionalists and religious groups.

Competitors of A Supermarket who trade ethically are also likely to adopt a holier-than-thou approach to gain favourable publicity, perhaps to the point where they deliberately draw the attention of the media to any deficiencies.

Ethical trading is part of the wider context of social responsibility which refers to a company's obligations to maximise its positive impacts and minimise its negative impacts upon society.

Whilst up to now these obligations have been largely a matter of choice, increasingly, societal pressures are being brought to bear and calls are being heard for legislation where necessary.

Strategies are therefore needed to address this situation.

2 Strategic approaches being taken by some competitors of A Supermarket

2.1 Reaction strategy

This is where you do nothing until exposed and you are forced into action. *Tesco* followed this strategy in the case of mangetout referred to above. This strategy can work but is highly risky. It also spurs the media on to find more instances as well as to check on the efficacy of the action taken. Worse still, you are seen to act only when forced, a stigma which tends to linger in the customers' minds.

2.2 Defence strategy

This is where you pre-empt the situation and take advance action to mitigate it. Tesco have recently set up a team of ethical advisors to assist in the monitoring of the goods it sells in its stores and to help to develop an ethical trading policy. Not only will this help to avoid further incidences of the mangetout variety, but also, in any future circumstance, Tesco can, in defence, point to its preventative mechanisms.

2.3 Accommodation strategy

This goes a step further and assumes responsibility for this issue in recognition of the growing pressure from consumer groups and indeed the environmental auditing already being undertaken by some financial investors.

The Co-op and some other major chains have signed up to participate in a project with the Fair Trade Foundation to investigate the mechanics of implementing independent auditing procedures which meet *international* trading standards.

2.4 Proactive strategy

This is where you assume responsibility without any outside pressure or threat of Government intervention, rather than making a virtue out of necessity.

Whilst to date no major UK supermarkets have gone wholly along this route, other chains like Boots and Bodyshop are seen to have adopted this strategy and been rewarded by images of consumer champions and trustworthiness, resulting in a high degree of customer loyalty.

Cafédirect have however, become a major force in ethical trading and consumerism by guaranteeing minimum trade prices which can occasionally be twice the going market level. Supermarkets have passed on the costs of these ethical business practices to consumers, who are clearly willing to pay a small premium if they feel the brand is operating more responsibly.

3 **Conclusions**

Social responsibility issues include ethical trading practices for which a number of strategies are possible, some of which are being adopted by competitors, as described above.

A Supermarket need a clear strategy to avoid adverse publicity and to benefit from the favourable differentiation that would result.

(b) **Marketing issues associated with ethical trading**

1 **Introduction**

There are a number of marketing issues associated with the development of an ethical trading policy, in addition to the strategies described above. These extend up to A Supermarket's Mission Statement and down through the marketing operations. Any time an activity causes consumers to feel deceived, manipulated or cheated, then a marketing *ethical* issue exists, irrespective of the legality of the situation.

2 **Marketing issues**

2.1 **Mission statement**

In order to demonstrate commitment at the highest level, A Supermarket's mission statement should contain the message that the company intends to fully accept its social responsibilities by trading both ethically and profitably.

2.2 **Objectives**

In addition to the normal sales and profit objectives, qualitative objectives can be set which reflect trading intent voiced in the mission statement. These could be extended and given greater substance by incorporation into a Code of Ethics which many companies now have.

2.3 **Operations**

Although not strictly marketing, items sold by A Supermarket should have been produced in accordance with the right safety standards, without excessive damage to the environment and without danger to the workers. This issue extends to suppliers selection, employment and payment policies. The essence is that of an honest and open approach in all operations as opposed to manipulation.

2.4 **Product and services**

Partly covered by 2.3 and legal obligations. However, A Supermarket should scrutinise all new product development from an ethical standpoint, particularly the packaging aspects.

2.5 **Price**

Price fixing and offer manipulation are marketing ethical issues which particularly affect A Supermarket and its suppliers as well as its customers. The extent to which a supermarket chain should squeeze its suppliers on price to make more profit for its stakeholders or even so as to offer lower prices to its customers, is a particularly sensitive issue.

2.6 **Promotion**

Given the development of an ethical trading policy, all the elements of the promotional mix can be deployed in communicating this to A Supermarket's target audiences. PR can be used to gain favourable publicity in the media; sales staff can emphasise the ethical aspects; advertising, mailshots, etc can be targeted at the more ethical market segments.

Kellog's All-Bran packets are currently featuring their pledge of £1m in working with the Cancer Research Campaign to help raise public awareness about how this disease can be prevented.

Needless to say, any misleading promotional messages, however clever or tempting, should be avoided.

2.7 **Place**

Marketing ethical issues also arise in this element of the marketing mix. In particular there are the questions of where to build new stores, where to lay down stocks and the even more contentious issues of transportation - noise, pollution, road congestion etc.

2.8 **Marketing research and the control aspects**

A Supermarket needs to conduct continuous environmental scanning in order to keep abreast of and anticipate future ethical issues. We also need to monitor trends of greed goods market shares.

Audits must be made regularly, to establish the extent to which our ethical codes of practice are being adhered to and also to ascertain the level of our ethical trading image.

3 **Conclusions**

Other supermarket chains are already implementing *independent* auditing procedures. A Supermarket should follow through an ethical trading policy with full attention to the above marketing issues if it is to avoid being accused of paying only lip service to its societal responsibilities.

(c) **Recommendations on a distinguishing ethical stance**

1 **Introduction**

Since no UK supermarket chain has yet established itself positively on the ethical spectrum, A Supermarket clearly has an opportunity to do this in a way which differentiates it from the others and hopefully gains a *sustainable* competitive advantage.

Benchmarks could be established with reference to best practices by other chains both in the UK and abroad. The Boots Company and Bodycare have already been instanced in this respect.

2 **Current situation**

A Supermarket already have a positive positioning on its price image, due in no small way to its powerful TV advertisements. This image appears to have been achieved without A Supermarket having the reputation of being unnecessarily harsh on its suppliers.

3 **Marketing research**

A Supermarket would need to know more about the extent of public feeling on ethical issues and which issues were the most important and/or growing. Research would then be able to establish how A Supermarket rates against these crucial issues in the public eye. It should also be possible to estimate how many customers would be likely to switch from competitors to A Supermarket, given substantially higher ratings. Again case studies with regard to non-supermarket chains performances could help.

Some pre-testing and post-testing of the ethical communications programme would also be necessary.

4 **Repositioning**

Bearing in mind the operational aspects detailed in section (b), events would have to be carefully scheduled over a considerable period of time. Some actions would have priority depending on their potential impact and the difficulty of competitors to copy. Concomitant with the ethical action would be a powerful promotional programme.

The repositioning objective would be to place A Supermarket as the most ethically and socially responsible supermarket with the greatest range of ethically sourced products and services, in the public's mind.

5 **Marketing objectives**

The sales and market share objectives would be increased commensurate with the investments needed and the results of the marketing research.

Targets would also be set with regard to unpromoted awareness and acceptance of the re-positioning.

6 **Marketing strategy**

New targets market segments would include the green/dark green consumers currently shopping with competitors.

New products and services would also be introduced to meet the needs of these new customers and also in response to demand from existing customers following the repositioning campaign.

7 **Tactics, evaluation and control**

These would be very much in line with those stated under section (b) above, modified as necessary by marketing research findings.

8 **Conclusions**

It would seem that A Supermarket have a window of opportunity in which to exploit the relative absence of ethical market leadership in the supermarket sector.

Failure to grasp this opportunity would mean that A Supermarket would be likely to gravitate towards a reactive strategy, losing considerable face in the eyes of the general public, especially if competitors adopt a more aggressive approach to their social responsibilities as Tesco appear to be doing.

56 Ford and Honda

(a) **Report**: From Marketing Consultant – Automobile Industry

Subject: (i) Centralisation versus Decentralisation

(ii) Marketing mix implications – globalised versus customised

Introduction

The arguments for and against centralised structures have been made over many years. That the debate continues is evidenced by some centralised organisations recently deciding to decentralise and vice versa. Many companies adopt a piecemeal approach with regard to functions, for example centralising finance but decentralising marketing.

Part of marketing may be centralised eg branding whilst others such as pricing and selling decisions may be operated regionally.

In these ways organisations seek to achieve a balance between centralised and decentralised decision taking in order to gain the best of both worlds and maximise the available benefits.

Centralisation – Advantages and Disadvantages

A centralised organisation is characterised by all the important decisions being taken by top management, usually from some geographically central location or head office. People at a lower level are expected to carry out these decisions without question rather than participate in the decision making process. Ford seem to have adopted the basics of this approach when restructuring in 1993.

Advantages

A more disciplined structure in which all staff are clear about the limits of their responsibilities.

Less argument and confusion in making important marketing decisions.

Ensures a consistent global marketing strategy is applied.

Is more efficient in the utilisation of scarce resources.

Customers and suppliers of marketing services know who and where the decision takers are.

Lessens risk of rogue decisions at regional level.

Helps in achieving an integrated marketing strategy and an integrated marketing mix.

Disadvantages

In the absence of a top manager, damaging delays in taking decisions can occur.

Initiatives at a lower level are likely to be stifled.

People below top management can become demotivated and leave.

There is likely to be an over-dependence on top management so that even minor decisions are referred upwards.

Product-service offerings are not adapted to local needs, leading to loss of potential market share.

Problems cannot be addressed on the spot, causing a potential loss of customer goodwill.

Opportunities which arise locally or even regionally may receive too slow a response or be overlooked.

Decentralisation – Advantages and Disadvantages

A decentralised organisation is one where decision making is devolved outwards from head office to the region and delegated downwards from top management to middle management. This is the situation that Ford believed in pre- 1993, when hitherto it had operated on a regional basis and cars were tailored to individual country/market needs. Honda has decentralised in recent years so as to achieve more customised marketing strategies.

Advantages

Encourages initiative at regional and local level.

Results in quicker and possibly more effective decisions at regional/local level.

Makes for greater motivation of middle management.

Local and regional opportunities are exploited.

Greater and quicker response to customer needs, thus maximising market share.

Disadvantages

Possible decision overlap and contradictions in neighbouring regions.

More difficult to achieve integration of marketing strategies and particularly tactics.

Less standardisation can cause loss of economies of scale and reduced profits.

Loss of central control and increased risk of poor decisions.

Corporate image can suffer in the eyes of large key customers who might want greater global consistency.

Communication becomes more complex.

Conclusions

As the case illustrates, firm conclusions on whether or not to centralise are difficult to draw. Decision making is affected by both internal and external factors: specifically macroenvironmental forces, competition, corporate objectives and cultures, resources and stakeholders.

Differences in management styles between Ford and Honda are illustrated in the case. At different times both companies have favoured decentralised strategies. It could be argued that with increased market segmentation fuelled by sociological and technological changes, at least a degree of decentralisation is desirable in today's international car market.

(b) **Introduction**

Centralisation lends itself to a global marketing strategy, whereas decentralisation is more suited to a customised marketing strategy. Dibb et al describe globalisation as treating the whole world as one single market and standardising products in the same way everywhere.

Companies attempt to standardise the marketing mix for all markets in order to gain the profit and competitive rewards attributed to globalised marketing strategies. Ford cards have been standardised and marketed in much the same way everywhere. However, not all elements of the marketing mix can easily be standardised.

Some companies have moved from customising products for a particular region in the world such as Europe, to offering globally standardised products with technological advances, extended guarantees, greater reliability and lower prices. Some Japanese car manufacturers have adopted this approach.

Dibb et al state that traditional international marketing is based on products *customised* according to cultural, regional and national differences, so that the degree of similarity among the various environmental and market conditions is what ultimately determines the feasibility of globalisation. Honda have clearly decided that Japan, Europe and the USA are sufficiently disparate to rule out the globalisation approach in favour of customised marketing strategies.

Marketing mix implications of Ford's global strategy

(i) **Product**

Each of the five vehicle centres will market the cars for which they are responsible in the same basic designs and with the same basic features across the world. In this sense product is fixed for all markets.

(ii) **Price**

This is one part of the marketing mix that is very difficult to standardise on account of such regional/country variables as taxes, import duties, currency fluctuations and other oncosts. Nevertheless Ford will endeavour to standardise price insofar as possible and particularly in such large markets as the USA and the EU.

(iii) **Place**

Distribution will be, to a large extent, standardised through the Ford dealer network worldwide. Transportation, handling and standards of preparation of the cars are all sub-elements of place that lend themselves to a large degree of uniformity.

(iv) **Promotion**

Certain elements of the promotional mix can fairly easily be standardised globally, whilst other are more difficult. Branding, corporate advertising and messages can be applied on a global basis, but media and certainly language will have to be adapted to suit regional and country markets.

Showroom layout, point-of-sale material and special offers can be standardised through appointed dealers to quite a large degree apart from language changes.

As regards personal selling, features and benefits should apply globally but campaigns based on mailshots and telemarketing are likely to need some adjustments.

PR principles can apply globally but the media and the target audiences could vary considerably between country markets.

Marketing mix implications of Honda's customised strategy

(i) **Product**

In contrast for Ford, Honda cars, whilst having much the same names around the world, are becoming less standardised – so much so that their latest generation Accord family cars differ in all three operating markets: Japan, US and Europe.

(ii) **Price**

In addition to differentiating its cars for various markets, the implication of Honda's strategy of customisation is that price will reflect individual market conditions. Factors impacting on local market prices will include economic conditions, competition and transfer pricing.

(iii) **Place**

Strategies of decentralisation and customisation also imply a propensity to vary distribution in the chosen markets. This may extend to channels other than that of dealerships, but is certainly likely to result in more dealerships and greater freedom for the dealers to maximise sales.

(iv) **Promotion**

Honda no longer needs to sing the same song for the Accord in all three of its current markets. For example, if lower prices were offered in Europe relative to the US, then the predominant message might be value; whereas if the product was made more luxurious for the US, then the quality might be emphasised to mitigate the higher price. The important point here is that the promotional messages as well as the media can be varied according to individual market factors.

The whole of the promotional mix: advertising, sales promotion, personal selling and PR, can be tailored to suit each of the Honda Accord's three markets whereas this would be unified across the three markets under a global strategy.

Conclusions

Whilst globalisation brings benefits of economies of scale and tighter control, both of which may operate favourably on profitability, sales and market share increase opportunities may be lost, which may have a compensatingly negative impact on profitability. This swings-and-roundabouts effect is leading car manufacturers like Ford and Honda to adopt dual or hybrid strategies. That is to say, they adopt as much globalisation as the market will allow and as is profitable. A term for this is **glocalisation** meaning a global strategy with local management.

Certainly, as customers become more individual, more wealthy and more demanding, and as technological advances enable smaller batches to be produced economically, we can expect a greater degree of customisation to be applied in the car market. We have already reached the point where customers can choose the colour, the engine size/type and the interior upholstery for a given marque; they can also see a virtual car of their choice on a computer screen and make adjustments to the virtual image on the screen by changing the feature mix. The next step might well involve a choice of body shapes and even greater freedom to customise your own car.

57 Air Products

Part A

1 Introduction

Good morning all. Over the next 30 minutes I would like to review for you the major differences between industrial and consumer markets and perhaps more importantly - to show how such differences might influence Air Products' marketing mix. I am quite willing to take questions during the presentation, but have allowed 15 minutes for these at the end, bearing in mind your tight schedule this morning. As you can see I am using slides and you have a handout covering the main points before you.

2 Differences between industrial and consumer markets

Industrial markets, also known as business-to-business markets, are characterised by dealing in products which are bought directly to be used in the operations of another organisation. In Air Products' case we are talking about industrial gases and associated equipment sold to food manufacturers.

The major differences between industrial and consumer markets can be classified into three main aspects.

2.1 **Market structure**

	Industrial	**Consumer**
Demand	Derived	Direct
Buying unit	Group	Individual
Geography	Concentrated	Diffuse

2.2 **Buying behaviour**

Customer mix	Small	Large
Order size	Large	Small
Order frequency	Infrequent	Frequent
Buying motives	Professional	Personal
Contractual penalties	Common	Uncommon
Buying power	Strong	Weak

2.3 **Marketing**

Approach	Relationship	Transactional

Of course there are others and there are different degrees of difference according to the particular product-market we are talking about, but in the case of Air Products we could say that the distinctive features are:

- Few, large customers hence the need to build long-term relationships through excellence in key account management
- Roles of the decision making unit/buying centre leading to the need to identify the various influencers on the purchase decision and the targeting of appropriate marketing activities towards these
- High risk/high cost purchase usually involving long-term contracts with built-in guarantees and a high degree of maintenance/after-sales service
- Constant competitor pressure highlighting the need for excellence in MkIS/ intelligence and particular vigilance in monitoring re-buy/new-buy situations
- Geographical concentration combined with relatively few large food manufacturers makes it relatively easy to identify potential new customers in Europe, the region I now intend to concentrate on

3 Implications for Air Products' marketing mix in Europe

3.1 Products/services

Linked products, ie gas and equipment, sometimes of a complex and hazardous nature give rise to a need for a high degree of service which includes technical advice, installation and testing as well as built-in maintenance and guarantees. Additionally, especially where new plant is concerned, delivery on time is critical. Conforming to European specifications is of course necessary and operating instructions need to be in appropriate languages.

3.2 Pricing

Each contract has to be individually priced and providing the specification is adhered to, the tendency for European food manufacturers is to accept the lowest bid. Often fixed-price tenders will be sought when food manufacturers are building new factories. However, value enhancement is preferred to price cutting as part of Air Products' strategy.

3.3 Promotion

Personal selling is of paramount importance, with the need for relationship management referred to above. Despite the use of key account managers, systems selling calls for a team approach involving technical and safety engineers.

Advertising in the main European food trade journals is largely of a prestige nature referring to successful contracts and designed to mitigate against the buyer fear inherent in placing large high-risk orders on a long-term basis.

Sales promotion is also important in industrial marketing. European buyers considering Air Products like to see a physical presence at the major food exhibitions ideally with working models. These can be supplemented by visits to working plants in some circumstances and the use of videos. Technical literature is of course necessary for complex equipment.

PR and publicity are important in building a strong brand image in Europe. A multi-language website is a necessary prestige builder and particularly useful for initial enquiries from the small specialist food manufacturers. Internet and email communications can also help in these initial stages prior and/or to supplement personal contacts.

Call centres are increasingly being used to handle initial/standard enquiries from smaller prospects.

Sponsorship is also a good image builder in the European region and I know that Air Products are already active in this form of promotion at various sports grounds.

Delivery on time and in good condition are essential and direct distribution is used for plant and equipment. Standard gas supplies can however be provided through distributors for the smaller accounts. It is of course necessary to maintain stocks of gas cylinders and spare parts at strategic geographical points in order to service the European region effectively.

4 Conclusions and questions

Well, ladies and gentlemen, I hope enough has been said to agree that whilst the general principles of marketing apply to both industrial and consumer goods - industrial marketing characteristics and particularly those applying to Air Products' markets in Europe are sufficiently different to warrant a distinctive approach to the marketing mix, an approach I would very much like to develop with you.

So now I would welcome your questions and comments …

Part B

1 Introduction

Thank you very much for your obvious interest in the first half of my presentation. I would like to adopt the same format for the second half which examines the likely composition of the decision-making unit (DMU) in a prospective food manufacturer in continental Europe and how each member might be persuaded to select Air Products as the preferred supplier for gases and associated equipment.

2 Likely composition of the DMU

Research has shown that in industrial markets the larger, riskier and more complex the purchase, the more likely it is to be a group decision. The numbers and types of members of the group will vary according to the particular product-market, but for a European food manufacturer considering placing a contract with Air Products, this is likely to be composed of:

2.1 **Gatekeepers**

These are essentially the people involved in the first stage of the process, ie gathering information on prospective contractors and are likely to be procurement clerks, secretaries and junior technicians, or perhaps buying agents where outside resources are being used.

Persuading gatekeepers to select Air Products to bid for a contract is a matter of ensuring they have our literature in their files; that they are continually reminded of our presence in this market by mailshots, emails, useful freebies such as files, desk diaries etc; and last but not least by personal visits supplemented by telemarketing.

2.2 **Users**

These are almost certain to be production engineers and operatives involved in the food manufacturing process. They could even be the initiators of the enquiry where existing plant has become unsatisfactory. The more democratic the company the more likely are users to influence or even decide the specification.

Persuading users towards recommending Air Products should ideally be by factory visits, technical assistance and onsite demonstrations. Word of mouth can also be a powerful influence. For production engineers rather than operatives, technical literature and invitations to exhibitions/workshops are also important.

2.3 **Influencers**

Apart from users, there are quite a number of other potential influencers in the DMU. Often forgotten are the trade unions and their European equivalents, also the hygiene and safety officers who can be consulted, particularly in our case of potentially hazardous gases and equipment. Works managers and maintenance engineers are others who clearly have an interest in the specification.

In persuading influencers, some research may be necessary through our key account managers to establish who these are and the type and degree of influence. Having done this, specially tailored letters and telephone calls can be made which focus on the particular interest held.

2.4 **Buyers**

The actual buyer/procurement manager/purchasing officer may not always be the decider but clearly care must be taken not to tread on this person's toes. In any case the buyer will be the person who actually places the order and oversees the official documentation.

The buyer should therefore be targeted as a very important person to persuade and personal contact is imperative here. The buyer may or may not be technically qualified in our sort of products so that the level of technical pitch needs to be adjusted accordingly. Third party references can be extremely persuasive when dealing with buyers for the first time, allied with invitations to exhibitions and factory tours. Videos of successful installations working, and including interviews with highly satisfied customers, can also be very effective.

2.5 **Deciders**

For our purposes there are clearly the most important members of the DMU and could be the chief buyer, senior technical engineer, a consultant, the managing director, the finance director or the production director. The greatest diplomacy needs to be exercised in finding out who will make the final decision.

Having done so, persuasion strategies need to be subtle and based upon the researched buying motives of the decider. Some form of social activity is usually employed such as a lunch, a specially convened conference, joint meetings at a senior level etc. It is quite likely that at this stage, the preliminary offer analysis will have been carried out at a lower level and the choice narrowed down to perhaps just two potential suppliers. Some efforts by the decider to negotiate terms or secure last-minute concessions can be expected, which offer opportunities to secure the contract. We should therefore plan very carefully and have some carrots to offer which are thought to be capable of persuading the decider in our favour.

3 **Conclusions and questions**

In conclusion, I should emphasise that the DMU is likely to be different in the detail for each potential contract and then not always fixed for a given contract. For example new European regulations can apply or funding difficulties arise which alter the circumstances and composition of the DMU.

We do therefore need to be extremely well informed and flexible in our approach.

We have about 5 minutes left, so are there any more questions or comments, please?

58 ICI Dulux Trade Paints

Examiner's comments. The SWOT analysis was generally reasonably answered, with evidence of understanding of internal and external factors. There was some confusion over the components of the audit. The best answers achieved the following:

- Intelligent application of the case situation
- Coverage of macro, micro and internal dimensions
- Summarised all into a SWOT analysis

(a)

To: The Marketing Manager, Dulux Trade Paints
From: Marketing Consultant
Subject: Marketing audits and the SWOT analysis

1 **Introduction**

Following your recent briefing, I am pleased to advise on the aspects of a marketing audit that your Senior Brand manager should monitor and to explain how these factors may be logically summarised in a SWOT analysis, prior to developing a brand marketing plan.

A marketing audit is a comprehensive, systematic, independent and periodic examination of a company's - or a business unit's - marketing environment, objectives, strategies and activities with a view to determining problem areas and opportunities and recommending a plan of action to improve the company's marketing performance (*Kotler*).

The audit should cover three major areas - the macro environment, the micro environment and the internal environment as follows.

2.1 **Macro environment**

Changes in the world at large or the macro environment will inevitably eventually affect all companies and should therefore be continuously monitored. A good framework for this audit is PESTLE: Political, Economic, Sociological, Technological, Legal, (Green) Environment.

For example, local governments set and change regulations covering the paint protection of street furniture decoration of council houses. Certain ingredients may not be permitted on anti-pollution grounds whereas others may be technological improvements affording greater corrosion protection. Social changes in tastes and fashions give rise to demand for new ways to enhance aesthetics and as you know, for paint products offering special effects.

2.2 **Micro environment**

This is the operating environment and includes customers, competitors, suppliers, distributors and the public at large.

Some customer segments may be more receptive than others to new products in general and special effects products in particular. During our briefing, you mentioned professional specifiers - within these some will be more innovative than others and therefore more receptive to the Dulux special effects brand. It might therefore pay dividends for your Senior Brand Manager to identify these subsegments and monitor their sizes and growth trends with a view to targeting these, rather than less promising groups such as general independent home decorators. The key is to win over the opinion leaders first and the rest will follow.

Obviously a close watch needs to be maintained on competitors like *Crown* and *Polyvine* so that retaliatory action can be taken as appropriate.

Some distributors will welcome special effects products more than others and be willing to cooperate in displays and instore demonstrations. Concentrating on these should result in better returns on the brand investment.

Distribution channels also need to be monitored for changes in brand shares, number of outlets, consolidation and so on, in order to retain control of the market situation and be one step ahead of the competition.

2.3 **Internal environment**

This breaks down into five sub-audits.

2.3.1 **The marketing strategy audit**

The Senior Brand Manager needs to audit past and present brand objectives and strategies to ensure that these are in tune with the external environmental changes. Questions such as - How is the brand positioned in the marketplace relative to competitors? And - Are we targeting the right segments with the right messages? - should be addressed at regular intervals.

2.3.2 **The marketing organisation audit**

'Structure should follow strategy'. Do we have the structural capability to implement the strategies needed for success? To what extent do we need to regroup, recruit and/or retrain staff?

Without frequent monitoring of the organisational aspects and appropriate actions, Dulux are likely to find strategies are not being implemented effectively and objectives are not being achieved.

2.3.3 The marketing systems audit

This generally breaks down into information, planning, control and new product development systems, the latter being particularly relevant in this context. Having developed these new products, do we have systems in place to modify these and to go on producing future winners?

To what extent are our computer systems up to data and able to cope with developments such as e-tailing?

2.3.4 The marketing productivity audit

This looks at the profitability of the marketing programme and the cost-effectiveness of marketing expenditure.

2.3.5 The marketing functions audit

This evaluates each element of the marketing mix individually and then as an integrated whole. It established the objectives of each element and the extent to which it is in harmony with other elements. For example to what extent are people to pay a premium price for special effects and will they expect to find these only in upmarket outlets?

3 The SWOT analysis

The data from the marketing audits proposed above can be conveniently categorised into strengths, weaknesses, opportunities and threats. Generally speaking opportunities and threats emanate from outside the company; from events out the company's control. For example competition is nearly always a threat, whilst technological breakthroughs can represent either an opportunity or a threat, depending upon the situation.

By contrast, strengths and weaknesses are inherent in the company itself and within the company's control. A strength could be the brand and a weakness, a lack of effective market segmentation.

Major strengths

An established and respected umbrella brand name
Intensive distribution
Technical expertise

Major weaknesses

High prices
Viewed as overlarge and impersonal
Confused product line branding

Major opportunities

E-tailing
Demand for differentiation
The EU - increased specification and higher environmental standards

Major threats

Changes in fashion, eg minimalism
Crown's Colourfects brand relaunch
Economic depression

> *Examiner's comments.* The better answers took their lead from the word 'brand' and brought in competitive advantage, target markets and brand positioning. The lowest marks were awarded when there was only a tactical plan on offer and no consideration of the business-to-business context.

(b) **Report - Marketing strategic and tactical plan**

1 **Introduction**

The SWOT analysis acts as a blueprint for the marketing plan in that actions can be taken to correct weaknesses, avoid threats, exploit strengths and opportunities.

The marketing audits and SWOT analysis lead naturally on to the drawing up of a brand marketing plan for the next three years as illustrated in the following process.

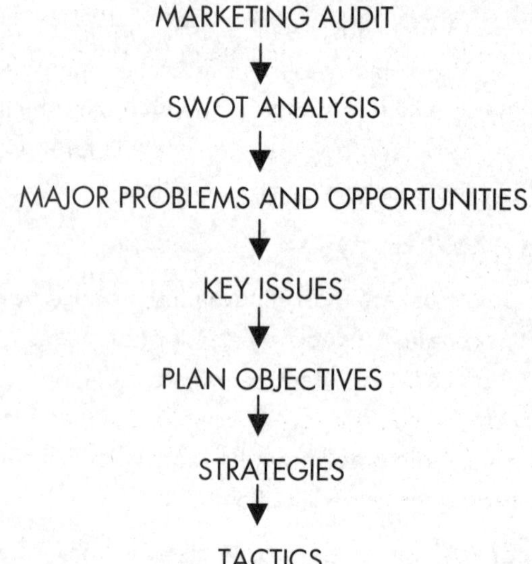

Whilst you and your senior brand manager are of course extremely familiar with the mechanics of marketing planning, you did brief me to put forward some ideas on strategy and tactics.

2 **Marketing strategy for the brand**

2.1 **Background**

The opportunity arose from a dramatic growth in the popularity of broken colour decorative paint effects stimulated by publicity in the media, including home improvement programmes on TV. Research shows that this new demand has not yet peaked and is likely to increase for the next 3 years albeit at a slower rate. Dulux Trade Paints overall objective is to secure as large a share of this market as possible, consistent with achieving the statutory minimum return on capital employed.

As predicted by the PLC model, the stage of increased competition has been reached with new entrants into this lucrative market segment, among them Crown and Polyvine. Whilst the trendsetters have been convinced, there are still some early adopters worth targeting.

2.2 **Segmentation, targeting and positioning strategies**

Subject to research confirmation, the largest potential market segment consists of homeowners and specifiers. Within this is the DIY subsegment which can be targeted directly, but the other subsegment is those aspiring home owners who can be influenced by (and also influence) their decorators.

The consumer profile is likely to be young, aware, ambitious, social and wanting to stand out from the crowd; keen to impress their friends and possessing a higher than average disposable income. The consumer is also likely to have a working partner, no children and be short of time.

Positioning has to be top of its class; highly differentiated if not unique; recommended by professionals, and premium priced.

2.3 **Porter's generic strategies**

These would be differentiation and focus. Differentiation is inherent in the product features but will be enhanced by the benefits emphasised in the brand image. Focus would be on the niche segment outlined above.

2.4 **Brand values**

Rational brand values would include unique end results, professional finish, design superiority, second to none technical advice and support.

Emotional brand values would include progressive, modern partnership, admiration of friends, self expression, environmental enhancement.

3 **Tactical plan**

3.1 **Product**

The current range to be retained but new effects such as metallics, mother of pearl and slate. Packaging to be revamped to give more on-tin impact.

3.2 **Pricing**

Premium pricing policy to be retained. Competitive pricing to be used only when products are similar and in special circumstances such as trade sampling.

3.3 **Place**

The existing channels to continue, but a feasibility study to be conducted on e-tailing direct to consumers and home decorators.

3.4 **Promotion**

The major new initiative here to be the setting up of special websites using the Dulux portal which walk visitors round the special effects range in various settings; offer advice and training for both consumers and home decorators, and facilitate the ordering of sample kits. General public visitors to the website would be able to locate a list of experienced special effects decorators in their region and all visitors would be able to interrogate an online panel with questions.

The overall promotion strategy would be to pull demand through home owners whilst pushing demand through the decorators and the retail trade. part of the pull approach would be a determined effort to obtain more TV and radio bites featuring the Dulux special effects brand. Part of the push approach would be the provision to home decorators of a promotional video to show to interested home owners.

The promotional campaign would be further supported by a series of regional exhibitions and sampling events, particularly at summer fetes and the like.

4 **Conclusion**

This report has endeavoured to highlight the importance of the marketing audit and to show how it can be transformed into a SWOT analysis, to form the basis of a brand marketing plan.

For maximum effectiveness, the SWOT needs to be prioritised (not all weaknesses are of the same weight or importance). I have some experience of applying Kotler's approach to prioritisation which I should be pleased to put at your disposal. You might also wish me to talk over some of the strategic/ tactical ideas broached above, with your Senior Brand Manager.

59 Volvo cars

> *Examiner's comments.* On the whole this question on promotional practice was well answered. A common mistake was to misinterpret the question, often including threats (which were not asked for). Excellent answers provided a detailed discussion of the pros and cons of the link between Volvo and CNN.

(a)

To: Senior Vice President for Marketing
From: Marketing Consultant
Subject: Programme Sponsorship Evaluation

1 **Introduction**

Volvo sponsor the CNN music programme 'World Beat', aired weekly to more than 213 million households.

Volvo's commercial branding on this programme includes opening and closing credits, programme break bumpers, spot advertising and Volvo branded vignettes. There is also an online version available, with Volvo as the sole partner and car advertiser.

2 **Programme sponsorship as a communicator of brand values**

Coulson-Thomas highlights that 'Sponsorship can put a name across and promote an image'. *Dibb et al* define it thus – 'Sponsorship is the financial or material support of an event, activity, person, organisation or product by an unrelated organisation or donor'. They go on to state that the popularity of corporate sponsorship has grown dramatically and point to Volvo's involvement with tennis as an example. In exchange for the sponsorship, the sponsor receives exposure of its name or brands. Sponsorship forms part of the promotional mix within the elements of the marketing mix.

2.1 **Strengths**

- An organisation's target audiences can be communicated with through sponsorship
- Sponsorship allows integration of the promotion and product elements of the marketing mix as it develops and reinforces brand values, for example through the Internet link and the advertising vignettes.
- The Volvo brand name is an acknowledged world wide symbol for safe, high quality vehicles. By collaborating with a global media company such as CNN, Volvo should be able to maintain and develop this solid, consistent image.
- Music is a big part of many people's lives

- It is very cost-effective in terms of reaching the target audience on a regular basis
- It increases awareness of the Volvo brand
- Image enhancement in terms of upbeat and global programme positioning
- An additional benefit can be to raise the morale of Volvo's employees by association with a modern and global promotion
- Being the sole car advertiser means that there are no competing brand messages

2.2 Weaknesses

- Sponsorship effectiveness can be measured by looking at either sales or communications effects on the target audiences. However, sales effects are much harder to measure as sponsorship is more concerned with long-term brand or corporate image development
- If the sponsorship programme is poorly produced or unsuccessful, this could have a negative effect
- Over time, viewing figures may be lower then predicted as audiences seek new forms of entertainment
- Upbeat entertainment may detract from the more traditional, safety brand values
- The mix of music types may make a clear positioning difficult to achieve

2.3 Opportunities

- Improved relationships with different publics
- Increased sales (audience of more than 213 million households)
- Sampling (test drives or on-line interactive experiences)
- Database building through appointment viewing
- Creative opportunities including the engagement of an audience in a relaxed atmosphere of goodwill
- Greater media exposure eg radio links
- Public relations spin-offs
- Sales promotion links with music industry and top-ten albums eg in-car radio/stereo

3 Conclusions

Sponsorship can prove to be a very cost-effective promotional tool, especially good for awareness raising and building image. It is most effective when integrated firstly with brand strategy and secondly with associated advertising, sales promotion, direct marketing and public relations activities, and with the overall marketing mix.

(b)

Examiner's comments. There was a suggested answer structure in this question, but it was handled less well. The best candidates referred to the strategic importance of relationship management and placed their answers firmly in the context of car dealerships with some examples of retention initiatives. Poorer answers focused on the marketing mix and standard responses about acquisition activities, thus missing the point of the question.

To: Senior Vice President for Marketing
From: Marketing Consultant
Subject: Corporation Customer Retention Plan for a Volvo Dealership

1 **Introduction**

The local dealerships need to be supplied with details of Volvo's corporate clients, including their particular needs and key evaluation criteria. Any opportunities to tailor the offering pre and post sale should be communicated by the Area Manager to the Dealer Principal.

The Area Manager should develop a number of initiatives with the Dealer Principal following a full analysis of the dealership's strengths, weaknesses, opportunities and threats.

2 **Objectives**

The core philosophy behind customer satisfaction is relationship building. A Volvo dealership should fervently promote the idea that it will go out of its way to meet Volvo owners' needs, whether that means despatching shuttles for service calls, providing courtesy cars, or personalising service consultation. Specific targets should be set for:

- 100% achievement of 'good' rating on all aspects of pre and post servicing aspects or an immediate follow-up call to assess why the dealership fell below this level
- 75% achievement of 'very good' rating on all aspects of pre and post servicing
- 100% repeat servicing business on lifetime of fleet cars or a follow-up call to assess why the client has not booked a service with the dealership

3 **Relationship marketing mix**

3.1 **Product/services**

- Courtesy car wash
- Service details
- Volvo merchandise range
- Courtesy cars and shuttle services
- Pick-up and deliver to home

3.2 **Place/physical evidence**

- Business office or quiet room
- Children's play area with mini Volvo cars
- Coffee and drinks machines
- Product details and displays
- Television
- Toilets with baby changing facilities
- Consistent dealership layouts

3.3 **Promotion/communications**

- Sales and service departments to constantly monitor work by the use of business reply cards, questionnaires, and follow-up telephone calls
- Business newsletter that will include bonus coupons, service tips and sales information
- Feedback and customer letters posted in a presentation, loose-leaf and leather-bound binder in the main showroom
- Corporate client loyalty scheme

3.4 **Price**

- Discounts on private sales and servicing through loyalty scheme
- Invoices directly to corporate head office

3.5 **People**

- Volvo dealership dress code
- Dedicated account managers for each customer

4 **Implementation**

A series of support measures needs to be implemented in addition to the marketing mix in order to realise the full potential of the corporate customer retention plan.

- Customer care training programme
- Employee incentive scheme – for highest satisfaction scores for dealerships, and 'most improved' competitions with suitable rewards
- Selection and appointment of corporate customer account managers
- Establishment of corporate clients' needs with regard to internal communications including details of Oncore and Care programme changes
- Dealer principals to attend at conferences to encourage full take-up and enthusiasm for the philosophy of customer retention initiatives
- Suggestion scheme for improvements to the programme
- Setting of appropriate targets, control mechanisms and budgets

5 **Conclusions**

A properly formulated plan is essential to the achievement of Volvo's core philosophy behind customer satisfaction – that of relationship building.

It is also proposed that the plans proposed by the area managers are approved by their immediate superiors and reviewed at quarterly intervals.

60 The BBC goes digital

(a) Report: UK Government
From: Marketing Consultant
Subject: Environmental challenges and not-for-profit constraints for the BBC

1 **Introduction**

The future launch of new digital services, recently announced by the BBC is crucial to its survival as a licence=charging, publicly accountable body. Fortunately, this initiative has been predicted on extensive and independent public consultation.

Nevertheless, in conducting this launch, the BBC faces a number of challenges from its marketing environment, not the least of which is fierce competition, and in doing so is handicapped by the constraints which affect not-for-profit organisations, particularly those which are publicly accountable.

2 Challenges in the marketing environment

2.1 Macro Environment

The framework adopted here is PESTLE standing for Political, Economic, Sociological, Technological, Legal and (Green) Environmental factors. A certain degree of overlap is however, inherent.

2.1.1 *Political*

The present government has made the improvement of public services its main priority for the current term and its re-election will depend on the extent to which this is seen to be accomplished by the voting public. Politics is involved in the selection of the BBC's Director General and its governors. Strong pressures can be expected both from the Government and the Opposition and possibly from the EC depending on the amount of political integration which takes place.

2.1.2 *Economic*

There is a range of economic factors which affect the demand for and diffusion of digital technology, not the least of which is affordability by the target market. This will in turn be affected by the forthcoming budgets; the price of housing; the cost of financing and so on. Economic slowdown affects people's propensity to invest in new technology applications.

2.1.3 *Sociological*

People's cultural interests change and with them their TV viewing and radio listening habits. Education also plays an important part, which in itself is undergoing radical overhaul. The new BBC 4 and Playbox channels face challenges from other alternatives such as the Internet and outdoor pursuits. Also there is the challenge of demographic change which is reflected in the provision of special radio programmes for black and Asian audiences. There are also moral and social responsibility issues involved here.

2.1.4 *Technological*

Mention has already been made of alternative technologies such as the Internet and the cost-benefit challenges. Further challenges arise from the pace of technological change in this market. We have, for example witnessed the evolution of broadcast music from vinyl records to tapes to CDs to videos, and now to digital CDs. Inevitably further technological progress will challenge the BBC's new channels.

2.1.5 *Legal*

A great deal of legal challenge can arise in the way of patents, intellectual property rights and the interpretation of its charter, which can work to negate the BBC's initiatives, not only in the provision of channels, but also in their development and content. The new Children's B provision for 6-13 year olds will be particularly sensitive to the censorship regulations.

2.1.6 *(Green) Environmental*

The viewing and listening publics are increasingly concerned with green issues and a variety of protecting organisations have developed in this context. There are for example concerns over the potentially harmful effects of radio waves; on the damage that might arise from overuse of mobile phones and over-exposure to TV monitors.

2.2 **Macro Environment**

2.2.1 *Competition*

This is by far the BBC's biggest challenge with fierce competition from other national and global commercial broadcasters using new and old technologies such as BskyB, ITV digital, Discovery, Virgin, TalkSport, with (no doubt) others to emerge. It needs to be recognised that the financial and political power of large multinational broadcasters affords them some advantage and this is compounded by the constraints that the BBC has to work under. Applying Porter's 5 forces model, we have already seen that competition is fierce and rising. The threat of new entrants is also quite high, since the capital costs of entry and the barriers are relatively low. The threat of alternative or substitute products is clearly high. The power of suppliers is substantial as they are not reliant upon the BBC and can sell to higher bidders as in the case of football in particular and sport in general. The power of buyers in the form of the general public seems intrinsically low but measured in terms of viewership/listenership ratings is conversely high.

2.2.2 *Customers*

Fortunately for the BBC, patterns of consumer behaviour change relatively slowly. The BBC is, after all, known as Auntie and has a nucleus of loyal customers. Nevertheless this nucleus is ageing and younger consumers are less loyal. The market in common with others is fragmenting.

Being essentially a public body, the BBC has a wide variety of publics, which include the Government, the Opposition, the Ombudsman and other watchdogs, the Arts Council and other vested interests. It is very difficult to please all of these customers all of the time.

3 **Not-for-profit (NFP) constraints**

As intimated above, there are a number of constraints on all NFP organisations which do not necessarily apply to their commercially oriented competitors.

3.1 *Stakeholders*

NFP organisations like the BBC have a wider variety of stakeholders than their commercial counterparts. In addition to the target audiences and obvious stakeholder groups such as employees and Governors, the BBC has the general public, the Government, the Opposition, watchdogs and regulatory bodies. This can give rise to conflicting objectives and certainly constrains decision taking.

3.2 *Financing and budgets*

Budgetary constraints are a serious limitation when trying to compete with private sector, which has open access to funding facilities and can increase budgets more easily and with less bureaucracy. The costs of marketing have to be justified.

3.3 *Transparency*

The BBC along with other NFP public bodies have to be much more open about its strategies than private sector profit-orientated competitors. Secrecy is more difficult to maintain and this makes them more vulnerable to competitor reactions.

3.4 *Quality*

The BBC cannot lower quality without a chorus of complaints from a host of ever-watchful critics. Its programmes are reviewed daily as a matter of routine by various media. It also has to be seen to give fair play to competing interests, such as the amount of time and scheduling devoted to political party broadcasts.

3.5 *Ethics and Social Responsibility*

It almost goes without saying that the BBC has to exercise a great deal of responsibility and discretion in deciding which topics to air, which programmes to sponsor and what they should contain, particularly where children's programmes are concerned. The commercial channels do not suffer from these constraints to the same degree and indeed are almost expected to exercise more latitude.

3.6 *Service Marketing and Expertise*

The BBC's products mostly lie at the intangible-dominant end of the product-service spectrum although there are some tangible offshoots such as videotapes and literature. Service marketing is acknowledged to be more difficult than that required for pure products. Compounding this constraint is a relative lack of expertise compared with the profit-oriented private sector, caused by the BBC being unable to offer competitive remuneration packages.

3.7 *Bureaucracy*

As for most public sector bodies, the BBC is constrained by bureaucratic, procedure-driven structures and policies, making it slow to respond to market changes.

(b) 4 **Approach for the further development of the new channel BBC4**

4.1 *Introduction*

Public consultation, although commendable, is not sufficient in itself, nor can it be regarded as a substitute for rigorous new product development (NPD) procedures. It is unclear how the screening of ideas is conducted. There is a need to adopt a more structured approach to NPD and to pursue further stages after the initial formulation of the concept and some concept testing. The NPD process generally used for products can be applied to BBC4 as follows.

4.2 *Statement of the NPD strategy*

The BBC needs to be clear as to what it wants to achieve from the launch of BBC4. How will it contribute to overall objectives and what position it will occupy in the product portfolio? The current segmentation/positioning is unclear in aiming at 'everyone interested in culture, arts and ideas. Surely this will subsume viewers of other intended channels such as BBC3's 16 to 34 year old and the 'young at heart'? The extent to which overlap and substitution will cause wastage needs to be more thoroughly investigated. More specific positioning statements and maps need to take into account the offerings of the BBC's competitors.

4.3 *Ideas generation and initial screening*

Whilst a start has been made on these parts of the process, they are iterative as the propositions develop and are fine-tuned. For example what proportions of BBC4's airtime should be devoted to culture as opposed to arts as opposed to ideas and what forms should the contents take?

4.4 *Concept development and testing*

After the concepts have been more fully developed, they should be tested on a representative sample of the target audience. This can be done either symbolically or physically. Since about half of all UK households are now connected to the Internet, virtual programmes could be shown and viewers interrogated on the Net. Alternatively the existing channel rating mechanisms and respondents could be employed.

4.5 *Development of the marketing strategy/business analysis*

Initial viewer targets, promotional strategy, outline marcoms plan and budgets, competitor response forecasts, confirmation of feasibility, further product development as necessary.

4.6 *Market Testing*

Consider text marketing on a regional basis and/or conduct further research on the finalised proposition.

4.7 *Commercialisation and Launch*

Launch BBC4 according to the following outline plan.

5 Outline launch plan for BBC4

5.1 *Situational Analysis*

The BBC is taking up the challenge of digital technology in order to improve its service to identified target groups. Parts of this initiative is the launch of the new channel BBC4 as detailed above and refined by the NPD process recommended.

SWOT analysis

STRENGTHS

- Good reputation
- Quality products
- Loyal viewers
- Government support
- Licence income
- Dedicated staff
- BBC brand

WEAKNESSES

- Lack of adequate funding
- Fragmentation of decision taking
- Other constraints as in 3. above

OPPORTUNITIES

- To establish the BBC as a leading innovator in digital broadcasting
- Withdrawal of franchise
- Anti-BBC elements in the establishment

5.2 *Objectives*

- To gain a 90% trial of BBC4 by the target audience within the first 6 weeks of transmission

- To achieve a 60% retention of trial viewers, measured by repeat viewing (minimum 2 programs weekly)
- To become market leader in terms of TV ratings in this target segment

5.3 *Strategies*

- Porter's Differentiation
- Ansoff's NPD
- Boston's question Mark
- Branding = BBC4 under the umbrella of BBC
- Segmentation/Targeting 'Everyone interested in culture, arts and ideas'. Demographic, geographic psychographic and lifestyle variables as established by further research
- Positioning – BBC4 as the flagship of the BBC – intellectual and sensual stimulation for all

5.4 *Marketing Mix*

This will be based upon the 7Ps for services marketing:

PRODUCT

The range of programmes will be extremely broad-based and flexible so as to take in topical events. It will of course include music, dancing, painting, literature etc plus ideas on improving the environment.

PRICE

Costs will have to maintained within existing budgets initially but there may well be sponsorships available later, together with a possibility of pay slots for special programmes.

PLACE

Initially the UK but eventually global.

PROCESS

BBC4 will be produced and disseminated by existing processes modified by NPD as detailed above.

PEOPLE

Existing staff co-opted for dedication to BBC4 plus outside agencies and creative consultants. Panels representing the general public.

PHYSICAL EVIDENCE

As existing but supplemented by special promotional tangibles –see below.

PROMOTION

Heavy advertising on existing TV and radio channels. Media publicity releases, general press and targeted media for cultural aware. Special website. Poster campaigns. Selected celebrity support including the Prime Minister. Sponsorship of mailshots and other campaigns by organisations with a vested interest in culture and the arts.

IMPLEMENTATION/BUDGETS

An action schedule to be drawn up detailing action items, dates, people responsible and the resource implications.

CONTROLS

Research feedback as in 4 above. Monitoring of trial viewing and repeat viewing figures and of complaints/suggestions. Qualitative performance indicators - viewer panels etc. Competitor response forecasting and monitoring.

CONTINGENCIES

Plans to be drawn up to counter competitor response and to initiate emergency action in the event of poor viewer ratings.

61 Reebok International

Report to: The Board, Reebok Retail Development
From: Advisor
Subjects: (a) Types and sources of information for European markets assessments
(b) Proposed outline marketing plan for German market

Part (a)

1 **Introduction**

Information is the starting point of any international marketing plan. It feeds into market selection decisions; then supports market entry mode decisions; finally advising on the best marketing mix for the target markets selected in light of the existing competition.

European markets outside the UK are many, varied and proliferating with the expansion of the EU. It would be unwise to assume that the successful formula developed for the UK will apply equally well to any other European market, there being differences in culture, consumer buying behaviour, language, currency and economics.

Bearing in mind the importance, cost and risk factors of these decisions, the information gathered should be assessed for reliability and timeliness.

2 **Types of information**

2.1 Preliminary screening of market potential

- Political, economic, sociological, technological, legal and environmental factors impacting upon the markets
- Competition, customer base and buying behaviour
- Size, age structure and composition of the population
- GDP, disposable income distribution, ability to buy, economic growth potential
- Accessibility – barriers on trading/distribution, infrastructure
- Consumer attitudes to fashion/sport/lifestyles/social responsibility, global brands
- Cultural compatibility with brand and clothing ranges, effects of climate and geography
- Initial assessment of profit potential (market prices compared with costs)

2.2 Detailed analysis of market potential

- Market access – tariffs, regulations, codes of law/conduct, taxation, planning regulations
- Product potential –customer segments, competitive strengths/weaknesses, suppliers of supporting services/products
- Other potential barriers – trade unions, prevalence of shoplifting/vandalism/burglary/arson

2.3 Detailed analysis of company sales and profit potentials

- Sales volume forecasting, similar indigenous retail outlets assessments
- Costings – landed costs, internal distribution/storage, slippage, maintenance, returns, staffing price levels, credit practices, exchange rates, promotional pricing etc.

3 **Sources of information**

3.1 Initial desk research on secondary/published sources

- Online search engines and websites
- Other desk research into government published statistics – economic, consumer expenditure, population and so on
- Acquisition of commercial export marketing research reports and syndicated surveys
- International institution reports (OECD, EU, UN, IMF)
- Consultants (EIU), trade associations, banks
- Sports and other media articles/reports

3.2 Followed by primary research

- Overseas trade missions
- Interviews with government bodies
- Customer research into cultural factors – brand awareness/image, preferred store layout, buying intentions, concept testing and so on
- Observational research into competitors' merchandising techniques and reactive behaviours
- Country-based specialist research agencies (eg focus groups, face-to-face interviews) for merchandise ranging insights, styles, colours etc and test marketing
- Geodemographical studies into prime retail sites

Part (b)

1 **Introduction**

The acquisition of information as specified above would be pre-requisite to the determination of the actual detailed marketing plan. It is appreciated that Reebok have considerable in-house research resources and may wish to use these to the utmost in preference to agencies, so as to maintain confidentiality and minimise costs.

The following outline plan for the launch of a chain of Reebok stores in Germany, is therefore tentative and although based on some initial research, assumes positive outcomes from the more detailed enquiries outlined above.

2 Situation analysis

2.1 *External*

The PESTLE factors for Germany are overall as good, if not better than other developed European markets such as France. The political situation is likely to become more stabilised after the forthcoming elections; English is widely spoken; enthusiasm for sports and fitness is high; quality is prized, disposable income is likely to grow and there is a strong buy-in to the social responsibility policies which are now an established feature of Reebok's corporate strategy.

Competition will of course be fierce, but no more so than in the USA and the UK – and confidence can be had in Reebok's competitive advantages – see 2.2 below. A 5 forces analysis indicates that the power of suppliers will be very low; the risks of substitutes fairly negligible; barriers to new entrants are low, competitive rivalry is no stronger in Germany than other European markets such as Italy; but the power of buyers is high.

2.2 *Internal*

Reebok has a high degree of brand equity and values which constitute considerable competitive advantage. It has established itself as a socially responsible company. Unlike some of its competitors, it sees itself as a brand that is honest and human, and being about fun and enjoyment.

To the above strengths should be added a skilled and dedicated management team which is innovative – witness the forthcoming introduction of the interactive console to facilitate customer access to merchandise variety details.

3 Objectives

To successfully launch a chain of stand alone retail stores in Germany, the quantity and timings to be established on the basis of further research. However, the opening of a test store in Munich is projected to take place within the next 12 months, leading to a minimum of 12 stores within the next 5 years.

Sales/profit and market share objectives will be based upon the results of the first flagship store in the UK due to be opened shortly.

4 Marketing strategies

Reebok will adopt strategies appropriate for a market challenger, attacking the current market leaders. The market life cycle position in Germany is that of growth but approaching maturity. A GE matrix analysis (market attractiveness versus company capabilities) confirms that Reebok's growth strategy of market development in Germany is the right one.

The target market having been selected from the European segments, the German market itself now needs segmenting based not only on the usual demographic factors, but also on consumer attitudes to foreign entrants; social responsibilities; lifestyles; environment; and particularly on the heavy users of sports clothing.

Reebok's successful brand positioning should be maintained for Germany.

5 Retail marketing mix

5.1 *Merchandise*

The current range to be maintained but adjusted to suit German sizes, colour tastes and so on. Packaging to be environmentally friendly and biodegradable where possible.

5.2 *Store location and layout*

In Munich in the city centre at a site popular with both the citizenry and tourists. Décor and in-store atmosphere to project the Venus Williams image consistent with style and fashion.

5.3 *People*

Staff uniform to be in accordance with the above store ambience ie 'Reebokised' but modified in accordance with German tastes. Appropriate training will be needed.

5.4 *Process*

Store traffic inducement system as defined by research and built around the new interactive console. Customer enquiry system to have a manual alternative. Order processing to be standard, modified to the Euro and adjusted to allow for a greater incidence of cash transactions in accordance with German culture.

5.5 *Physical evidence*

This will be a function of the store ambience and particularly of the window displays, staff demeanour, cleanliness, logical layout and so on.

5.6 *Price*

Based on value and distinctiveness and expressed in Euros. Store management discretion to be exercised with regard to competitive pricing and promotions, subject to Boston guidelines.

5.7 *Promotion*

Major elements of the promotional mix will be sponsorships arranged through headquarters and a PR programme appropriate for the German market contracted out to a German agency. There will be advertising in the Munich media; in poster sites and in media used by visitors, as identified in the research programme.

Fascias and windows will feature prominently in promoting Reebok's wares. There will of course be a continuing programme of in-store promotions, merchandising displays and so on.

Staff will be trained in appropriate sales techniques.

Direct mailshots will play an important part in the initial pre-store opening, publicity campaigns. Although not yet a prominent medium for the German public, the Munich store will have its own website which will feature other stores as they are opened.

6 Budgets

It is anticipated that the programme for the Munich store and its followers in Germany will cost approximately the same as the programme for the UK chain plus an inflation rate of 3%.

7 Implementation

The Munich store is targeted to open in May 2003 with subsequent openings at the rate of 2/3 per year to 2006. This schedule could be accelerated depending upon the test store results and resource allocations. A special market development team will be dedicated for this purpose by HQ, but this will draw heavily upon the experience and staff of the team already chosen to develop the UK chain.

8 **Controls and contingencies**

Critical path analysis will be the main control for the opening of the Munich and other new stores. Once opened, the Munich store will operate to the budgets laid down, plus a contingency of 8%. Sales, costs and profit targets will be as defined by the research but eventually benchmarked to the best European performer, with appropriate incentives for all staff.

Should the Munich store fail to produce the minimum results laid down after 6 months despite having used the 8% contingency resource, then an exit plan (already in existence for all stores) will be invoked.

Conclusion

I would be pleased to receive the board's comments and suggestions and to answer any queries resulting from this initial report.

62 Derby Cycle Corporation

Report to: The DCC Managing Director
From: Marketing Consultant
Date: 5 December 200X

(a) **Components of the DCC marketing plan**

1 **Corporate mission/objectives**

The mission statement clarifies for DCC stakeholders what business we are in; what are our aspirations/aims and what are our ethical/societal responsibilities. It confers upon our stakeholders a shared sense of purpose, direction and opportunity (Kotler).

DCC's corporate objectives will convert this generalised mission into more specific objectives of profitable growth for the planning period in question, ideally quantified and time-scaled. These define the overall objectives for all functional plans including the marketing plan.

2 **The marketing audit**

This consists of three main elements – the external macro environment, the external micro environment and the internal audit.

The macro environmental audit covers what are known as PESTLE factors, namely **P**olitical, **E**conomic, **S**ociological, **T**echnological, **L**egal and (green) **E**nvironment.

The micro environmental audit covers customers, competitors, suppliers and distributors.

The internal audit evaluates our company's marketing performance under the five headings of the marketing – strategy/organisation/systems/productivity/functions.

All these audits can be summarised into the so-called SWOT analysis which categorises the internal factors into **S**trengths and **W**eaknesses and the external factors into **O**pportunities and **T**hreats, so as to form the basis of the DCC marketing plan.

3 **Business and marketing objectives**

Whilst the overall DCC corporate objective might be profitable growth (quantified and time-scaled), this could be broken down into the business (or functional) objectives of lower production costs, fewer staff, a more profitable product mix and so on. Marketing objectives for DCC are likely to be expressed in terms of specific increases in sales/market share/customer satisfaction for the next three years.

4 **Marketing strategies**

There is a wide range of models which can be used to help decide marketing strategy for DCC. Among these, probably the most helpful would be Porter's generics, Ansoff's growth strategies and Segmentation/Targeting/Positioning strategies.

Porter suggests that we choose from one of three generic strategies or risk being 'stuck in the middle'. Probably the best Porter strategy for DCC would be focused differentiation, to enable us to focus on the UK, Europe and the USA with the Diamondback youth imagery.

Ansoff offers four basic growth strategies with increasing levels of risk, namely existing products for existing markets; existing products for new markets; new products for existing markets; and new products for new markets.

Clearly DCC are into new products with the Diamondback, accessories and apparel and are seeking to expand existing markets in the US and EU via acquisition.

With regard to segmentation, the market segments into the different needs of young and old. DCC are targeting the youth segment and will position the Diamondback brand to be more modern and exciting than its competitors.

5 **Marketing tactics**

These are the detailed ways in which the strategies can be implemented using the extended marketing mix elements of the 7Ps – standing for **P**roducts, **P**rice, **P**romotion, **P**lace (distribution), **P**eople, **P**hysical Evidence and **P**rocess. The last three of these apply to services rather than to products but as DCC have elements of service in its customer offering, these have been included here for completeness.

6 **Marketing budgets**

Costs will be involved in implementing the above strategies and tactics. In the case of DCC there will be considerable product development and promotional costs, to which must be added budgets for marketing research to test marketing objectives set.

7 **Implementation, monitoring and control**

No plan is complete without an action plan, scheduling action items and allocating responsibilities. Progress against this and the marketing objectives set must be monitored at at least monthly intervals and corrective action taken where necessary. Contingency plans need to be drawn up to cover large deviations from the objectives set caused by unforeseen events such as competitor response or big upsurges/downturns in the market.

(b) **Main challenges in the marketing environment and limitations of information**

The macro and micro environmental factors have been identified and explained in 2 above. The main challenges emerging from these that are likely to impact on the Raleigh and Diamondback brands over the next two years are as follows:

Macro

Political factors will represent a challenge for all companies including DCC. The increasing regulation/harmonisation of standards by the EU will affect product development of the two brands.

Economic factors impacting are of course the income levels and interest rates in the target markets over the next two years.

Sociological factors will include attitudes of publics in the target markets towards bicycles as an alternative mode of transport and a means of leisure/exercise.

Technological factors will continuously affect product development of the two brands as, for example, lighter-weight and stronger metal alloys are developed, together with recent micro and nano technology breakthroughs. Other important aspects here are increased computerisation and worldwide use of the Internet.

Legal factors representing a challenge for these brands will be the increasing concern for health and safety and the ensuing plethora of regulations. The current vogue for claiming compensation for accidents must also be an increasing concern for the faster (more dangerous) Diamondback brand.

Environmental (green) factors are likely to impact favourably on these two brands which are seen as being 'anti-pollutionist' in nature. The challenge will be to make the most of this favourable positioning in the brands' communications mixes.

Micro

Customers will become even better informed and choosy over the next two years, also more influenced by celebrities' endorsements and the green issues. They are also more likely to become more computer literate and users of websites.

Competitors will be more numerous and aggressive as globalisation continues to develop and trade barriers are lowered. The threat of substitutes is likely to be low in the short-term.

Distributors DCC intend to expand through acquisition in the US and Europe which will present challenges as well as opportunities for distribution and logistics of the two brands. Consideration must also be given to database sharing and the opportunities represented by the developing electronic technologies.

Suppliers The power of suppliers is likely to increase with stakeholder concern about who to do business with reflecting ethical and social responsibility issues. There are also the matters of scarce resources/labour exploitation in the case of rubber/leather materials used in bicycle assembly.

Critique

Whilst the macro environmental factors affect all businesses in the long-term and need to continuously monitored, the direct effect on DCC's operations in the next two years is not likely to be critical. The response of business to challenges from the macro environment is therefore likely to be gradual and incremental.

Challenges from the micro environment are on the other hand more obvious and direct and will affect DCC operations in the short-term to a greater degree. Management does therefore need to monitor the micro environment on a more frequent basis and to be ready to respond immediately to, for example, a price attack from a major competitor.

Limitations of market information – external audit

In the context of wishing to expand within the enlarged European Union, there are a number of countries where DCC could experience the following difficulties:

- Non-availability of secondary data for comparison with existing developed markets such as the UK and the USA
- Where comparative secondary data does exist it may be less reliable or out of date.
- Some governments might be reluctant to release secondary data in their possession.
- The above limitations would make it difficult for DCC to establish such basics as gross national product, disposable income, proportion of population owning bicycles, amount of cycling lanes etc, which are valuable aids in determining market size, growth rates and other measures of attractiveness when deciding which new markets to enter.
- As a consequence of being obliged to conduct original primary research, DCC would encounter considerable extra costs.
- There are limitations in conducting primary research in certain countries and communities within countries. Germans, for example, are less willing to be interviewed in the street or within shopping malls and the large Turkish community within Germany might object to their women being approached by strangers. These problems are likely to be greater in particular East European countries where languages and cultures are more different still.

(c) **Planned growth strategies and associated risks**

DCC's planned expansion through acquisitions in the US and Europe and by offering accessories and apparel can best be identified and explained within the context of Ansoff's growth strategies matrix as illustrated below:

	Current Products	New Products
Current Markets	**Market Penetration** ■ More frequent purchasing ■ Gain customers from competitors ■ Convert non-users into users ■ Reduce loss of customers to competitors	**Product Development** ■ Product modifications ■ Different quality levels ■ Entirely new products
New Markets	**Market Development** ■ New geographical markets ■ Developing new market segments/niches ■ Establish new distribution channels	**Diversification** ■ Horizontal integration ■ Vertical integration ■ Concentric diversification ■ Conglomerate diversification

1 **Market penetration strategy**

There are three main ways of increasing sales of existing products to existing customers:

1.1 Get customers to buy more frequently, ie to buy a new bicycle more often.

1.2 Gain customers from competitors with the use of consumer, salesforce and dealer incentives. Also by recruiting competitors; sales staff with good dealer contacts.

1.3 Convert non-users into users. Campaigns could be run, perhaps with help from government agencies to get more people to use bicycles, so as to grow the existing market.

A fourth way is to stem the loss of existing customers by ensuring top of class products, value for money and developing better customer relations.

2 **Market development strategy**

There are again three main ways:

2.1 Entering new country markets as indeed DCC are doing

2.2 Identifying and targeting new market segment within these countries such as supplying school, cycling clubs etc, offering ancillary services etc

2.3 Establishing new distribution channels eg marketing direct via an interactive website.

3 **Product development strategy**

There are different degrees of newness.

3.1 Entirely new products.

DCC are planning to add two new product ranges to their bicycles – accessories and apparel/clothing, presumably to be marketed under the Raleigh and Diamondback brand names. Whilst these are not 'new to the world' items, as far as DCC are concerned, they are entirely new products.

3.2 Different quality levels

Rather like cars, DCC cycles could have different marques which vary in the detail of finishes and included features.

3.3 Product modifications

These are usually relatively minor such as different sizes, colour schemes, saddles etc and include minor improvements/changes to handlebar grips, bells and the like.

4 **Diversification strategy**

DCC is in effect already employing this highest of all risks strategy in that they are involved with both new products and new markets – see above. There are four main types of acquisition/integration:

4.1 **Horizontal integration**

Acquiring a similar business or competitor ie other bicycle producers

4.2 **Vertical integration**

Buying backwards or forwards into the distribution channel – possibly in our case forwards into the distribution channel – possibly in our case forwards into dealerships

4.3 **Concentric diversification**

Buying another business with technical or marketing synergies such as bicycle accessories and apparel.

4.4 **Conglomerate diversification**

Seek a completely fresh challenge for our marketing skills.

Associated risks

Some writers suggest that the risk rises exponentially in the sequence used for these four growth strategies with comparative ratios quoted as extreme as 1, 2, 4, 16.

However there is relatively scant evidence for such extreme claims except that some studies have established that as many as 9 in 10 new products fail in the sense that they are no longer on the market two years after launch. Certainly most researchers agree that market penetration carries the lowest risks, whilst new products represent a higher risk than market development, so that a combination of these latter two results is the highest risk of all. This is the strategy boldly being adopted by DCC. Steps need to be taken to reduce these risks wherever possible and one of these is to ensure an efficacious marketing mix – a challenge which is addressed in the ensuing section of this report.

(d) **Marketing mix recommendations for Diamondback apparel range.**

The marketing mix needs to be integrated around the Diamondback brand image which is both global and consistent with West Coast USA youth imagery. This brand essence and its brand values need to pervade the entire marketing mix as suggested below.

Product – the quality of the apparel as well as its nature and design needs to accord with that of the Diamondback bicycle. Clearly the colour ranges will need to harmonise. Fashion will be important in product design and some allowances made for market segmentation, particularly that between adults and children and between males and females. A degree of limited editions for loyalty clubs and other niche markets would seem appropriate. Packaging would also need to be consistent with and add value to the brand essence.

Price – this would have to represent value for money in light of global competition. However, premiums would be appropriate for limited editions and for up-market versions to match the best of range Diamondback bicycles.

Promotion – as previously suggested, celebrity endorsements are likely to be an important component in achieving the desired cachet for the brand. These would be at their most effective when using international cycling start, particularly in Europe. Media would have to be chosen with the target market segments in mind and the messages would need to align with the AIDA principle of **A**ttention/**A**wareness; **I**nterest; **D**esire; **A**ction. Sales promotions should be integrated in the form of consumer/dealer competitions and considerable time and effort should be given to obtaining favourable publicity and PR.

Place – existing and new dealers in the chosen markets should form the basis of distribution and logistics, but in keeping with modern trends a multiplicity of channels could be used. Dealers not wishing to add apparel to bicycle stocks could be offered a degree of sale or return and/or to act as mail order agents. Any remaining gaps could be filled by a direct internet ordering facility built into DCC's website provision.

Summary of report

As this report indicates, these are challenging times for DCC and a considerable degree of risk is entailed in pursuing the chosen strategies. Under these circumstances an objective and informed opinion can be found valuable. It is therefore hoped that our co-operative relationship will continue and perhaps be extended.

63 Starbucks

Examiner's comments: The answer identifies the challenges facing Starbucks coffee shops in their quest for growth. Section (a) looks at the impact of the macro and micro environment on the brand and the importance of marketing information. Section (b) uses Ansoff's matrix to guide business expansion and section (c) considers the importance of the brand and the extended marketing mix decisions.

(a) **Report: The Impact of the Macro and Micro Environment and the Starbucks' Brand**

From: Marketing Consultant
To: Marketing Director, Starbucks
Date: December 20X3

1 **Executive summary**

This report highlights three key areas for evaluation to provide a secure framework for future growth of the Starbucks' brand. Starbucks' future is not just with coffee house outlets but with the continued expansion and diversification into new markets, such as health and sports leisure and with new product development in response to changing consumer behaviour, such as caffeine free drinks.

2 **Critical appraisal of challenges in the marketing environment**

2.1 **Macro Environment**

Political - issues are wide and varying with pressure from health and environmental organisations. Crucially Starbucks perceived trading standards and policies to their suppliers is important, as much of their raw material is sourced in developing countries.

Economic - issues regarding personal disposable income and the impact on employment are important influence on the choice of location for retail outlets.

Sociocultural - analysis of trends and changes have impacted on Starbucks. A younger generation of consumers are more aware of healthy living, where caffeine for instance has been recognised as a habit similar to smoking. The important challenge is to identify the correct segments of the marketplace for each of the product offerings.

Technological - Internet café opportunities as a distribution channel need to be considered for younger consumers as possible extensions to their offering. The Internet provides an excellent marketing communications opportunity to increase awareness to the wider consumer groups.

Legal - trade barriers in certain countries together with labelling, classification and promotion of healthy goods are important. Accurate information for consumer and valid assertions of low fat, reduced fat and healthy living products should be carefully marketed.

Environmental - the use of green packaging and biodegradable materials should be considered with a message of sustaining natural resources used in their products.

2.2 **Micro Environment**

Threat of new entrants - very likely as there are low entry barriers, therefore more need to concentrate on differentiation of brand. Positioning and target issues are important.

Bargaining power of customers - high volume of buyers and high disposable income and expectation of service performance.

Competitors - will impact on price, quality and range of products and consistency of standards. Proliferation of high street coffee shops.

Bargaining power of suppliers - limited number of coffee producers poses a threat on coffee retailers and profitability.

Threat of substitute products - tea, chocolate, juices and soft drinks. Level of competitive rivalry - consolidation and expansion are features of the sector. The consumers are varied with differing requirements. There is potential high growth in the older age sector, but a noticeable decline in the healthy younger aged market.

3 **Critical appraisal of role of marketing information**

The role of external information for full assessment of each situation within a market audit is very important. It will help to formulate the marketing plan for the Starbucks brand and provide a basis on which to set the objectives to achieve growth. However, it is necessary to consider the reliability of published data in certain countries and the difficulty of accessing reliable and relevant information. Primary data collected for the purpose of this work can be researched and gathered by Starbucks directly or with the help of an external agency on Starbucks' behalf. Secondary data can be obtained from Government offices, national statistics sources, existing industry reports etc to assist in the process. However, there could be difficulty in analysing information which has been formatted in different ways and that is not relevant to the research objectives. Having gained the marketing information it can then be used as a basis for undertaking a SWOT analysis to gain a greater understanding of their market environment.

(b) **Introduction**

Ansoff proposed the idea of product/market scope to aid in the formulation and selection of strategies, particularly for those companies with growth objectives. The matrix comprises 'markets' on the vertical axis and 'products' on the horizontal axis. Each axis is divided into new and existing and each segment of the matrix represents a different strategic alternative in achieving growth.

		Product	
		Present	New
Market	Present	Market Penetration	Product Development
	New	Market Development	Diversification

Market penetration is a strategy of expanding sales based on existing products in existing markets. Where the total market is growing the strategy may be achieved through natural market growth.

Market development is a strategy of expansion based on entering new markets with existing products, such as entering an export market for the first time.

Product development is a strategy of developing and launching new products for sale in existing markets.

Diversification involves the company expanding with new products into new markets such as an airline entering into the car insurance market.

Identification of most appropriate growth strategies for Starbucks

Starbucks would most likely consider the most appropriate growth strategy to expand their business within the next two years to be market and/or product development. Market Penetration is not a likely option as the market is becoming saturated and Diversification could be considered in terms of stretching the brand (such as clothing etc) but is very risky and is not particularly realistic.

A market development strategy would consider further segments of affluent 'grey' clients and or new countries. It may also consider developing into public services or corporate markets to improve brand preference and attract loyalty. Serving Starbucks products at conferences or on trains could increase sales and customer growth for existing products.

Conversely a product development strategy would consider the potential for new products or product/brand extensions. They could consider a caffeine free range of products targeted at healthy living customers and younger aged groups.

(c) **Consideration of role of branding in relation to planning for growth**

A brand is a name, term or symbol which is used to identify the goods or services from one seller and to differentiate them from those of competitors. For Starbucks defining the role of branding as a strategy to differentiate products is important and should be incorporated into their mission statement. The key areas to investigate are to invest in the brand and to consider the implications for brand stretching and links to value proposition.

Application of the Marketing Mix for growth strategies

Using Ansoff's matrix there are a number of possible strategies for growth of the Starbucks' brand. We have decided to adopt a product development growth strategy and apply the extended marketing mix decisions.

Product - the introduction of caffeine free and low fat coffee ranges to outlets have been decided upon. These are specifically targeted at city centre outlets where there the existing and potential customer segments include those people aspiring to live a healthy lifestyle and for younger aged customers.

Promotion - the new ranges need to promoted to increase general awareness and have a high impact with our targeted customer segments. The use of advertisements on television at key times, appearance of advertisements at health, sports and leisure clubs and in selected magazines is crucial. The use of the Internet for advertising is also important, together with SMS promotion. An introductory offer would also attract further attention, including 'trials' of the new ranges. Packaging of the new range must reflect the Starbucks' brand and the messages for healthy lifestyle and younger customer likes.

Price - the healthy alternative would attract a premium. However close attention must be given to the sensitivity of demand and a review of the prices must be considered. At the introductory phase discounts would be used rather than a low price approach which would be increased at a later stage. The higher price approach is linked to the perception of value by the target customer segments.

Place - existing outlets would be used, although non-smoking zones would be introduced to reinforce the healthy living message. A high emphasis should be placed on tidiness and clearing up after customers have left the shop.

People - staff training of the attributes of the new ranges must be incorporated into the existing training procedures.

Physical evidence - staff uniforms should be upgraded in line with the new brand image. The outlets would also benefit form a reinvigoration of the shop fittings and to introduce more fashionable furniture to give a fresher feel to the coffee shop.

Process - customer loyalty cards with bonuses and offers for regular and repeat use of Starbucks shops should be introduced. Performance measures should be introduced to assess waiting times, product quality and customer satisfaction.

Summary

The report is designed to bring forward options and alternatives to develop a two year growth strategy. Further study, analysis and discussion are required to develop the launch details and the roll out programme across the Starbucks' outlets.

Test your knowledge

1 When does a marketing opportunity exist?

2 What are the main internal organisation factors used to analyse marketing opportunities?

3 What are the external marketing (macro) environmental forces?

4 What distinguishes industrial/business to business marketing from consumer marketing?

5 How might the promotional mix for industrial products vary from that for consumer products?

6 What are the four basic characteristics of services?

7 What are the six major parts of a comprehensive marketing audit?

8 Give the sub-structure of both the marketing systems audit and the marketing productivity audit.

9 Briefly describe Michael Porter's three generic strategies.

10 What are the four levels of involvement in international marketing?

11 What are the structural choices which relate to the levels of involvement?

12 What sorts of information would you seek with regard to foreign market access?

13 Give the essential features of the marketing control process.

14 What two major forms of analysis would you use when evaluating marketing performance?

15 What sorts of *analyses* are recommended before determining core target markets?

16 What is corporate strategy?

17 Describe a marketing audit, including its primary purpose.

18 Briefly describe Ansoff's four competitive strategies.

19 State the contents of a 'detailed plans and programmes document'.

20 What are the major categories of constraints on marketing decisions?

21 Define marketing ethics.

22 What is the nature of social responsibility?

23 State four basic consumer rights.

24 Briefly distinguish between market segmentation, targeting and positioning.

25 What are the basic consumer characteristics or segmentation variables?

26 Give three basic strategies for dealing with social responsibility issues.

27 Categorise the contributions which IT has made to distribution.

28 What is internal marketing?

29 What are the 7Ps for services marketing?

30 State what difficulties exist, and why, when trying create a competitive edge for services.

31 What is non-business marketing?

32 What are the five stages in sequence of the marketing planning cycle?

33 What are the six competitive marketing strategies which can be used to attack market leaders?

34 What are the five stages of Wilson, Gilligan and Pearson's cycle of control?

35 Distinguish between price skimming and penetration pricing.

36 Define strategic marketing as fully as possible.

37 Which one of the following statements is true? According to *product life cycle theory*, profits:

- A And sales peak during the growth stage.
- B And sales peak during the maturity stage.
- C Reach a peak during the growth stage, but sales peak during the maturity stage.
- D Never actually peak.

38 List at least five benefits of the process of marketing planning.

39 What are the major bases for segmenting industrial markets?

40 Which stage of the new product development process is missing?

- Idea generation
- Screening
- Concept development testing
- Marketing strategy
- Product development
- Market testing
- Commercialisation

41 Fill in the missing phrases. The General Electric multifactor portfolio model is a two dimensional matrix with __________ on the vertical axis and __________ on the horizontal axis.

- A Market growth rate, relative market share
- B Market attractiveness, competitive position
- C Competitive position, market attractiveness
- D Industry attractiveness, business strength.

42 List four financial and four non-financial criteria which can be used in making the strategy selection decision.

43 Distinguish between intensive, selective and exclusive distribution channel strategies.

1 A marketing opportunity exists when circumstances allow an organisation to favour an opportunity for taking action to generate sales from particular groups of customers.

2 Factors are as follows.

- Organisational objectives
- Financial resources
- Managerial skills
- Organisational strengths and weaknesses
- Cost structures

3 Forces are as follows.

- Political forces
- Legal forces
- Regulatory forces
- Societal/green forces
- Economic forces
- Competitive forces
- Technological forces

4 In industrial marketing products are sold to be used directly or indirectly in producing other products. The buyers are other businesses rather than the general public. Buying motives therefore differ.

5 The *promotional mix for industrial selling* is likely to emphasise personal selling. Advertising is usually low key. Sales promotion is largely literature and exhibitions rather than sales incentives/competition, PR is mostly confined to publishing technical articles and arranging factory visits.

6 Characteristics of services are as follows.

- Intangibility - cannot be seen, touched, tasted or smelled
- Inseparability - produced at the same time as they are consumed
- Perishability - services cannot be stored. They are instantly perishable
- Heterogeneity - no two services can be exactly the same

7 The six major parts of a comprehensive marketing audit are:

- The marketing environment audit
- The marketing strategy audit
- The marketing organisation audit
- The marketing systems audit
- The marketing productivity audit
- The marketing function audit

8 *Marketing systems audit*

- Marketing information system
- Marketing planning system
- Marketing control system
- New product development system

Marketing productivity audit

- Profitability analysis
- Cost-effectiveness analysis

9 Porter's three generic strategies are as follows.

(a) Cost leadership - the development of low cost structures so as to allow the company to achieve high returns even when competition is intense.

(b) Differentiation - developing superior products or services either in quality or unique features so as to obtain a distinctive competitive advantage.

(c) Focus - the company concentrates on particular market segments so as to meet their specific needs better than competitors.

10 Levels of involvement are as follows.

- Casual or accidental exporting - occasional, unsolicited orders received
- Active exporting - active effort to sell existing products overseas
- Full scale international marketing involvement
- Globalisation of markets - company operates as if the world was one large market

11 *Structural choices*

- Exporting
- Licensing
- Joint ventures
- Trading companies
- Direct ownership

12 *Market access information*

- Limitations on trade - tariffs, quotas
- Documentation and import regulations
- Local standards/practices and other non-tariff barriers
- Patents and trade marks
- Preferential treaties
- Legal considerations - investment, taxation, employment etc.

13 The essential features are as follows.

- The development of objectives
- The establishment of performance standards
- The evaluation of actual performance
- Actions to reduce difference between actual performance and performance standard

14 These are twofold.

(a) *Sales analysis,* for example, sales volume, sales turnover and market share, all reported by product/product group and/or by region/area.

(b) *Marketing cost analysis:* marketing costs per activity to gain a certain level of sales. For example, selling costs, advertising costs, sales promotion costs.

15 Analyses leading to strategy determination include the following.

- Customer needs, market segments, brand positioning
- Analysis of the marketing environment and trends
- Competition and competitors' strategies
- Marketing opportunities/trends
- SWOT

16 Corporate strategy is the set of decisions on resources and utilisation of resources covering all the functional areas: production, finance, research and development, marketing and personnel, so as to achieve agreed organisational objectives. Corporate strategy could also be said to co-ordinate the functions in achieving corporate objectives.

17 *A marketing audit* is a systematic examination of all an organisation's marketing activities, from the setting of objective through strategy to performance in the market place. It is essentially an evaluation of marketing operations designed to identify weaknesses, with a view to correcting these. A thorough marketing audit will include examinations of the macro and micro environments in which marketing operations take place.

18 Ansoff's four competitive strategies are as follows.

- Market penetration (existing products for existing markets)
- Market development (existing products for new markets)
- Product development (new products for existing markets)
- Diversification (new products for new markets)

19 Contents are as follows.

- Company mission
- Product/market background information
- SWOT analysis
- Statement of objectives
- Strategies (target, markets, competitive edge, brand positioning)
- Marketing programmes (sales targets, detailed marketing mixes)
- Allocation of resources, task, responsibilities
- Financial implications/budgets
- Operational implications and implementation
- Appendices (supportive information)

20 Categories are as follows.

(a) Legal constraints, such as on advertising, monopolies and mergers, restrictive trade practices etc.

(b) Regulatory constraints imposed by government/non-government agencies, such as the Ministry of Agriculture, Fisheries and Food

(c) Voluntary constraints: non-legal such as the codes of practice adopted by professional bodies like the CIM

(d) Ethics and social responsibilities: moral values and societal expectations which prevail against abuses such as pollution.

21 'Marketing ethics are moral principles that define right and wrong behaviour in marketing. The most basic ethical issues have been formalised through laws and regulations to conform to the standards of society' (Dibb, Simkin, Price, Ferrell)

22 Social responsibility in marketing refers to an organisation's obligations to society. Whereas ethics relates to individual decisions, social responsibility concerns the impact upon society of an organisation's decisions. The society expects organisations to act in a way that maximises their positive impacts and minimises their negative impacts.

23 The four basic consumer rights are as follows.

- The right to safety
- The right to be informed
- The right to a choice
- The right to be heard

24 *Market segmentation* is the process of dividing customers in a heterogenic market into smaller more similar or homogeneous groups or segments.

Targeting: when segments have been identified, a decision can be made about how many segments and which segments should be earmarked or targeted for action.

Positioning: this is the distinctive marketing mix tailored for a given market segment which positions the product in the mind of the target customer, eg pricey, prestigious, long lasting, readily available etc.

25 Basic consumer characteristics are as follows.

- Demographics - age, sex etc
- Socio-economic - income, education etc
- Geographic location - country, type of housing etc
- Personality, motives and lifestyle - extrovert, status seeking, yuppy etc.

26 The three basic strategies are as follows.

(a) Reaction strategy: allowing a situation to go unresolved until the public gets to know and then reacting.

(b) Defence strategy: the company tries to minimise or avoid the problem by legal and other manoeuvring

(c) Accommodation strategy: the business assumes responsibility for its actions.

27 Categories of IT's contribution to distribution are as follows.

- Computerised ordering systems
- Computerised stock control
- EPOS and EFTPOS
- Databases
- Journey planning and queuing control
- Electronic signage on motorways

28 Internal marketing is about getting everyone in the organisation from top to bottom to accept the focal importance of the customer. This means striving to ensure that all functions (not just marketing) work *wholeheartedly* together to provide maximum customer satisfaction.

29 The 7P's for services are as follows.

- Product: ie characteristics of services provided
- Promotion: selling, sales promotion, advertising, PR
- Price: basic prices plus add on
- Place: distribution, timing
- People: services provided by people for people
- Process: stages in service provision
- Physical evidence: the tangible elements of service

30 A *competitive edge* or differential advantage is more difficult to achieve for services owing to their intangibility and the central role of people. These lead to problems in protecting unique service features and in maintaining the quality of services.

31 *Non-business marketing* is that conducted by individual and organisations to achieve objectives other than profit, market share, return on investment.

Non-business marketing can be divided into non-profit organisation marketing and social marketing.

32 The marketing planning cycle includes the following stages.

- Development/revision of marketing objectives
- Assessment of marketing opportunities and resources
- Formulation/revision of marketing strategy
- Development/revision of the plan for implementation and control
- Implementation of marketing plan

33 Frontal Attack, Flank Attack, Encircle Attack, Bypass Attack and Guerrilla Warfare.

34 Stage One
Where are we now? (Beginning)

Stage Two
Where do we want to be? (Ends)

Stage Three
How might we get there? (Means)

Stage Four
Which way is best? (Evaluation)

Stage Five
How can we ensure arrival? (Implementation & Control)

35 Price skimming is where price is set high in order to generate large profits. Penetration pricing is where prices are set low in order to generate large sales.

36 Your definition should include as many of the following key elements as possible,

'Strategic marketing is a process of: strategically analysing environmental, competitive, and business factors affecting business units and forecasting future trends in business areas of interest to the enterprise; participating in setting objectives and formulating corporate and business unit strategy; selecting target market strategies for the product markets in each business unit, establishing marketing objectives, and developing, implementing, and managing program positioning strategies for meeting target market needs.'

37 According to product life cycle theory, profits reach a peak during the growth stage, but sales peak during the maturity stage (c).

38 The process of marketing planning has a number of benefits which include the following.

(a) It motivates staff and improves commitment
(b) It secures participation and involvement
(c) It leads to better decision-making
(d) It requires management staff to state assumptions
(e) It prevents 'short-termism'
(f) It ensures a systematic approach to the future has been taken
(g) It creates a climate in which change can be made

(h) Standards of performance are established
(i) Control systems can be designed and performance assessed more objectively

39 Major segmentation bases for industrial markets are: demographic, operating variables, purchasing approaches, situational factors and personal characteristics.

40 Stage 5, Business Analysis, is missing.

41 The General Electric multifactor portfolio model is a two dimensional matrix with industry attractiveness on the vertical axis and business strength on the horizontal axis (d).

42 Financial and non-financial choice criteria include the following.

Financial	Non-financial
Liquidity	Sales volume
Value-added	Market share
Earnings per share	Growth rate
Shareholders value	Competitive position
Share price	Consumer franchise
Profit	Risk exposure
Cost leadership	Customer satisfaction
Cash generation	Reliance on new products
Profitability	Sustainable competitive advantage

43 Intensive distribution is where products are placed in as many outlets as possible. Here the image of the outlets is not the key criteria, coverage is, whereas with selective distribution, products are placed in a more limited number of outlets. This strategy seeks to show products in the most promising or most profitable outlets only. Exclusive distribution is where only one distributor is used in a relatively large geographic area.

Professional Diploma
(formerly Advanced Certificate, Stage 2)

Marketing Planning

3 Hours Duration

This examination is in two sections.

Part A is compulsory and worth 50% of total marks.

Part B has four questions, select two. Each answer will be worth 25% of the total marks.

DO NOT repeat the question in your answer, but show clearly the number of the question attempted.

DO NOT OPEN THIS PAPER UNTIL YOU ARE READY TO START UNDER EXAMINATION CONDITIONS

PART A

Case Study

The 2008 Olympics in Beijing

In 2008, China will be hosting the Olympic Games. China is calling these games the "People's Olympics", and they are to be hosted in Beijing, which is ready to become a truly international city. Beijing is showing a new, vigorous image through its on-going economic reforms.

By hosting the People's Olympics, there will be an emphasis on the value of human talent, ambition and achievement. Indeed, the organising Committee sees the Olympic Games as a catalyst for exchange and harmony between various cultures and people.

China aims to strengthen public awareness of environmental protection and promote the development and application of new technologies via the Olympics. The Chinese people love sports and the nation's athletic enthusiasm is evident in wide participation in sports activities among its 1.25-billion population with distinctive achievements of Chinese athletes at previous Olympic Games.

Celebrating the Games in Beijing in 2008 will offer a unique opportunity to inspire and educate a new generation of Chinese youth with the Olympic values, and to promote the Olympic spirit and the cause of sport in China and the world.

The Olympic Organising Committee

The Beijing 2008 Olympic Games Bid Committee (BOBICO) is in charge of all matters related to Beijing's bid for the 2008 Olympic Games. BOBICO was founded on September 6, 1999. The committee is made up of 10 departments. Its members include athletes, personnel from the education, science and culture circles and contributors from other social sections, as well as officials from the Beijing municipal government, the State General Administration of Sport and departments of the Central Government.

Sponsorship

More than US$600 million is expected to be raised from the international sponsorship of the 2008 Games. A similar amount could be expected to be raised from domestic sponsorships within China from companies wanting to become anything from the official airline, bank, insurance company, telephone company, petrol company and travel agent, down to the official supplier of ice cream and waste management services. The committee aims to have the major corporate sponsors signed up before the 2004 Games in Greece, well ahead of the event.

Indeed the games are seen to be the biggest ever marketing opportunity for China and they are currently starting to develop the marketing plan. The plans for the marketing programme include a nation-wide contest in China to design a new logo for the 2008 Olympics to replace the well known logo which was used for the Beijing bid. It aims to generate a new look with fresh marketing potential.

Preparation for the games in Beijing is everywhere in evidence, from signs in shop windows to pins on the lapels of shoppers. New roads, bridges, and stadiums are planned, a massive environmental protection programme is underway, and technological modernisation, from cell phones to Internet access, is expanding to every corner of the city.

'The Olympics have already speeded the pace of change in Beijing and across China,' says Mr. Liu Jing-min, Vice Mayor of Beijing and Executive Vice President of the Beijing 2008 Olympic Games Bid Committee. "The survey demonstrates that the people of Beijing embrace these changes, welcome the world to our city, and are prepared to host a great Olympics."

The above data has been based on a real live organisation, but details may have been changed for assessment purposes and does not reflect the current management practices.

Source: Olympic Games website.

PART A

Question 1.

You have been appointed as a Marketing Consultant to assist the Beijing Olympic Organising Committee. Write a report for the Committee that:

(a) Assesses the potential impact of macro-environmental forces on the marketing plan for the Beijing Olympics, specifically considering the role of culture, ethical approaches, and social responsibility.
(15 marks)

(b) Explains the role of the Beijing Olympic brand and explain the importance of the brand in attracting the targeted sponsorship required, critically identifying the methods, which could be used to develop the Beijing Olympic brand
(15 marks)

(c) Explains the concept of service quality and recommends an effective extended marketing mix in relation to the service delivery and service encounters for the consumers during the Olympic events.
(20 marks)

(50 marks in total)

PART B – Answer TWO Questions Only

Question 2

You have been appointed as a marketing consultant to a small business to business company who is looking to gain financial funding.

(a) Explain the components of a marketing plan which the company will need to write, discussing the synergistic planning process. (15 marks)

(b) Explain the role of the marketing plan in relation to the company's business objectives. (10 marks)

(25 marks in total)

Question 3

You are a marketing management consultant and have been asked to undertake a marketing audit for a double glazing and window frame company.

(a) Explain the different processes and techniques used for auditing the marketing environment. (9 marks)

(b) Explain the potential impact of wider macro-environmental forces on the business, such as ethical and social responsibility issues. (6 marks)

(c) Explain the concept of segmentation, targeting and positioning which this company could consider. (10 marks)

(25 marks in total)

Question 4

During a recession, an organisation of your choice has an objective to expand its market share by developing a market penetration strategy.

(a) Explain how such a strategy could be achieved at an operational level and contrast this with a market development strategy. (15 marks)

(b) Explain how pricing decisions can help to achieve the organisation's objective. (10 marks)

(25 marks in total)

Question 5

You are a brand manager for a consumer product of your choice, which appears to be in decline. You plan to rejuvenate and reposition this product in the market.

(a) Explain how you will reposition this product and justify which segments will be targeted. (10 marks)

(b) Explain how you will integrate the marketing communications mix to achieve this new positioning . (10 marks)

(c) Explain one method for evaluating your marketing plan. (5 marks)

(25 marks in total)

Suggested answers

DO NOT TURN THIS PAGE UNTIL YOU
HAVE COMPLETED THE TEST PAPER

1

> *Examiner's comments:* This answer covers the issues specifically referred to in the question fairly well, it does not include any reference to the PESTEL (Political, Economic, Social, Technological, Environmental and Legal) factors of the external environment. The three aspects of branding required by the question – its role, how it might be used by sponsors, and methods which can be used to develop the brand are covered. This answer achieves a pass standard through its practical application of the extended marketing mix to the Case Study scenario. A basic knowledge of SERVQUAL is evident, though more marks would have been gained through an explanation of the unique characteristics of services – intangibility, perishability, heterogeneity, inseparability and lack of ownership - and the associated problems

Report to: Beijing Olympic Organising Committee
From: Marketing Consultant
Date: 9th June 20X4

I write these reports as a consultant, providing you with the benefits of my experience and to offer advice to ensure the commercial success of the 2008 games. There are three sections that cover macro environmental forces, the Beijing Olympic brand and service quality.

(a) **Report on the impact of the macro Environment for the Beijing Olympics, specifically considering the role of culture, ethical approaches, and social responsibility**

It is important to examine the external macro environmental forces that will effect our planning. These forces are not under our control, though we may be able to influence some of them. By assessing them now we can take account of them and use them to our advantage. These include Political, Economic, Societal, Technological, Environmental and Legal issues (PESTEL).

Macro Force	*Considerations*
Political:	Impact of potential war, restrictions or agendas from central Chinese government or regional influences
Economic:	Local economy in Beijing and economic reforms
Societal:	International approach to such games and impact on communications. Response from local Chinese to hosting games.
Technological:	IT links, impact of IT on service offering. IT capability to support Games
Environmental:	Noise and waste pollution including green issues
Legal:	Consideration of international legislation or regulatory influences

As an extension to this analysis, culture, ethical approaches and social responsibility will be discussed.

Culture

One of the main areas to assess for impact is the cultural influences. It is important to realise that the games bring a cultural feel unique to itself, whilst at the same time there will be an expectation of strong cultural influence from China.

People will be coming from all over the world bringing with them their own values and expectations. We must manage and anticipate these expectations if our marketing plans are to succeed.

Chinese culture has some Western influences but it is still very far from the Western world and it is important to realise that most overseas visitors will be Western. However, some countries (eg USA) have poor records on environmental protection and the choice of this area to highlight could be seen as a little antagonistic if not handled properly (unless that is the plan). All plans must be developed remembering that China is looking for overseas investments, as well as a means to increase awareness of its own brands rather than just manufacturing under licence.

Ethical approaches

China has a human rights image problem. This will have an influence on any wording or tone used to appear ethical. What may seem ethical in China may not in other regions.

A commitment to doing what seems ethical (as well as legal) will help the plan. Any opportunities that arise for unethical behaviour must be managed by an ethics team who will have the right structure, culture and personality traits.

Green/environmental considerations are also very important to Westerners at the moment. The environmental protection found in China should be highlighted.

Social responsibility

This covers responsibility to the environment, employees and of the future for all involved. Macro forces such as political desire to do things quickly could result in unnecessary damage to the environment or employment uncertainty.

(b) **Role of the Beijing Olympic brand**

With 600 million US dollars at stake it is important that this is positioned correctly. As a consultant I can advise you of the best steps to take and help you identify the best options for brand building. Brands are used in marketing to embody the essence of a product or service in order to make them easier to sell. The Beijing 2008 brand will be critical in developing a co-ordinated and strong marketing campaign with consistent messages to reach our target audience.

The logo is a key part of the brand and any logo used must balance the design positioning of China with its environmental / technological aims with that of the history, culture and feel of the games.

The logo will be seen all around the world and will be interpreted differently everywhere. The wrong colour or shape could cost in corporate sponsorship. A sponsor may not wish to be associated with anything overtly communist for example.

The problem of balancing a communist image with the look of 'new China' with its international trading, new technology and openness will need to be solved by the branding.

Elements of the brand

The colours, strap-lines, imagery and logo will all manage to create the brand. The emotive experience, awareness and memories will all be formed by this. Sponsors will require colours, imagery and meanings to work with on their own artwork. The brand will be, it seems, aimed at technology companies.

Developing the brand

To summarise the above:

- **Logo development** - approved or modified version of competition winner with considerations for sponsorship at forefront.
- **Imagery** - consistent with values and desires of games, China and sponsors.
- **PR** - activities aimed at developing the right China/international look and feel of the games, especially considering problems likely to occur from human rights protests.
- **Colours** - careful use of red. The colours of the rings would be more suitable and expected allowing sponsors to choose the best match.

It is important to remember that to some extent China will not 'own' the brand. It is merely being borrowed for these particular games.

(c) **Service quality**

Service quality is best summarised using the model below which helps identify the areas to concentrate on as well as being a useful checklist tool. The model is Western and will be most suitable to the majority of visitors.

SERVQUAL

- understand consumer expectations
  gap 1
- service specifications
  gap 2
- service delivery
  gap 3
- service expectations

By researching what people expect by way of service when at the games and then recording these as a set of specifications we can avoid *gap 1* appearing therefore meeting people's expectations. This will take us to a theoretical level, but because of the involvement of people in the service delivery we also need to monitor *gap 2* between the specifications and the actual delivery. This can be done by special staff selection and training.

China has a good reputation for structured obedience (military precision). People will have high expectations. They will also be focused on the games and won't want poor service to get in the way. This can be managed by the information in the following section.

The extended mix

There are three key areas to concentrate on to ensure high service quality.

1 People
2 Physical evidence
3 Processes

Service delivery and encounters will rely on getting the mix of these three areas correct (along with the rest of the mix - place, price, product and promotion).

People

The interaction between service providers and visitors is vital. Problems with language, culture and expectations will be high. People must be well-trained, have a good appearance, appear polite, sincere, and honest and give a reliable, responsive service. They must be full of empathy when required.

They will need to be carefully selected and trained, an area of strength for China. Training will need to include Western service standards, norms of behaviour and some language skills.

Physical evidence (ambience)

All consumer areas will need to be kept tidy. Any areas of layout that are peculiar to China will need to be identified and redesigned/signed to assist foreigners. Knives and forks should be provided as well as any other elements that will be expected and provide comfort to the consumers. Cleanliness, comfort and a sporting ambience must be the themes used in the design and layout of all venues.

Processes

Again, this is somewhere I would expect China to excel. People will be wanting to move around quickly, and will expect information to be readily available. China can demonstrate its new technologies in these areas by using them to improve certain processes.

Public transport will be a major element. People and athletes must arrive on time. Special routes and timings will need to be laid on. The cleaning of all areas must also be systematic.

Security processes must be watertight. Expect terrorism and human rights campaigners to try and gain publicity. Problems must be dealt with in an acceptable and open manner.

In summary, the political, environmental, societal, technological, economic, green and legal influences in the environment will need careful reviewing and management to ensure they do not negatively affect the plan.

Branding is a critical importance to the games and its sponsors. Any mismatch of culture/ethics must be carefully handled to ensure the brand is protected.

Consumers will have high expectations of service and through identification of problem areas and using the areas I have outlined in this report I am confident that all expectations can be met.

It is positive that planning has started as there are likely to be many challenges ahead.

2

Examiners comments: It is important to discuss the key issues facing small businesses, such as the company would have limited resources and on the way in which its marketing would therefore be constrained. The answer should include the components of a marketing plan and their relationship to the company's business objectives.

(a) **The marketing plan and the synergistic planning process**

To: Steve Hamblett, Managing Director
From: Oliver Bruce, Marketing Consultant

To effectively market your business it is important to carry out a comprehensive marketing plan using the following framework.

1.1 Executive summary
1.2 Situation analysis
1.3 Marketing strategy
1.4 Numerical forecasts
1.5 Control

The Synergistic Planning Process includes the following approach:

2.1 Determine desired outcomes

2.2 Analyse the current situation

2.3 Decide on possible routes to the desired outcome

2.4 Decide what course of action to take and how to get there

1.0 The marketing plan components

The marketing plan is the framework that outlines all the marketing activities and initiatives for an organisation.

1.1 Executive summary

The executive summary gives a brief overview of the whole plan. This details how the need arose to develop a plan, what the aims and targets are. It gives an overview of where the company is at now in terms of markets, products and customers. It also briefly outlines any proposed actions including the timescales and funding required to fulfil these plans.

1.2 Situation analysis

The situation analysis analyses the position of the company at present moment in time. There are various parts in this analysis.

- **Macro environmental analysis**

  This investigates the wider market in which the company operates. It can be analysed by looking at political, economical, social, technological, environmental (Green) and legal factors.

- **Micro environment**

  The Micro environment analysis investigates the markets within which the business operates. It can be analysed by looking at Porter's five market forces.

  Customers - who are they, what are their perceptions and attitudes, how many are there?

  Suppliers - their capabilities and capacity

  Competitors - who are they, how successful are they?

  Threat of new entrants to the market - which may decrease market share

  Threat of substitutes - who may provide products which replace the business's products

  These factors can be analysed via a SWOT analysis which identifies opportunities and threats to the business.

- **Internal appraisal**

  This is looks at the business's own capabilities and can be assessed by looking at the 5 M's.

  Men - the capabilities of the workforce
  Money - the financial situation of the company
  Machinery - the fixed assets
  Materials - the supply and production processes
  Markets - the market share, growth, trends

These can also be analysed using the SWOT technique to identify strengths and weaknesses.

1.3 Marketing strategy

This will outline the marketing actions needed to be taken to achieve future aims. It sets out:

- the marketing objectives - smart
- the target markets - who to sell to
- the products position - where the product is now
- the marketing mix to achieve objectives - this will focus on aspects of price, product, place, promotional strategies to achieve objectives
- marketing research - in order to carry out the strategies

1.4 Numerical forecasts

These include turnover, market share, growth, trends, costs and break even analysis which are required to assess the situation and project forecasts for future.

1.5 Control

This ensures how the company gets to where it wants and includes:

- performance measures
- roles and responsibilities
- implementation milestones
- contingency plans

2.0 The synergistic planning process

There are four components to this.

2.1 Determine desired outcomes

This is the setting of objectives of where the business wants to be.

2.2 Analyse the current situation

This is the macro and micro environment analysis plus the internal appraisal.

2.3 Decide on possible routes to the desired outcome

This is the marketing strategies for how to achieve the objectives.

2.4 Decide what course of action to take and how to get there

This is the selection of the best strategy and the control mechanisms to ensure the objectives are achieved.

(b) The marketing plan and its relationship to the overall business plans are illustrated below. The corporate business plan and mission statement outlines the direction that the whole organisation wants to take for the future. From this, corporate objectives are developed.

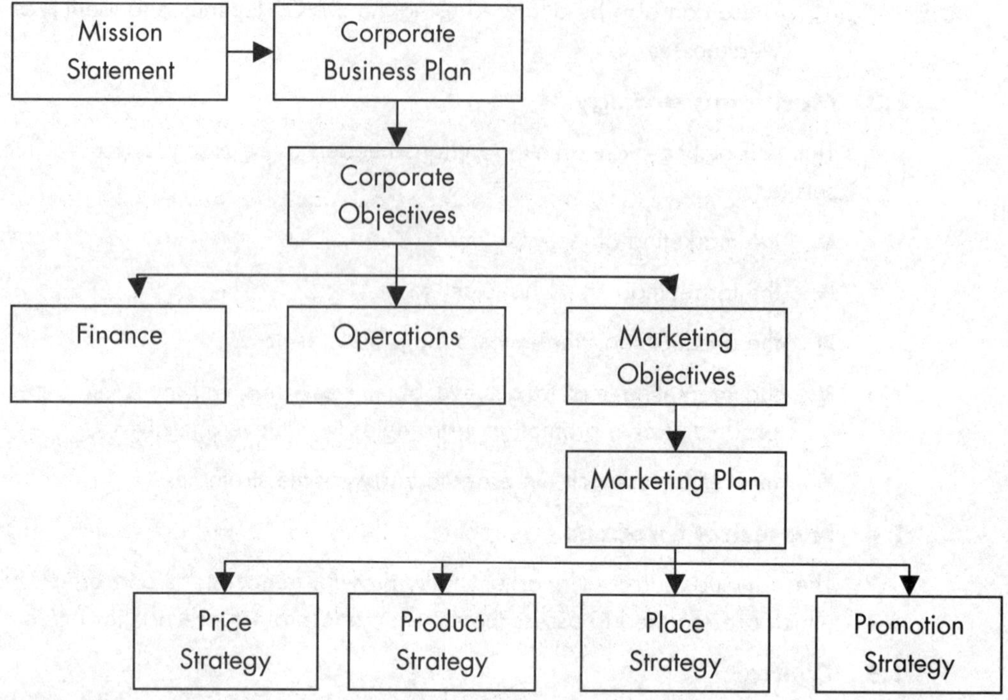

Each business function will develop objectives which will contribute to the overall attainment of corporate objectives. These objectives need to be integrated across all the functions to ensure success. Therefore the marketing function has to determine sets of objectives to achieve corporate success. This allows the marketing plan to be developed to achieve the marketing objectives. From the marketing plan individual strategies can then be drawn up for the components of the marketing mix, ie price, products, place and promotion.

3

> *Examiner's comments.* This question is set to assess knowledge and understanding of the processes and techniques available for conducting a marketing audit, ethical and social responsibility issues and segmentation targeting, and positioning in the context of a double glazing and window company.

Marketing environment and segmentation analysis for double glazing

To: Senior Management
From: Marketing Management Consultant

This report will detail the processes of an audit and all the factors surrounding it. It will include the following:

1.0 The marketing environment
1.1 Porters five forces
1.2 Swot analysis
1.3 Boston Consulting Group

2.0 The macro marketing environment
2.1 PESTEL issues
2.2 Social responsibility and ethics

3.0 Segmentation

4.0 Targeting

5.0 Positioning

(a) There are three main areas that make up the wider marketing environment. These are the micro environment, the macro environment and the internal environment. In the wider marketing environment there are a number of techniques for auditing the various areas.

1.0 The marketing environment

This is the environment in which the firm operates. It can be assessed in market share, growth, trends and uses such tools as:

1.1 Porter's five forces

Customers - this analyses who customers are, what their attitudes are, their opinions on the company, their buying behaviour.

Suppliers - is looks at suppliers' ability to supply component products, their effectiveness, efficiency and whether they cost their products appropriately. It also analyses whether suppliers will be able to continue supplying in the future for its alternatives may need to be found.

Competitors - who are they? How successful are they? What is a market share, has the market share grown?

Threat of new entrants - this is the possibility of new members entering the markets; may affect the market share.

Threat of substitutes - this is the possibility that new products may enter the markets or existing products change which may provide a better replacement for the current double glazing and frames.

1.2 SWOT analysis

This analyses the strengths and weaknesses in company. It also looks at the opportunities such as a competitor going out of business or threats such as a competitor winning a major contract.

1.3 Boston consulting group

This process allows you to review your products and compare them with those of your competitors. The diagram below compares market share to market growth. If you then realise that your low market share in a particular area is draining your resources you can pull out or use harvesting prices and then pull out. Resources and time can then be focused on the areas that are left.

		Market Share	
		High	Low
Market Growth	High	Star	Problem Child
	Low	Cash Cow	Dog

(b) **2.0 The macro marketing environment**

This analyses the wider market forces that can affect the business.

2.1 PESTEL issues

- Political issues such as the local government announcing plans to refit their council properties may affect the business.
- Economical issues such as an increase in interest rates may affect the ability of potential customers to enter into credit agreements.
- Social issues such as the safety of its products.
- Technological issues such as better class production methods can impact on the business
- Environmental issues such as the public awareness to consider heat and save energy may impact on the business
- Legal issues such as changes to health and safety law may affect working conditions for staff

2.2 Social responsibility and ethics

The company has a moral obligation to ensure that the public do not come to any harm. This includes the possibilities to its employees to ensure that they have adequate and safe working conditions. It also has responsibility to its customers that provide safe high-quality products. There are safety standards to follow to ensure the glass is safe if it smashes.

(c) **3.0 Segmentation**

This divides the entire market into groups of people who have similar needs and wants, characteristics or patterns of behaviour. The business segments its customers according to their needs for example:

- industry customers
- domestic customers
- local government

They will have different needs which the company can distinguish between.

4.0 Targeting

Targeting involves selecting segments of the markets which are appealing to the business in which the business can provide for. There are three approaches to targeting:

1 Undifferentiated, when segments are ignored and the products are solved to everyone in the market.

2 Differentiated, where the company still sells the whole market, but the products are developed specifically to meet the needs of the different segments.

3 Focus, where the company focuses on just one segment in the market, or forms a niche.

In this case, the double glazing company may wish to follow a differentiated targeting technique, by providing specific products and services to each of the key segments of industry, domestic and local government customers.

5.0 Positioning

This relies on how the public perceive the organisation. An organisation can decide on its position by using a perceptual positioning map, whereby two variables are used to access the customers' perceptions of the product eg.

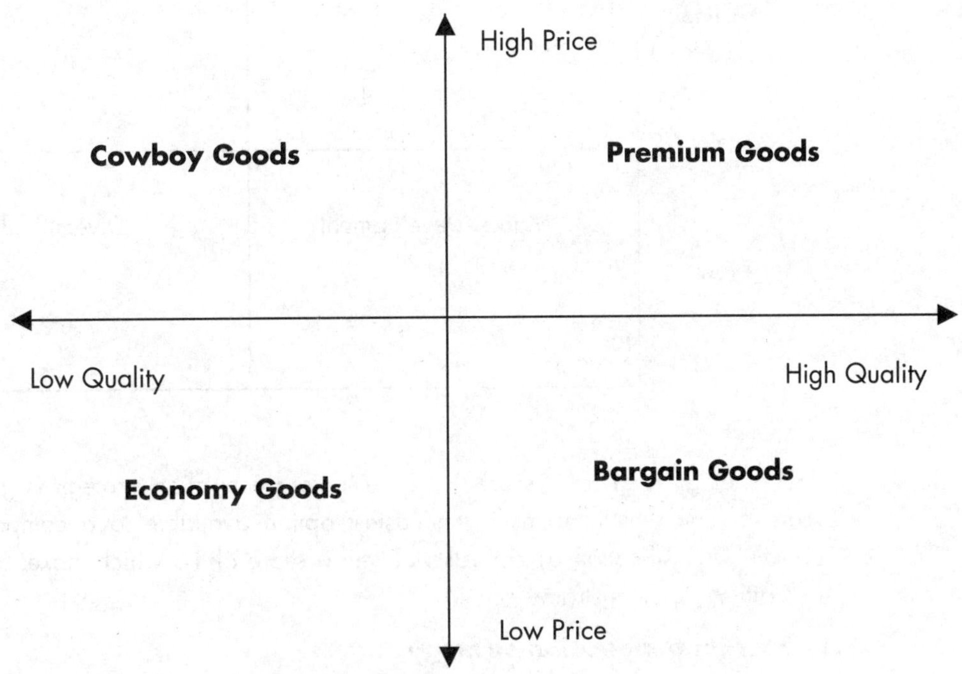

The double glazing company can assess its competitors place on the map and find a gap. For example, the competition may be focusing on providing high price but high-quality premium goods, and there may be a gap for the double glazing company to fill the high-quality, low price bargain goods section of the market.

Another method is to assess the market and either follow the 'me too' positioning strategies whereby the company aims to produce products in direct competition with other firms. Or they can adopt differentiation strategies to make their products more attractive to customers via altering them to meet the customers' needs better.

For this purpose, it may be best to use positioning maps to assess the gaps in the market, and establish their double glazing products as different from competition.

4

> *Examiner's comments:* This question is set to assess candidates' understanding of growth strategies using Ansoff, and ways in which the marketing mix might be adapted for two named options – market penetration and market development.

(a) **1.0 Introduction**

The organisation chosen is a regional brewer. Ansoff identifies four different strategies for growth.

		Product	
		Existing	New
Market	Existing	Market Penetration 1	Product Development 4
	New	Market Development 2	Diversification 16

Each strategy is given a score 1 - 16. Market penetration strategy is given the lowest score of one which makes it the easiest option available to a company to achieve growth. Diversification by contrast is given a score of 16 which makes it the most risky and difficult growth strategy.

1.1 Market penetration strategy

During the recession a brand of a regional brewer has been losing market share. As the marketing manager I have identified three strategies available to the company to increase market share – the brand sponsors Ben Cohen and Northampton Saints.

1. Get current loyal drinkers to drink more. This could take the form of a sales promotion. An on-pack offer on bottles or cans where consumers have the ability to send an entry to win a free trip to Six Nations in 2005 and lower their prices of rugby merchandise. There would be data collection on the back of the entry form to add to and build into the database for future direct marketing.
2. Encourage those that currently drink competitor brands but do drink in the category to switch to our brand. Again sales promotions coupled with advertising to raise interest and awareness would be used.
3. Get non-users to start drinking in the category and drinking our brand. This would involve heavy use of advertising to raise awareness and generate trial. Emotional features and benefits would need to be stressed. Research into these drinkers needs to be carried out to identify their likes and wants. Could potentially use a celebrity endorser who this segment identify and associate with to promote the brand - source credibility/attractiveness and power. Target innovators and opinion leaders with messages first so they spread positive word of mouth to like-minded friends and colleagues.

1.2 Market development strategy

The two main strategies identified to target drinkers into the brand by a new development strategy include:

1. **New target market**. This would involve research into different market segments, identification of possible suitable new market segments, the targeting

of these chosen segments with various communications mix and the positioning of the brand at these new target markets in line with their attitudes, beliefs and values but not to the detriment of core drinkers.

2 **Geographical expansion**. Again research into new segments, the identification of new segments by geographic locations - ale drinking is big in the Midlands and the North so these are potential areas. Would need to investigate channel to market availability - the use of intermediaries and potential new retail/wholesale listings to ensure product available. Need to advertise and promote brand in these new regions not previously available.

These two different strategies involve significantly different operations and a decision would need to be taken between the two as both cannot be pursued.

(b) **Pricing decisions**

When an organisation sets its prices this will have an affect on demand and thus profitability of the product and so pricing decisions need to be given careful consideration. Factors that need to be considered when setting prices include:

1 **Demand**. During a recession, demand for luxury goods such as premium ale fall considerably with consumers buying cheaper alternatives if any at all. Therefore when times are hard, a penetration pricing strategy could be considered to significantly reduce price for a period to increase market share. The company would need to the careful here though as if price was caught for too long, consumers would come to expect it.

2 **Channel to market**. During a recession the organisation may want to consider cutting expensive distribution channels. The company still needs to get product to retail outlets (direct delivery via the Internet is not an option) so it is available to buy. However, cheaper alternatives may be available, look to share resources with another company, or invest for long-term in own distribution fleet.

3 **Stage in product life cycle**. If the product is in the introductory or growth stage - penetration pricing for a short period could be considered. If the product is in the mature stage, we could look to price cut permanently to differentiate in a saturated market. If the product is in the decline stage then either premium price to get the maximum profit available with on-pack offers to reward and retain loyalists, or manage decline and phase product out.

4 **The competition**. Especially during recession, may want to follow suit with what the competition are doing. Do not want to start risky price wars that could force company out of the market - only a regional brewer, not a big national player.

5 **PESTEL factors** will also want to be taken into the equation.

6 **Buyer perceptions** will play a significant role in pricing decisions that market research could reveal. It could be that during a recession, loyal drinkers of which brand x has a large number still seek the brand out and are prepared to pay the normal price. Therefore price reduction and promotion is costly and unnecessary.

Conclusion

It is clear from looking at the numerous factors that influence pricing decisions that careful consideration, research and planning needs to be given to setting prices process to ensure appropriate price is set to meet the company's objectives.

5

> *Examiner's comments.* This question explores the concepts of repositioning and segmentation as well as the appropriate marketing mix to achieve repositioning, and control mechanisms for evaluating the success of this plan. It is set in the context of a consumer product, which candidates may select and use as an example. This answer uses the example of a soft drink to illustrate some of the key aspects of repositioning a brand including the product life cycle, the selection of an appropriate segment and a perceptual map showing the proposed position.

Report: Repositioning, the mix and evaluation
From: Brand Manager
To: Marketing Director
Date: June 20X4

This report is to outline a plan to reposition Sunny D from being a kid's drink to a teenager/clubber refreshment.

Declining sales following bad PR surrounding sugar content and additives have resulted in declining sales despite repositioning as a healthy drink with no sugar added options.

It is worth noting that Fantas 'Freekie/Freekin' drink have faced positioning problems whilst looking at the same market. I believe that by taking a well-known brand name and embracing its properties we can see sales back to their peaks. By selecting segments based on age and lifestyle we can reposition it as an energy drink full of flavour. This will require some product reformulations.

Age groups: 15 - 25

This encompasses a wide range of individuals with disposable income. Likely to be very active, care less about long-term health and will purchase own products rather than rely on parents who recognise problems with product contents.

Socio/psychographics

This includes sports fans, clubbers and outdoor activity types, and are likely to be leaders. They will encourage take-up by followers, therefore providing valuable personal recommendations and the 'cool' factor that is so important to this age group and lifestyle types.

Repositioning will see it fall into the following perceptual area.

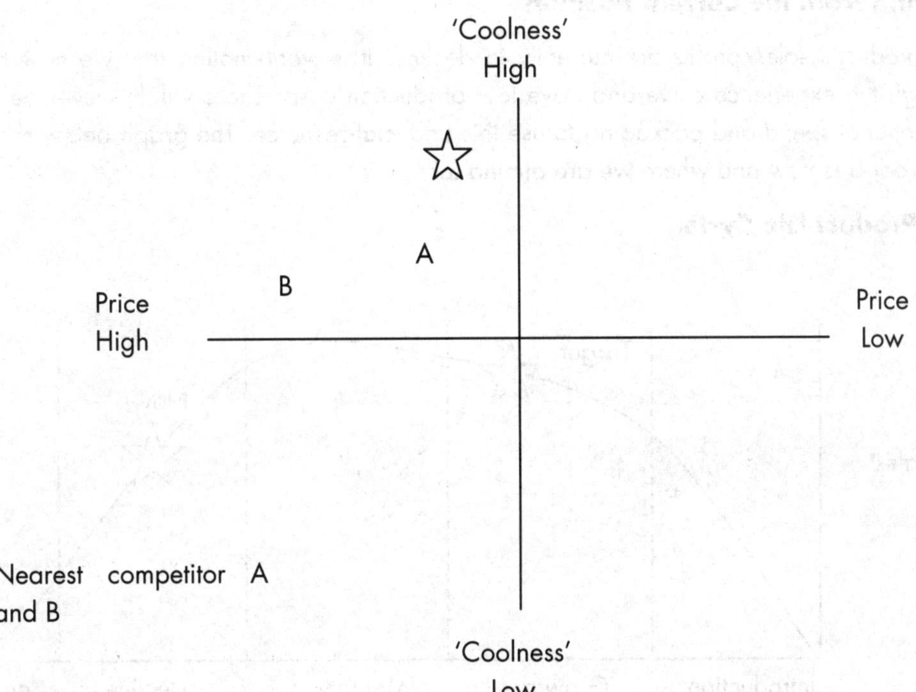

The integration of the mix

Overview of the marketing mix

(a) **Place**

Vending machines
Sports clubs
Bars (as a mixer)
Clubs
Supermarkets
Note: incentivise wholesalers

(b) **Price**

Reasonably high. Paying for cool factor.

Positioned slightly above nearest competitor to skim at first. Market penetration later when 'coolness' takes off.

(c) **Product**

Multicolours
Packaged as now and new sports packs like Lucozade
new flavours (market research)

(d) **Promotion**

Use the multicolours and packaging to appear in trendy magazines

Get away/dump the image of product bought by mums for their kids

Appeal to the disaffected youth through ads on selected Sky channels and relevant consumer press

Moving from the Current Position

The product's sales/profits are currently in decline. It is worth noting that we now have gone through the experience curve and have low production costs. There will however be additional promotional spend and packaging to use this financial resource. The graph below shows where the product is now and where we are aiming for.

The Product Life Cycle

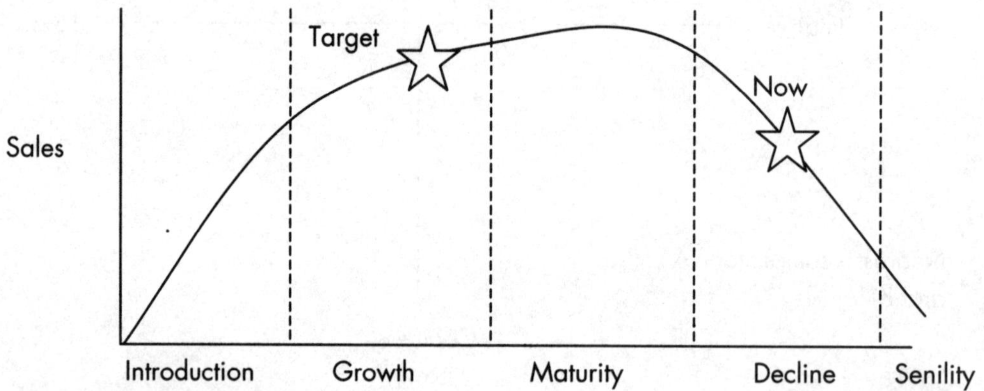

Details

We will run TV advertisements and a direct mail/e-mail campaign over a two-month period. This will be supported by on pack offers, price reductions (initially) and endorsements by leading figures relevant to each of our target markets. A website will be created to support the rebranding/position and allow consumer feedback.

Evaluation of plan

To evaluate the success of the plan we have various options ranging from quantitative to qualitative. As your brand manager, I would advise the use of the PIMS database. (Profit Impact on Marketing Strategy). This will give us figures that will be compared to our competitors. It will also showed trends over time for further analysis. (A qualitative method would be to measure brand awareness before and after the repositioning. Focus groups could be used both before and after for comparison.)

We can examine our profits and sales as a result of the repositioning activity.

Summary

This repositioning will require cross functional co-ordination, which, as brand manager, I am well placed to manage. I can ensure consistency and the overall management and development of this activity are done to the highest standards. We have an existing well-known brand name which we could reposition 'cleverly' to use the problems it has had to our advantage. There is a high risk of failure but product is in decline.

Topic index

See overleaf for information on other
BPP products and how to order

Mr/Mrs/Ms (Full name)

Daytime delivery address

Postcode

Daytime Tel　Date of exam (month/year)

		2004 Texts	2004 Kits	Passcards
PROFESSIONAL CERTIFICATE IN MARKETING				
1	Marketing Fundamentals	£19.95 ☐	£9.95 ☐	£6.95 ☐
2	Marketing Environment	£19.95 ☐	£9.95 ☐	£6.95 ☐
3	Customer Communications	£19.95 ☐	£9.95 ☐	£6.95 ☐
4	Marketing in Practice	£19.95 ☐	£9.95 ☐	£6.95 ☐
PROFESSIONAL DIPLOMA IN MARKETING				
5	Marketing Research and Information	£19.95 ☐	£9.95 ☐	£6.95 ☐
6	Marketing Planning	£19.95 ☐	£9.95 ☐	£6.95 ☐
7	Marketing Communications	£19.95 ☐	£9.95 ☐	£6.95 ☐
8	Marketing Management in Practice	£19.95 ☐	£9.95 ☐	£6.95 ☐
PROFESSIONAL POST-GRADUATE DIPLOMA IN MARKETING				
9	Analysis and Evaluation	£20.95 ☐	£9.95 ☐	£6.95 ☐
10	Strategic Marketing Decisions	£20.95 ☐	£9.95 ☐	£6.95 ☐
11	Managing Marketing Performance	£20.95 ☐	£9.95 ☐	£6.95 ☐
12	Strategic Marketing in Practice	£26.95 ☐	N/A	N/A

SUBTOTAL £

CIM Order

To BPP Professional Education, Aldine Place, London W12 8AA

Tel: 020 8740 2211. Fax: 020 8740 1184

email: publishing@bpp.com

online: www.bpp.com

POSTAGE & PACKING

Study Texts and Kits

	First	Each extra	Online	
UK	£5.00	£2.00	£2.00	£
Europe**	£6.00	£4.00	£4.00	£
Rest of world	£20.00	£10.00	£10.00	£

Passcards

	First	Each extra	Online	
UK	£2.00	£1.00	£1.00	£
Europe**	£3.00	£2.00	£2.00	£
Rest of world	£8.00	£8.00	£8.00	£

Reduced postage rates apply if you **order online** at www.bpp.com

Grand Total (Cheques to *BPP Professional Education*) I enclose a cheque for (incl. Postage) £

Or charge to Access/Visa/Switch

Card Number

Expiry date　Start Date

Issue Number (Switch Only)

Signature

We aim to deliver to all UK addresses inside 5 working days. A signature will be required. Orders to all EU addresses should be delivered within 6 working days.

All other orders to overseas addresses should be delivered within 8 working days.

** Europe includes the Republic of Ireland and the Channel Islands.

REVIEW FORM & FREE PRIZE DRAW

All original review forms from the entire BPP range, completed with genuine comments, will be entered into one of two draws on 31 January 2005 and 31 July 2005. The names on the first four forms picked out on each occasion will be sent a cheque for £50.

Name: ______________________ **Address**: ______________________

____

____

How have you used this Kit?
(Tick one box only)

- ☐ Self study (book only)
- ☐ On a course: college______________
- ☐ Other ______________

Why did you decide to purchase this Kit?
(Tick one box only)

- ☐ Have used companion Text
- ☐ Have used BPP Kits in the past
- ☐ Recommendation by friend/colleague
- ☐ Recommendation by a lecturer at college
- ☐ Saw advertising in journals
- ☐ Saw website
- ☐ Other ______________

During the past six months do you recall seeing/receiving any of the following?
(Tick as many boxes as are relevant)

- ☐ Our advertisement in the *Marketing Success*
- ☐ Our advertisement in *Marketing Business*
- ☐ Our brochure with a letter through the post
- ☐ Our brochure with *Marketing Business*
- ☐ Saw website

Which (if any) aspects of our advertising do you find useful?
(Tick as many boxes as are relevant)

- ☐ Prices and publication dates of new editions
- ☐ Information on product content
- ☐ Facility to order books off-the-page
- ☐ None of the above

Have you used the companion Study Text for this subject? ☐ Yes ☐ No

Do you intend to use the new companion Passcards for this subject? ☐ Yes ☐ No

Your ratings, comments and suggestions would be appreciated on the following areas.

	Very useful	*Useful*	*Not useful*
Introductory section (Study advice, key question checklist etc)	☐	☐	☐
Short questions	☐	☐	☐
Exam standard questions	☐	☐	☐
Content of suggested answers	☐	☐	☐
Index	☐	☐	☐
Structure and presentation	☐	☐	☐

	Excellent	*Good*	*Adequate*	*Poor*
Overall opinion of this Kit	☐	☐	☐	☐

Do you intend to continue using BPP Study Texts/Kits/Passcards? ☐ Yes ☐ No

Please note any further comments and suggestions/errors on the reverse of this page.

Please return to: Glenn Haldane, BPP Professional Education, FREEPOST, London, W12 8BR

REVIEW FORM & FREE PRIZE DRAW (continued)

Please note any further comments and suggestions/errors below.

FREE PRIZE DRAW RULES

1. Closing date for 31 January 2005 draw is 31 December 2004. Closing date for 31 July 2005 draw is 30 June 2005.
2. Restricted to entries with UK and Eire addresses only. BPP employees, their families and business associates are excluded.
3. No purchase necessary. Entry forms are available upon request from BPP Professional Education. No more than one entry per title, per person. Draw restricted to persons aged 16 and over.
4. Winners will be notified by post and receive their cheques not later than 6 weeks after the relevant draw date. List of winners will be supplied on request.
5. The decision of the promoter in all matters is final and binding. No correspondence will be entered into.